JESUS WHO BECAME CHRIST

Peter De Rosa was born in north London in 1932 and educated at the Jesuit College of St Ignatius. He read Philosophy and Theology at St Edmund's College and, having graduated from the Gregorian University in Rome, he lectured for five years at St Edmund's. He was Vice-Principal of Corpus Christi, London, an international institute for religious education, for five years, and is currently a radio producer.

JESUS
WHO BECAME
CHRIST

Peter De Rosa

Fountain/Collins

First published in the United States of America 1974
by Dimension Books, Inc., Denville, New Jersey
First published in Great Britain, in a revised edition, 1975
by William Collins Sons & Co. Ltd, London
First issued in Fountain Books 1977

Copyright © 1974 by Peter De Rosa

The quotation from 'The Dry Salvages', one of T. S. Eliot's
Four Quartets is reprinted by permission of Faber and Faber

Made and printed in Great Britain by
William Collins Sons & Co. Ltd, Glasgow

This book is for Mary
who came when the night was dark
and with me saw the dawn.

Contents

Contents

Contents

Introduction
A word to my fellow-snakes

My intention in writing this book was not to shock my fellow-Christians. I realize, though, how inevitable it is that many Christians will be shocked and exacerbated – I hope only initially – by some of the ideas expressed in the pages that follow.

How can I help it if many believers cling tenaciously to a picture of Jesus Christ that is quite incompatible with the latest scriptural research and our present understanding of man and the world? It saddens me that the gap between 'devotion' and scholarly findings has been widening dangerously for so long a time; and I would be content if I could reduce it by just a little.

The gospels are still too often taken as essentially a literal narration of what actually happened before, during and after Jesus' lifetime. Worse, patristic and medieval speculation on the basis of this inaccurate interpretation of the gospels is identified with Christian doctrine. I would not want to deny that, enfolded in these often bizarre imaginings and fanciful modes of expression, the truth about Jesus Christ as God's Word to men – to use a scriptural metaphor – has been in essence preserved and preached. Nonetheless, this truth can only reach us today when these colourful elements are accepted for what they are, namely, the wrappings of truth and not the truth itself.

A NON-HUMAN CHRIST

Most Christians, when they are honest with themselves, are forced to admit that Jesus can be classified only with the utmost difficulty as a member of the human race. He seems to be an amalgam of God and man. He is credited with a duality of minds and wills. He is thought to be simultaneously compounded of infiniteness and finiteness, omnipotence and weakness.

This composite image has arisen out of a prosaic, occidental reading of scripture and it is not lacking in a certain plausibility. In the New Testament, Jesus comes to our notice as someone who can walk on water *and* sweat blood in the garden, predict his passion in detail as though he had precise foreknowledge *and* be ignorant of the day when the Son of Man is to appear.

The medievals, considering the inadequacy of their exegetical equipment, made gallant attempts to harmonize the apparently contradictory data of the gospels. St Thomas More was being perhaps a trifle severe when he complained that reading the scholastics was like milking a billy goat into a sieve.[1] Thomas Aquinas – to name the greatest scholastic – was a man of immense humility and depth, simplicity and breadth of vision. His attempt to integrate all the admittedly sparse results of scientific research in his time with his Christian faith will remain as a monument to the industry of the human spirit, despite the fact that for his pains three Archbishops of Canterbury, in obtuse succession, condemned him.

For all that, the medieval world, with its weird metaphysical conjectures about Christ, is even further removed from our day than the world of the New Testament that antedated it by a thousand years and more. The reason for this is not hard to find: the concrete story-presentation of religion will always outlive the pretentious abstractions of academic theologians, just as the work of artists – poets, painters, sculptors – remains of perennial interest when the tomes of scientists are laid to rest in museum archives.

It is reasonable to ask: since we no longer avail ourselves of medieval sciences, why should we be afraid of *dispensing altogether* with medieval systems of theology? Common sense, not impiety, recommends that we should. Theology is not an independent discipline but part of the close-knit fabric – social, political, ideological, scientific – of any particular age. If we do not feel compelled to copy medieval politics, medieval drainage-systems and medieval means of locomotion, why should we think it worth while, even necessary, to feed our minds on medieval theology and devotion? Theology is not faith; it is the attempt to make faith contemporary. Of its nature, the finest theology is as ephemeral as the generation that produced it. The mentality illumined by, and dependent on, medieval theology has disappeared almost as completely as a pebble dropped from a jet-plane into the ocean.

How can we find the Christ who will satisfy us today? Is it inevitable that he comes across to us as a hybrid, a superman, a man with God inside him, a man with an internally divided human mind as well as a duplicate or shadow divine mind? Must he remain a man with whom we cannot really identify? To evade the heavy hand of the past we must first of all investigate the literary 'form' of the gospels.

The spontaneous reaction to modern New Testament exegesis may well be that it is both suspect and dangerous. Only further reflection reveals how responsible it is and how, without it, Jesus Christ will never be relevant to our time.

THE CHRIST OF FAITH

Scripture scholars are agreed that the gospels are not biographies but confessions of faith in Jesus who became, by his death and resurrection, the Lord and the Christ (Acts 2:36). The gospels do not set out to tell us with exactness what Jesus said and did as if this in itself were of value to Christians. Gerhard Ebeling writes: 'The direct passing on of what Jesus himself taught played only a secondary part in the message of early Christianity.'[2] Otto Betz, a solid, middle-of-the-road scholar, suggests: 'Without the historical Jesus, the Christ of the Church is shallow, a radiant shell, a mythical hero without historical weight. On the other hand, anyone who clings to the historical Jesus alone is blind, for without the light of the Easter creed he is swallowed up by the darkness of the cross.'[3] According to J. M. Robinson, the gospels 'retain a concrete story about Jesus, but expand its horizon until the universal saving significance of the heavenly Lord becomes visible in the earthly Jesus'.[4] Statements like these could easily be multiplied.

It is commonly agreed that the Easter message has not led to a distortion of the gospel; on the contrary, it has *constituted* the gospel as the good news. It is the Easter faith of the disciples that makes the gospels, from beginning to end, contemporary stories of the communion between Jesus Christ and those who believe in him.

This present book lays no claim to comprehensiveness. My aim is only to spotlight the effect of Easter faith upon some of the more important matters dealt with in the gospels so as to modify the reader's judgement on the gospels as a whole. I have selected for this purpose the infancy narratives, the miracles of Jesus – with a heavy emphasis, for the sake of illustration, on Jesus' walking on the water – and the resurrection stories.

MYTHICAL ELEMENT IN THE NEW TESTAMENT

Modern exegesis enables us to resolve many of the traditonal scholastic dilemmas – often referred to in reverent tones as 'mysteries of faith' because they are so puzzling – and to see, via the mythological elements of the New Testament, the truth about God and man there contained.

Certain believers may be distressed that the word 'mythological' is used at all in reference to the gospels. This is *fact*, they want to assert, and not *fiction*.

It is a pity, as Mircea Eliade has pointed out, that the word 'myth' is associated in many people's minds with fable, invention, fiction. The consequence is that many Christians, if asked, would claim that Christianity is not only a religion without myths but the best religion *because* it is without myths.

In fact, there never has been or could be a religion without myths properly so-called. According to Eliade, ' "myth" means "a true story" '. It is a story that is 'a most precious possession because it is sacred, exemplary, significant'.[5]

God is Mystery, the Unfathomable One. Only through the

myth, the parable, the story, can we approximate to the reality of God and the depths of man who is made in God's image. R. A. F. McKenzie writes: 'Myth is always an attempt to express, and thereby to make comprehensible, some truth about the world and man's existence in it, a truth inaccessible and unknown in itself, but capable of being expressed in and by symbols.'[6] It is 'dogma' that is abstract, time-conditioned, easily exhaustible, a constant temptation to idolatry – as if we, or the clergy, could know God, describe him and predict his ways.

The dogma is related to religion rather in the way that a subsequent explanation is related to a funny story. Such an explanation, when it is called for, sometimes illumines or spells out the humour contained *in* the story but it is hardly comparable to the experience of seeing for oneself the humour *of* the story. Further, dogmas are often totally lacking in religious warmth just as so many books on humour by, say, Freud, Bergson and Priestley are so painfully unhumorous. Jesus, it is worth remembering, did not speak in dogmas.

Of course, Jesus was a real historical character like Aristotle or Julius Caesar. The gospel is not to be compared *tout court* with the magnificent Genesis myths which we inherited from our Jewish forebears, myths that describe no historical happenings whatsoever. But how else can we interpret the incarnation, resurrection and ascension except in the terms of mythical thought?[7]

For example, the eternal Word of John's gospel existed 'up there' in the timeless time before time, 'before' he came down, entered into time by becoming flesh. This is a superb mythological conception based to a considerable degree on the current Jewish cosmology, not at all like Einstein's, in which heaven, the abode of God, was up there beyond the heavens. But unless it is understood to be mythological, twentieth-century man is bound to misunderstand the theological meaning it was intended to convey, namely, that Jesus is one with God, his actions are God's actions and his words God's words. The mythical category of Luke's rocket-like ascension is appreciated widely today though, for some reason, people balk at the mythical element in John's descension (called 'incarnation').

RESPECT FOR THE MYTHICAL

To demythologize – to use a modern term – 'is to reject not scripture or the Christian message as a whole but the world-view of scripture, which is the world-view of a past epoch, which all too often is retained in Christian dogmatics and in the preaching of the Church'.[8] Mythology is not for that reason to be eliminated. Mythology is not incompatible with theology but *the original form of theology*; it can still speak to us provided we grasp the kind of literature we are dealing with. We must not allow a first-century scientific-cum-mythological picture to function as a *description* of God and his doings.

R. H. Fuller makes two interesting, interconnected remarks relevant to our theme. First, 'demythologizing removes the adventitious stumbling block precisely in order to expose the real stumbling block with brutal clarity',[9] namely, the cross of Christ. Second, mythical language, far from being the most naïve, is one of the richest forms of religious expression to which man always returns. 'Myth *must* therefore be used in communicating and expressing Christian truth.'[10]

Any reader of the New Testament can see that the future coming of Christ on the clouds of heaven has already been demythologized in the fourth gospel in which Jesus Christ comes in judgement in his lifetime and throughout ours. Since the average Christian in the pew, without any prodding, demythologizes Jesus' ascension, it is disconcerting to find some theologians refusing to demythologize in any radical way, say, the resurrection of the body, the end of the world and eternal damnation. They are equally against demythologizing 'dogmatic myths' such as that Jesus possessed two minds and two wills! Many will not countenance the possibility that such statements are in any sense mythological. They take them as straightforward, matter-of-fact characterizations of Jesus' divine-human make-up. I am puzzled that theologians who would be distressed at the suggestion that Jesus might have had two heads are perfectly ready to accept that he had two minds.

WHY THIS BOOK WAS WRITTEN

This book may be seen as complementing my former *Christ and Original Sin*[11] in which I stressed the thorough manhood of Jesus. My emphasis on the Man, Jesus Christ, even then did not please all the critics. One of them – a lady of erudition – was so staggered by it she said she expected me at any time to announce Jesus' IQ. Grateful for this witticism I would like to characterize her opinion of Jesus by replying in the same vein:

> I know he was a man but please don't smile:
> He *was* a member of the Trinity.
> And while he couldn't run a minute-mile,
> He had an IQ of infinity.

In this present work I attempt to develop the scriptural basis for the Christology of *Christ and Original Sin*. Like Martin Luther, I propose to speak to the common man – by no means the unintelligent man – who for too long has been bemused and tormented by academic discussions about Jesus, God *and* man, infinite *and* finite, impassible *and* susceptible of pain, a being with two minds and two wills. I want to simplify the work of the dogmatic theologians of our time like Rahner and Schillebeeckx who seem, alas, to revel in writing prose of labyrinthine complexity.[12] Above all, I would like to abbreviate the findings of scripture scholars such as Bultmann and Fuller whose professional writings are to layfolk tiring in the extreme.[13]

JESUS, A FIRST-CENTURY JEW

A further preliminary warning. The Jesus who is emerging from recent scriptural studies – in so far as the historical Jesus can be detected through the medium of gospel preaching – is

a first-century Jew. He lived in a pre-scientific world in which
information on what was going on in his own village was
difficult to come by or to assess. He was a stranger to the
phenomena of radio, television, commercialism, pluralism, the
shrinking world, nuclear weapons, lunar probes. He never
read a word of print or rode in a car on a motorway or
marked a ballot paper in an election. By our standards, he had
unappealing ideas about the inspiration and authorship of the
Bible, demon-possession, the way God is accustomed to act in
human affairs, and the end of the world. As the eminent
exegete, the late C. H. Dodd, put it: 'Jesus was too deeply
concerned with the critical time in which he lived to be thinking
about us . . . It is part of this time-relativity that Jesus, like the
prophets, could not but make use of the thought-forms of his
age.'[14]

Jesus, a man; a first-century Jewish layman; a man belonging
to a barely recoverable age. He became the Christ. How can
he have anything to say to us? What is Christ for us today?[15]

MAKING CHRIST CONTEMPORARY

These are the questions that we, like our predecessors, go on
asking. The answers proposed must change, indeed they have
always changed in every generation, as the ever-renewed
fashions in theology demonstrate. But there is some continuity
in the theological flux, all the same. An example from the
sphere of technology will illustrate this.

There is continuity between the steam engine, the automobile
and today's rocket that propels men and heavy machinery to
the moon – even though these machines do not *look* alike.
There is, for example, no part of the design of a steam engine
built into the internal combustion engine to guarantee, as it
were, the continuity of thought and technical know-how
between the earlier and later vehicles of propulsion.

So it is with theology. To be strictly in historical continuity
with Chalcedon and Trent, with Augustine and Aquinas, we
may be forced to discard all the conceptual structures by means

of which they expressed themselves and build new ones out of new materials. This process of change is visible in the New Testament itself which is not a colourless reporting of events but an ongoing tradition and interpretation by the early Christian communities, such as the Palestinian and Greek, of what Christ meant to them in the changing circumstances of their lives.

We must not be frightened of this word 'interpretation' as if it inevitably means manipulation of the truth. In common with other exegetes and most modern historians, Ernst Käsemann has pointed out that mere cataloguing of 'what actually happened' would be of no use to anyone. We need to make sense of 'the brute facts' of the past just as, by organizing our sensible impressions, we make sense of our present experience. A developing tradition, and, in religious matters, a community interpretation, is essential to ensure that what happened once upon a time is of significance today.

Gerhard von Rad has shown this is true of the Old Covenant in his superb two-volume work, *Old Testament Theology*.[16] J. L. McKenzie approved this way of looking at things by commenting that the Hebrew story is 'a projection of God into history. The Hebrew story is an interpretation of events' formed according to their knowledge of God.[17]

Käsemann applies the same basic principle of interpretation to the New Testament: 'To state the paradox as sharply as possible: the community takes so much trouble to maintain historical continuity with him who once trod this earth that it allows the historical events of his earthly life to pass for the most part into oblivion and replaces them by its own message.'[18]

If this happened in the case of Jesus' words and deeds for them to become *contemporary* words and deeds, it would be naïve to think that the Church at a later date could manage to get by with mere *repetition* of ancient credal formulas. We have to take into account that our age may feel little or no cultural affinity with some earlier ages. Repetition, especially in religious matters, can be the most radical sort of falsification. Doctrines, like bread, need to be freshly baked. Failure to grasp this has led to Christians being fed with stale, non-biblical formulas such as 'the Trinity' and 'three persons in one nature', with the consequence that they have been led sometimes to imagine a heavenly triumvirate, and, despite protestations to the contrary, to 'believe in' three Gods.[19] As Käsemann puts it: 'Time and again, continuity with the past is preserved by shattering the received terminology, the received imagery, the received theology, in short by shattering the tradition.'[20]

Of course, the shattering is not to be taken as an elimination, a suppression of what is true in the past; the community's links remain. The new interpretation is consistent with the old and continuous with it even when it seems not to be. To return to the image of the steam engine and the automobile. Without the steam engine, there would be no automobile today. (It is scarcely conceivable that mankind should have passed straight from the horse and cart to the internal combustion engine.) There is a consistent line of development between them, and this is why we honour our ancestors who were brilliant enough to consider, project and finally perfect means of locomotion other than those dependent on wind and water, on animals and brute human strength.

This does not mean we have to go on riding in steam engines in the twentieth century out of reverence for James Watt and other geniuses who preceded us. Unfortunately, for many people, fidelity in religion is identified with the willingness to continue travelling *mentally* in the equivalent of the steam engine. These engines are the ancient dogmas. They were invented in a bygone age. Only expert mechanics, called theologians, really know how they work; *they* are able to take them to pieces and put them together again. Bishops are not in general so knowledgeable but at least they are able to manoeuvre the machines and have authorized driving licences stamped by God himself. The rest of the Christian community just has to submit to being taken for a ride.

Meanwhile the world whizzes past us wonderingly. Why, people ask, do Christians insist on trying to use words like nature, person, substance (as in 'consubstantial' and 'transubstantiation' – to name the most infamous) in ways totally at variance with normal usage, in a manner belonging to an era long since dead?

It is not right that the average Christian should have his religious life stunted, his thirst for relevancy unassuaged, on account of a *false* adherence to the past. We need to know not simply what past dogmaticians said but why they said it and in response to what kind of problem. And what they *would* have said had they been alive today in answer to *our* problems. Only when we know this are we in touch with our tradition.[21]

The New Testament statements about Jesus did not satisfy, say, the fifth-century world of Chalcedon; new terms and formulas had to be invented to satisfy a new generation. Isn't it reasonable to suppose that we cannot be content with the repetition of ancient Council dogmas? Or are these dogmas more adequate than scripture itself?

We have the task of thinking through and re-expressing Jesus' message today. But first we must locate the mythology and master the literary form of the gospels. This book, *Jesus who became Christ*, is offered as no more than a help to my fellow-snakes in commencing that important investigation.

MY FELLOW-SNAKES

Why do I address my readers, hopefully, as my fellow-snakes? Let me explain.

You must know that most animals shed their skin (or cuticle) in the course of their lifetime. This is how they renew themselves. They cast off the dead outer layer, having provided for their future by growing a replacement underneath, a kind of living underwear.

We humans undergo the same process, though, in our case, it is slow, continuous and, generally speaking, unspectacular. We keep on rubbing off the dead skin, wearing it slowly away. Only when we are sunburnt do we flake and peel.

The snake peels more remarkably than a banana: in one piece. Only when it is ill does the snake tear its skin off bit by bit.

When the snake is forming its new skin and preparing to

shed its old, its eyes become misty. A white, opaque liquid which is soon to be the new skin produces this temporary blindness. But when the new skin is perfectly formed, it becomes transparent and the snake is able to see again.

In the period of its 'blindness', the snake becomes indolent and lethargic; it sits coiled up – preferably in sunlight – all day long. When the time comes for the snake to slough off the old skin it breaks out into feverish activity. It gives enormous yawns in the attempt to break through the skin around the jaws. It rubs itself vigorously against any rough object, sticks, stones, the bark of trees. Flexing its muscles, it winds its way through shrubs and undergrowth and the forks of branches, dragging itself painfully out of its old covering, its past. Eventually, the skin lies there, discarded, inside-out, usually a drab-brown colour.

Contrary to popular report, snakes slough off their skin not once but many times. The first occasion is soon after birth. A new skin is produced every six weeks for two years, then at two-monthly intervals. Even when fully grown the snake manufactures a new skin twice every year.

The swiftly moving age in which we humans live demands that we, too . . . But need I say more, my fellow-snakes, except to ask you to read on and, while so doing, to diagnose with a pacific mind any peculiar symptoms you may show? Who knows, there may be some creative significance even in your yawns.

Part I

BEGINNINGS

1. WHAT A GOSPEL IS

The Swedish film *Elvira Madigan* is a long and beautiful visual poem. At the beginning, before the first pictorial frame, we are told that the movie is the true story of a nineteenth-century couple, a cavalry officer named Count Sparre and Elvira Madigan, a tight-rope walker, who were one day found together shot in the woods.

Why did the director, Bo Widerberg, choose to tell this to the audience? It is not customary to tell the public of the finale of a film before it has begun.

I presume Bo Widerberg wants to give this vital piece of information to eliminate any sense of apprehension or doubt about the outcome of events. This movie, he is intimating, is a tragedy of love, as inexorable as a Greek tragedy by Aeschylus or Sophocles.

Then the story begins to unfold. Count Sparre is, we discover, a married man with two children. In a conventional age, he deserts his wife, his children and his regiment to live precariously with a lovely young woman, Elvira Madigan. On the surface, there are times when it seems an idyllic love relationship. Except that the director has forewarned us there is no future in it. Death is to have the last word.

Because the ending has been anticipated, it is possible to watch this film unfold with utter peace. There is no need to try to guess the outcome of the liaison; it is known in advance. There is never a sense of indecisiveness, uncertainty, suspense, with the result that the movie-goer is never distracted for an instant from a perfect sympathy towards this couple in the hopelessness of their fragile love.[1]

The film director, by telling the ending of the movie before it begins, conditions the way we watch the film. This stratagem enables him to weave over us the spell of his choosing. He is implicitly saying: 'I am employing this particular artistic form and no other.' If a movie-goer enters the cinema one minute after the film has commenced he will follow every sequence of it quite differently from someone who reads and is influenced by the director's opening statement. In a profound sense, he will not be watching Bo Widerberg's film since he fails to appreciate the form in which the film is cast.

Is there a special form of the gospels? Have the evangelists, like Bo Widerberg, deliberately set out, before everything else, to influence us, to guide our reading, by telling us what the nature of their story is?

The answer to both questions is yes. The evangelists tell us, Mark does so in the very first sentence: 'This is the gospel of Jesus Christ.' Unless we realize this we will misread their writings; every sentence of them.

'Gospel' means 'good news' and is, therefore, primarily a spoken message. Never forget, each of the evangelists insists, that this story when written down as *a* gospel remains the proclamation – the preached message or *kerygma* – of the triumph of God in Jesus Christ. More expressly, the *kerygma* is: Jesus crucified is alive by the power of God.

Elvira Madigan was known in advance to end in tragedy. The gospel story is foreknown to be consummated in the death and resurrection of Jesus Christ, which is to say, it has no end. It is the proclamation of the presence of Jesus alive in the midst of this believing community that continues to live by him.

The resurrection and lordship of Jesus is not one item supplementing other items known about Jesus, for example, that he was born in Bethlehem, grew up in Nazareth, died on Calvary. It's not as if the evangelists want to tell us all these facts and, *in addition*, that Jesus was raised from death on Easter Sunday! The resurrection conditions the way the evangelists relate everything, even the story of the birth; hence it conditions the way they want us to *respond* to everything they tell us. They aim, above all else, to evoke faith in us and to guide the exercise of faith.

What is a gospel? In a word, it is a written proclamation of the resurrection of Jesus Christ from the dead. Everything subserves this end: to give testimony that Jesus of Nazareth was truly from God and that God has raised him from the dead. A gospel is, in its entirety, a document of faith.

2. WHAT A GOSPEL IS NOT

A gospel is not a straightforward biography or description of the life of Jesus and it is a mistake on our part to insist it should be to be worthy of credence. A gospel is certainly not an obituary of Jesus. He is the Christ; he is not dead but alive forever.

Christian tradition has often spoken of the gospels – indeed, of the Bible as a whole – as inspired and inerrant. This has often been taken to mean that the gospels are a source – the only source we have and, therefore, to be specially cherished – of precise, infallible information about Jesus. The evangelists, it has been assumed, have given us a detailed, more or less chronological description of the life of Jesus. The gospels' inconsistencies, on this view, can and should be harmonized, at least by scholars, without too much difficulty.

It was once argued, in the absence of the necessary research, that the evangelists were either witnesses of what they recorded or, like Mark and Luke, loyal scribes of eyewitnesses. It was presumed that they were all good and honest historians unwilling to 'falsify' their accounts of what Jesus, 'the God-Man', said and did while he was on earth.

In his dramatic way the Greek novelist, Nikos Kazantzakis, has given us a graphic representation of this now outdated notion of what a gospel is. In his book, *The Last Temptation*, Matthew, the despised and outlawed publican, is co-opted by Jesus into his apostolic group. Kazantzakis continues:

When the meal ended and all the others lay down to sleep, Matthew knelt below the lamp, drew out the virgin notebook from under his shirt, took his quill from behind his ear,

leaned over the blank pages and remained meditating for a
long time. How should he begin? Where should he begin?
God had placed him next to this holy man in order that he
might faithfully record the words he said and the miracles
he performed, so that they would not perish and that future
generations might learn about them and choose, in their
turn, the road of salvation. Surely, that was the duty God
had entrusted to him. He knew how to read and write;
therefore he had a heavy responsibility; to catch with his pen
all that was about to perish and, by placing it on paper, to
make it immortal. Let the disciples detest him, let them not
want to frequent his presence because once he was a
publican. He would show them now that the repentant
sinner is better than the man who has never sinned.

He plunged his quill into the bronze ink-well and heard a
rustling of wings to his right. An angel seemed to come to
his ear and dictate. With a sure, rapid hand he started to
write: 'The Book of the Generation of Jesus Christ, son of
David, son of Abraham. Abraham begot . . .'

He wrote and wrote until the east began to glow bluish-
white and the first cock was heard to crow.[2]

Kazantzakis assumes that Matthew, the publican, wrote the
first gospel that bears his name. This is considered by the
majority of scholars to be inadmissible for a number of reasons.
For example, the author of Matthew's gospel borrowed in
places from Mark word for word. Is it likely that an eyewitness
would 'copy' from a secondary source?

Kazantzakis also takes it for granted that Matthew is writing
an uncomplicated biography of Jesus and that whether he
wrote during Jesus' life or after his death makes no difference.
What Kazantzakis, together with most Christians in the past,
failed to notice was the effect that the death and resurrection of
Jesus had upon the disciples. It was only then that their eyes
were opened. Only then did their faith in Jesus as the Christ
finally mature.

We are forced to part company here with our predecessors
on an issue at once simple and of astounding consequence.

Whereas it was until recently presumed that the gospel stories *led up* to the resurrection of Jesus, today it is taken for granted that these stories *derive from* the resurrection, are completely coloured by the resurrection and are intended to witness to the resurrection.

Jesus' rising from the dead is the primary assumption of faith.[3] Jesus crucified is alive. In his death God has been glorified, hence Jesus is exalted to God's right hand. This being so, it follows that any judgement on Jesus' life, his ministry, his words and deeds, in order to be *Christian* must be 'informed' with that faith. Günther Bornkamm writes: 'We possess no single word of Jesus and no single story of Jesus, no matter how incontestably genuine it may be, which does not embody at the same time the confession of the believing congregation.'[4] All the gospels, from the beginning, speak of the conquest of sin and death at the resurrection of Jesus. They are not Requiems for Jesus but Alleluias to celebrate his victory, God's victory, over the forces of evil.

If the gospels are not biographies of Jesus nor in every respect exact descriptions of his life, must we not concede that in some places, at any rate, they have falsified what happened, distorted 'the facts'?

Only someone with an over-simplified view of truth would be worried by such a question. It was only after the disciples came to believe in the resurrection that they understood what had been 'happening' all along. Only when they believed in the triumphing character of Jesus' death did they grasp what 'the facts' really were: God had all the time been at work in him in ways they now began to marvel at. They had possessed eyes but they had not seen. The resurrection meant that it was not too late for them to see *for the first time*.

The preaching of the gospel – at length sufficiently developed to be written down by four editor-theologians in gospels – aimed to present what until Easter the disciples had been too foolish and slow of heart to believe (Luke 24:25): Jesus is the Christ. Earlier, they had been faithless; earlier, therefore, they had been *untrue* to Jesus. Now they have found faith. They will scrutinize everything he said and did, everything he hinted at, all the testimony that the scriptures (the Old Testament) gave to him. Out of all this will be woven, in a most creative way, the gospels: the primary documents of the Christian faith.

In brief, a gospel is not an exact description of the life of Jesus. This is no disadvantage, for if it were that and that alone it would not witness to Jesus as the risen one, the Lord. It would mostly lead up to the good news but it would not be the good news *in every verse*.[5]

3. BRINGING THE PAST UP TO DATE

There is a saying, 'What is past is past.'
And yet my thoughts of yesterday don't last.

The whole of our conscious life is a process of renewing or reshaping our judgements about what we have previously done or had done to us, accomplished or failed to accomplish. Without noticing it for the most part, we are continually bringing the past up to date, especially our own past.

What once we called tragedy, in the light of subsequent experiences, we may call a blessing. What initially we looked on as a blessing we may spend our lives bemoaning ever came our way at all. A riotous existence, exciting while it lasted, may seem in retrospect, after, say, a religious conversion, to be the most regrettable period of one's life. Nor is it so uncommon for a wedding day, or some other moment of great expectations, to be regarded afterwards as an illusion or a disaster.

In our personal life it is easy to see that some incidents are more crucial than others, even though the decisive appreciation of any incident may occur much later.

Take the case of a man who first met his wife at a party. The significance of that encounter lay in what was to follow and not simply in the events of the evening. At the time, it may have appeared as inconsequential as his talking to a number of other girls at parties before and since. But the development of their love, their subsequent marriage and raising of a family illumines and gives meaning to their original meeting. In fact, only what was to come proved what really happened in the first encounter. This is because life is a process, not a series of wholly disconnected incidents.

Imagine this man, in the company of a group of friends, saying: 'That first meeting with my wife was the most wonderful and meaningful thing that ever happened to me.' Imagine, too, one of the group replying: 'But, Harry, that's nonsense. You're romanticizing. I was with you that evening when you first met Rosemary. You hardly said a word to her that night. As I recall, you were in love with someone else at the time. Your only comment about Rosemary was that she's a very dull and plain-looking kind of girl.' Harry will hotly contradict his friend and he will be right. That meeting *was* the most important of his life even though he did not know it then. He is looking at the incident as the privileged 'insider' and with the eyes not of yesterday but of today.

We mark out a few moments of our lives as crucial turning points, but the normal process of reassessment we constantly engage in is unobtrusive. The changes are slow and cumulative as is the case with growing old; we realize we have become middle-aged not by looking more courageously than usual in the mirror on one particular morning but by comparing what we look like now with our appearance in an old photograph.

We are constantly surprised at the relativity and shifting nature of our judgements. A visit to an old school, so much grubbier and smaller than I imagined. The replay of an old film on TV – what must I have been like to have enjoyed it so much once upon a time? Old letters, especially love-letters; old papers, articles or books I have written which might just as well have been written by a stranger – did I *really* think and feel like that? The journey of life, in one sense, is so long we forget our origins; and most of the places we pass through are destined to be hazy memories.

Even the most prejudiced person changes his outlook and his judgements far more than he is prepared to admit. The bigot usually cherishes the illusion that in vital matters at least he has *never* wavered – a claim which, if true, would only testify to the sclerosis of the spirit. A detailed diary would probably reveal how absurd and dishonest his profession of personal immutability really is.

In the realm of literature, we come across a variety of ways in which the past is brought up to date.

Autobiography, for example, provides an author with a rare problem of interpretation. He looks back on the foreign land of his own past from the platform of this present moment. What he is *now* inevitably colours his appreciation of what he was before and how he became what he is now. We easily allow for this interpretative element in autobiographies.

Take Winston Churchill's interpretation of his youth in *My Early Life*. He there relates his first acquaintance with a Latin grammar. The teacher at his expensive private school left the young Winston alone with a well-thumbed specimen of this little-loved manual and warned him he would reappear in half an hour. In the meanwhile, Winston was to learn the first declension. '*Mensa*, a table; *Mensa*, O table; *Mensam*, a table; *Mensae*, of a table; *Mensae*, to or for a table; *Mensa*, by, with or from a table.'

According to Churchill's account, the master returned on time and the following conversation took place:

'Have you learnt it?' he asked.

'I think I can say it, sir,' I replied; and I gabbled it off.

He seemed so satisfied with this that I was emboldened to ask a question.

'What does it mean, sir?'

'It means what it says, Mensa, a table. Mensa is a noun of the first declension. There are five declensions. You have learnt the singular of the first declension.'

'But,' I repeated, 'what does it mean?'

'Mensa means a table,' he answered.

'Then why does Mensa also mean O table,' I enquired, 'and what does O table mean?'

'Mensa, O table, is the vocative case,' he replied.

'But why O table,' I persisted in genuine curiosity.

'O table – you would use that in addressing a table, in invoking a table.'

And then seeing he was not carrying me with him, 'You would use it in speaking to a table.'

'But I never do,' I blurted out in honest amazement.

'If you are impertinent, you will be punished, and punished, let me tell you, very severely,' was his conclusive rejoinder.

Such was my first introduction to the classics from which, I have been told, many of our cleverest men have derived so much solace and profit.[6]

It would be naïve to take Churchill's accounts as an exact description of what occurred on the day he first handled a Latin grammar. It would be more naïve still to be surprised at Winston's 'imaginativeness' or to accuse him of lying and duplicity. Winston, in a most felicitous and amusing way, is depicting himself most truly, telling us what we most want to know from his autobiography: the kind of person he is and, in a profound sense, always was.

Another example, this time from biography. Kim Philby, a British secret-service agent, was a counter-spy working for Russian Intelligence. Had a book or an article been written about Philby before he was detected, it would probably have been in the form of an appreciation of his services to the Crown. After his defection to Moscow, Philby was revealed as a long-term traitor. At this critical point, his whole career had to be reconsidered. Not so much his words and deeds as the interpretation to be put upon them had to be drastically altered. Even his unsuspecting wife had to reassess her marriage to Philby and ask herself, 'Why did he marry me? How sincere was he throughout our marriage in his protestations of love? Was he using me as one more pawn in his game of betraying his country?'

Any form of literature that purports to tell what 'really happened' – and this applies particularly to history – must allow for the interpretative element. There are innumerable presuppositions built into apparently simple notions such as 'getting at the facts' or 'recording what really happened'. Few historians today would agree with Lord Acton who said in his inaugural lecture at Cambridge (1895): 'We are still at the beginning of the documentary age which will tend to make history independent of historians.'[7] Such a phenomenon would be as remarkable as vision becoming independent of eyes! Contrary to what Acton thought, there never will be a golden age in which 'our historians will be sincere and our history certain'.[8] However touching our historians' sincerity may be, history will be none the more 'certain' for that. Even without deliberate concealment of evidence, no account is as unbiased, as uncoloured, as 'hygienic' as the writer likes to think. But there is nothing disturbing in this. Human beings are *never* neutral, uninvolved spectators or recording angels; they are participants in the events they judge by the very action of selecting them and judging them.[9]

It only remains to say that the gospels are a supreme example of the expressly acknowledged involvement of the early Christian community in the process of judging Jesus, of interpreting everything he said and did after he was 'unmasked' or detected as the Christ. With all the imagination and creative flair they had at their disposal, they brought the past of Jesus' life up to date, in the light of Easter faith, as the permanently saving word and deed of the Christ of God.

4. THE NATIVITY STORY IS PART OF THE GOSPEL

Sooner than born denied.
Should we pretend
He will not end
Abandoned, crucified?

Life is born in a cave.
Should we disguise
That he will rise
Glorious from his grave?

Swaddled, a manger his bed.
Who could forget
This babe is yet
Judge of living and dead?

The nativity story, related only by Luke and Matthew, is part of the gospel. It is, therefore, an Easter story since the gospel is from beginning to end the proclamation of Jesus' resurrection. The nativity story has the same depths to it as the accounts of the passion and Easter. To forget this is to misunderstand the special 'form' of the gospel which includes the process of 'updating' Jesus as the Christ. Unless we bring Easter faith to his birth, we may find ourselves indulging in pious talk about a delightful baby boy born in a setting called a stable but which, as many Christmas cards prove, would pass with minor modifications as a travel brochure for the blue grotto of Capri.

There are no sentimental overtones in the evangelists' accounts of the birth of Christ. On the contrary, they are asserting: Here we are dealing not with a repeatable, commonplace happening but with the decisive, saving word and deed of God. Here we are reflecting on the meaning and implications of God's Son sharing our weak, mortal human condition. Here is divine weakness that is ultimately stronger than men.

It was far from the evangelists' intentions to depict the Son's birth as picturesque, charming, heartwarming. This coming is a contradiction; it is brutal and searching like a two-edged sword because it is the breaking in of that folly of God which is wiser than the wisdom of all wise men. God's word is at work here judging history and all human affairs; and, despite all appearances, it is finally triumphant.

Sometimes at Christmas we try to pretend we don't know the end of the story. For the sake of the joyous festivities, we close our mind to the fact that this child is going to be crucified and rise again. What we try to forget or, at least, to put in parentheses, is precisely what the evangelists insist we remember. They want us to know that Jesus' life is, theologically speaking, all of a piece. This poor child in his crib is the crucified, the risen and the coming One; this is the Saviour of the world.

In the nativity narratives, the evangelists are preaching the Lordship of Jesus more obviously through symbols and the play of the imagination than in the passion and resurrection narratives. This is not to say these stories are less *true*. Exact description, we noted, is not the only way or necessarily the best way to depict the truth, especially the truth about God who is the Mystery.

The Church in its public prayers expresses the gospel character of Christ's birth. When we read the liturgical texts of Advent and Christmas we notice that we are not being oriented simply to the earliest moments of Jesus' existence. If anything, we seem to be directed more to the future than to the past, towards that crucified and risen One who is to come.

There is a fusing – to many a confusing – of the two comings of Christ. Which of the comings are we meant to focus on at Advent, the coming in weakness or the coming in glory? Both at the same time. Even this is not an adequate reply. We focus on both, together with a third coming that unites the other two. This third coming is here and now. Christ comes to us today.

Everything Christian has the threefold dimension of past, present and future. The future refers to a fulfilment to come, or better, a fulfilment in process of coming. To hope in the future, however dramatically we may paint this future, is really to have absolute confidence in God who, we believe, will allow himself to be found tomorrow as he let himself be found yesterday and today. He will never abandon us. He himself and his glory are our future.

Bornkamm remarks that the Church and its tradition centres not on yesterday but today. 'This today is not to be understood as a mere date in the calendar, but as a present appointed by God, and together with it a future made accessible by God.'[10] The Christian message only presents history in so far as it bears on today and opens up tomorrow.

An image springs to mind. The strands of past and future are gathered into the sliding knot of the ever-present. He who was born and crucified (past) and who is to come in glory (future) is with us now and always as the risen one (present).

5. A GOSPEL IS A PRESENTATION OF JESUS THE LORD

If he comes not now,
What if millennia ago he came?
He will not notice when my head I bow,
He will not hear me when I speak his Name.

If he comes at death,
If only at that hour he whispers, 'Look!
I am here to receive your last faint breath',
Today I will not find him in a Book.

If he comes for me,
Must he not come for me throughout each day,
And in the nights when I no longer see.
Then will he say, 'You have not lost the Way.'

A gospel, we have emphasized, is not and does not claim
to be an impartial piece of reporting. We now need to develop
the positive notion that a gospel is literally a *presentation* of
Jesus crucified, risen and to come. Unless Jesus is presented to
faith in his fullness we do not have the gospel (or good news)
which saves us but only accounts so unreliable that historians
may feel obliged to dismiss them as belonging to the realm of
fable or legend.

Jesus, for instance, is said to have healed a blind man. An
impartial historian committed to the sifting of evidence will
keep an open and essentially disinterested mind about this.
For the 'interested' believer, this story is part of the gospel
which affects his attitude to life. For him, the meaning of the
story, already spelled out in the fourth gospel, is: Jesus, the
Light of the world, who is to come and save us from that
endless night in which God cannot be found (future), healed
the blind man (past) and comes in his word to heal us (present)
of our blindness. The believer knows he is called upon to
think of himself as the blind man who recovers his sight at the
Lord's word.

The Sermon on the Mount is also an integral part of the gospel. Jesus taught the people and brought the law to fulfilment on the cross (past); he is to come as the judge of the living and the dead (future). In this sermon, the same Lord Jesus comes to me now (present), giving me the law of love to live by, a law by which I am already being judged.

Christians have never found it difficult to appreciate the threefold dimension of the Eucharist. In this sacred banquet, the victim of the passion, who is to be the food we everlastingly feed upon, is really present at our table. He fills our hearts today with peace and joy. Here is the real presence of him who was and is to come. C. H. Dodd writes: 'Past, present and future are indissolubly united in the sacrament. It may be regarded as a dramatization of the advent of the Lord, which is *at once* his remembered coming in humiliation and his desired coming in glory, both realized in the sacrament.'[11]

Christians should approach every passage of the Bible as they approach the Eucharist. In both Bible and Eucharist the same food, the ever-living word of God, awaits us.

To omit any of the three elements just mentioned is to lose something vital and essentially Christian. If we leave out the past as having no importance, Christianity becomes legend or abstract doctrines without any firm historical basis in the life of Jesus.[12] If we leave out the future, we Christians are people without hope. If we leave out the present, we are not ourselves touched by, or involved in the gospel story: our role is reduced to that of being passive spectators.

Most frequently, omissions occur in regard to Christ's miracles. The healing of the deaf, the multiplying of the loaves, the cleansing of the lepers – these, we are tempted to assume, were wonders that happened to other fortunate people a long time ago, a long way away. We then fail to see that built into them is this enormous saving hope: these wonders take place in us when we commit ourselves wholeheartedly to the resurrected Lord. The miracles of Jesus as presented to faith in the gospels indicate what life is all about and the rich possibilities hidden in life for us.

It could be said without excessive paradox that it is the real presence of the Lord to his disciples that enables them to comprehend the work that Jesus accomplished in his ministry. Historians to whom Jesus is not present in faith as their Lord will have no interest in what he is purported to have done so many centuries ago. 'Who cares', they might ask, 'about allegations of magic recounted in ancient writings of dubious reliability?' This objection shows that only the power of the gospel in our life today can open to us both the meaning and essential truth of the divine event that occurred two thousand years ago. More than that, the gospel will introduce us – in the sense of 'initiate' us – into that event.

Returning to Christ's nativity, we can say that, considered exclusively as an incident in the past, it loses those other two dimensions without which it is not the gospel: it does not speak of the hope to come; it does not particularly concern us today.

6. WHY THE INFANCY NARRATIVES AROSE

> Tell me about my Lord,
> Hide nothing, tell me all.
> Tell me about Mary
> And that birth in a humble stall.

Thoughts of Christmas take in not only Jesus' birth but also the present moment of each one of us to whom Christ the Lord comes now. It is the meaning of that birth – in continuity with Jesus' mission, death and resurrection – that the evangelists intend to highlight, so as to evoke faith in their readers. The Jewish Bible, the Old Testament, was the main source-book they used to explore the significance of Jesus' birth. In the course of this exploration, the Old Testament was not rejected or replaced but reassessed and brought up to date. The result was that the New Testament came into being. We are reminded again that in the eyes of the first Jewish-Christians, Jesus was the Jewish Messiah, the Son of David, the Son of God, and, as Luther says, every word of the Bible peals his name.

The evangelists did not have at hand enough hard facts about Jesus' birth to provide any biographical account of his infancy. Their aim, in any case, is never primarily to give information about Jesus but to express what they believe him to be in the hope that we, too, may believe. Theologians who used to read the gospels expecting to gain from them detailed and consistent information about Jesus' early life soon came across insurmountable difficulties. For example, the Benedictine, Abbot Vonier, a progressive scholar in his day, wrote in his book, *The Personality of Christ*:

> There is an apparent contradiction in the gospels in this matter of Christ's manifestations. His birth was surrounded with the elements of the miraculous; and not once is an appeal made to it in Christ's later career. It is hardly credible that the vision of the shepherds on the night of the nativity and the visit of the wise men from the East, left no traces on the popular imagination. After all, thirty years is not a long period, and for a nation like the Jewish nation, the marvellous is remembered with infinite care and delight. No doubt the traditions survived; perhaps even they acquired volume and strength with time. But there is one providential circumstance told in the gospels which alters the case completely: the rapid and prolonged change of abode of the family round which there had been the momentary glory. The disappearance into Egypt of the 'Holy Family' told by St Matt. (ch. 2) deprived the glorious tale of its hero, and instead of making the reputation of Mary's Son, it helped to swell the volume of fair legends that made everybody look to the immediate coming of the Messiah. Far from helping Christ's cause, they went against him, as the fact of his having been born at Bethlehem was not known.[13]

This remarkable fabrication shows what happens when the literary form of the infancy narratives is misunderstood. Vonier, supposing that they provide exact, historical information is at a loss to know why Jesus was not subsequently proclaimed by his people as divine.

An examination of the literary form shows that what we have in Matthew and Luke is not the record of a series of supernatural events which must at all costs be harmonized with each other and dated in the calendar alongside more ordinary happenings. Rather, the two evangelists, in the light of their Easter faith, are reflecting theologically upon the nativity of him who had shown himself in the end to be the Christ. Since they, like their Old Testament predecessors, thought in pictorial not abstract fashion they each tell an unforgettable story in which their readers are invited to discern the ways of God and confess their faith in him.

Even the genealogies drawn up by Matthew and Luke are literary devices to express their belief about Jesus. Nothing could have a more solid appearance of historical reliability than a genealogy, yet a comparison of Matthew's and Luke's shows that, out of seventy-six names recorded, there is agreement on only sixteen of them. The genealogy is part of the theology. Matthew traces Jesus' origin to Abraham to confess he is the fulfilment of Israel. Luke goes further back to Adam to indicate that Jesus is the head of a renewed humanity.

The angels, too, are part of the theological story which these authors are telling. The presence of the angels in the story is a way of representing God's mysterious presence in the humble event of Jesus' birth. To ask historical questions about angels is about as rewarding as the medieval disputations in the famed University of Paris when it was solemnly discussed whether Jesus ascended into heaven with or without clothes. If he wore clothes, what became of them when he got 'up there'? If he didn't, did he scandalously appear before his disciples naked?

A further literary device employed in Matthew's gospel is the dream in which Jews at that time supposed God revealed himself. Matthew uses this device to encounter objections that arose later on when the virgin birth was preached. Matthew's reaction is to say that Joseph had the same doubts about Mary's virginity and they were set at rest by God himself through a revelation in a dream. Matthew's constant stratagem – it was very Jewish – is to theologize through stories and images and to answer an objection to a part of his story *by developing the story*. Joseph's dream is a polemical stratagem by which Matthew answers the charge of illegitimacy brought against Jesus as a result of the story of the virgin birth.

An outline of the historical context may explain better the origin, scope and meaning of the infancy narratives.

When the gospel was first preached, interest centred exclusively on Jesus' death and resurrection, the crucial event by which Jesus became Lord and Christ. Of this, many witnesses survived for a considerable time. The death and resurrection of Christ, in their view, had paved the way for his coming from heaven, a coming to which they looked forward so longingly. When the Lord came, they believed, he would judge the living and the dead and bring about the general resurrection. This was already foreshadowed, even initiated in his own resurrection. He was the 'first fruits' guaranteeing a bumper harvest.

Later, the new converts wanted to know more about the Lord Jesus whose coming in glory was seemingly delayed. Stories, sayings, anecdotes about him began to circulate at different places and in various cultural settings. In preaching, teaching, legislating, a deed or parable of his was taken over and often adapted to suit the current local circumstances. This seemed to them a most reasonable thing to do in that Jesus, being risen, was everywhere among them. His word was God's word, alive and active; it contained the implicit answer to all their deepest needs.

The disciples who had been with Jesus – especially the apostles who had followed him throughout his ministry and witnessed his resurrection – must have recounted the stories of their Lord in the light of their Easter faith. It cannot be over-emphasized that only at Easter did the disciples fully pierce Jesus' disguise and perceive his life and, above all, his death as the final saving word of God. This explains why they could not simply describe straightforwardly what once they saw; their task was to preach what in unbelief they had *not* seen but what now they believed God had been doing all along in Jesus' life. 'Pure' description would have been distortion. Out of the shattering realization that Jesus had been not at all the kind of Messiah they had expected, the gospels ultimately emerged. *They are not about Jesus nor about the Christ but about Jesus Christ.* We will follow some of the more important ramifications of this discovery later on.

Many 'memories' – some authors speak of 'kerygmatized' memories of Jesus – were circulating in isolated fashion before the evangelists put them together for their own editorial purposes. The passion narrative assumed a final theological framework quite early. This is clear from Mark's more or less continuous account. His was the earliest, and even the fourth gospel does not elaborate as much on the passion as on the rest of Jesus' ministry. But for the most part, the order and siting of what Jesus said and did could not be recovered; the sources were too varied and unsystematic for that.

Later still, when the disciples wanted a kind of consistent life-story of their Lord, the nativity narratives were penned. There was a pious tradition once – though it had no foundation – that Luke received 'inside information' from Mary. In fact, the narratives reveal that there were no witnesses to supply data on the birth of Jesus when it had become a matter of interest.

A superficial critic might suggest the infancy narratives are, after all, only pious fables, fairy stories, uncontrolled conjecture. They are not. Based perhaps on earlier Aramaic sources, they contain some of the deepest, most developed theological reflection. They are pure gospel, the presenting in inspired pictorial fashion of what is believed about Jesus crucified, alive and to come.

7. THE MAGI

The gospel according to Matthew tells how wise men, the Magi, came from the East where they had seen the star of the king of the Jews. At Jerusalem, the Jewish capital, where their journey first took them, the star which they had seen in the East reappeared. It went before them to Bethlehem and came to rest over the exact house where the child was. Their joy knew no bounds when they found the child with Mary, his mother. They fell down and worshipped him, offering him precious gifts of gold, frankincense and myrrh.

There, in outline, is the story of the Magi. It seems a very simple, pious, legendary story – especially if the Magi are represented as kings, as is so often the case in paintings. Here is a tender picture of earthly kings worshipping the King of kings.

The critic can run riot if he wants to. An excellent example of a fable, he might say. We know that stars are not moderately sized lanterns hung from the vault of heaven. They cannot come close to the earth and, becoming footloose, conveniently guide foreign tourists to a little home in Bethlehem.

Even those Christians who are most keen to take the gospel text literally on every conceivable occasion would have to admit that the star presents something of a problem.

In the thirteenth century, St Thomas Aquinas affirmed the veridical character of the Magi's perception of a star while denying that what they saw was one of the stars in the heavens. He gave several reasons for the denial. The star went in the wrong direction, that is, from East to West; it appeared at midday as well as at night, which even the moon cannot do (which raises a doubt as to whether St Thomas had ever looked at the sky by day); it went into hiding over Jerusalem; it did not have continuous movement but rested when the Magi did; it came down low over the particular house where Jesus was, to indicate its whereabouts.[14]

The star's ability to give such exact directions prompted the medievals to speculate on whether the star was an appearance of the holy Spirit or perhaps an angel. St Thomas prefers to think of the star as created by God for the occasion; it was located not in the heavens but close to the earth and set in motion by the will of God.

Aquinas, following the exegetical methods of his age, insists on keeping to a star that did not appear in the gospel text. It is puzzling to know why Aquinas should go to such lengths to retain this star when it was *not* a star as we would understand the term. The obvious solution does not seem to have entered his mind as a possibility: the star is to be accounted for by the literary form of the evangelist.

St Thomas' exegetical method is, in essence, perpetuated in our day with greater astronomical competence by the Director of the Vatican Observatory, Fr P. J. Treanor, SJ, who writes: 'Among the several astronomical interpretations of the star of the Magi there can be little doubt that the one most worthy of serious consideration is the triple conjunction of Jupiter and Saturn in 7 BC, a date which fits in rather well with the most probable estimate of the birth of Christ. In that year, these two planets approached each other closely three times, a fact extremely rare in the annals of astronomy.'[15]

Fr Treanor is forced to admit the comprehensive limitations of his own hypothesis, 'the one most worthy of serious consideration'. The text says a 'star'; and can the association of planets be so called? The text says that the star disappeared and reappeared; can planets (read 'star') behave in such an irregular and astronomically reprehensible way? Further, since stars are not visible by day, must we presume the Magi only travelled at night?

It is staggering that in the twentieth century such learned irrelevancies are put forward as a possible way of interpreting the gospel. The attempt to keep literally to the text issues in wholesale manipulation of the text in any case. This being so, it is surely preferable to think that the star resulted not from the special creation by God of a suitably small heavenly body nor from the conjunction of two planets which the Magi noticed and fathomed so precisely but from the literary leanings of the evangelist. This explanation is simple and comprehensive.

Few Christians today are worried by it. I have only emphasized what modern exegetes take for granted to encourage the reader to look on the infancy narratives as a whole as first-century Christian documents, for that is what they are. This does not mean they are naïve. It is the literal interpretation of them in a fashion never intended by the authors that is naïve and often frivolous. Scholarly trimmings, whether from the fields of science, metaphysics or theology, are no substitute for literary criticism.

Now to a consideration of the theological meaning of the Magi.

8. THE THEOLOGICAL MEANING OF THE MAGI

Wise men came out of the East. They came from where the golden sun was daily born and whence came strange, exotic riches, carried by the traders. The East was the place of mystery, the uncharted region. The wise men came, then, from lands of sunrise and wandering stars and the mists of morning.

They are depicted by Matthew as star-gazers or astrologers. From the unmapped territory they are guided by a star.

If this can be surmised from the text, what is its most obvious theological meaning?

These men are truly wise. They are seeking the Word and Wisdom of God. They are guided by a star to indicate that this child is no ordinary child but king of the Jews. The star they saw in the Orient is *his* star. All the elements are obedient to this child and testify to him. We should remember that this story arose when Jesus was spoken of as one who calmed the winds and the waves. The whole earth darkened at his death in a terrible mourning, and the temple veil of Jewry was torn. Dead men walked around Jerusalem afterwards. All this startling imagery was created by the evangelist to help us penetrate the meaning of the crucifixion. The star, too, may not be a supernatural portent but it is significant, nonetheless.

The Magi came not simply out of the East but out of paganism. The star indicates something more wonderful than itself: the child. He is the one to be worshipped and not the eternal ever-glowing stars in heaven. The Magi are thus shown to belong symbolically to the very heart of the gospel message: the good news is for everyone, even for the star-gazing pagans. It knows no barriers of space or race. Israel's Messiah is the king and saviour of the Gentiles, too.

The Gentiles, in the persons of the Magi, rejoiced to be led to the king of the Jews. Pagans are seen, with tender irony, to be eager for Israel's Messiah to be born. They cannot wait for it. They travel from afar, from the earth's distant horizon. Yet at the time the gospel was written, Israel – here represented by Herod and the highest Jewish Council, the Sanhedrin, whom Herod consulted – Israel, though already on the spot and so well and long prepared, was showing no such eagerness. The Messiah, the Son of David, was born in David's city, Bethlehem. He had come home. And no one welcomed him. A solitary star had more effect on the Gentiles than had centuries of divine action and prophetic teaching on Israel. Matthew is saying this with sadness not bitterness.

The Magi confess their faith at the crib as another Gentile, the Roman centurion, confesses his at the cross: 'Truly this man was son of God' (Matt. 27:54). The Magi represent pictorially words of Jesus to that centurion whose servant he had healed: 'Not even in Israel have I found such faith. I tell you, many will come from the East and West and sit at the table with Abraham, Isaac and Jacob, while the sons of the kingdom will be thrown into the outer darkness' (Matt. 8:10–11).

The Magi bring both joy and sadness. Joy that all the world is eager to receive the Lord; sadness that Israel as a body was later to refuse to worship her king. It is understandable why in some Latin countries Epiphany is celebrated more lavishly than Christmas. It is our festival since on this day the light has shone on us Gentiles. In the story, the Gentiles come *to* Christ. This is a way of saying that Christ has come *for* the Gentiles; he has come for us.

To summarize: there are two superficial approaches to Matthew's Magi story.

The first is: everything must be accepted literally. The wise men did see something answering to the description of a 'star' in the East, understood its import, followed it from Jerusalem whence it led them to the stable in Bethlehem.

The Magi would have grasped the gospel message before it was ever preached by Jesus and fulfilled in his cross, presumably by means of some interior, 'prophetic' illumination. This would have been a highly miraculous portent to mark the advent of God's Son.

It would seem more reasonable, however, to assume this story arose to express the universalism of the gospel which only became clear to the Church after it had listened to Peter's and Paul's arguments and seen the effect of the first missionary preaching.

The second superficial approach is: the Magi are in no sense historical; it is rather silly, if not dishonest, to go on telling the story of Jesus' birth in this literally 'fabulous' way.

This view suffers from the illusion quite common in Western academic circles that there is only one definition of truth to which God or man can grant approval: the conformity of word (or thought) to empirical reality.

Both approaches ignore the nature of a gospel as a presentation (or making present) of the Lord Jesus Christ. Without the symbolism of the Magi the nativity is not complete as a gospel story, a story for now.

The Magi stand for the divine meaning of Jesus' birth: the Lord who came for all men's salvation and who is to come in glory, comes now to everyone – be he Jew or Gentile – who accepts him with a joyful and humble heart.

9. JESUS THE NEW MOSES

In the story of King Herod's slaughter of the innocents there is further evidence of the talent of the author of the first gospel. It is generally agreed that he constructed his gospel so as to depict Jesus as the new Moses.

Moses was the great saviour of his people. The book of Exodus tells how a tyrant king, the Pharaoh of Egypt, afraid that the Hebrews in his kingdom were growing too powerful and numerous, decided to wipe them out at source. He ordered the midwives to the Hebrew women to kill at birth every male Hebrew child. When the midwives refused to comply, Pharaoh decreed that all these children should be cast into the Nile. Moses, at the age of three months, was hidden by his mother in a basket made of bulrushes. Pharaoh's daughter found him by the river bank and adopted him as her own. This was the child who one day was to set his people free.

When he grew up, Moses had to leave Egypt for a time since he was afraid for his life. He knew he had been seen killing and burying in the sand an Egyptian who was beating one of his people. But he returned from exile. He led the Hebrews out of Egyptian bondage to become a new people in the exhilarating openness of the desert where God made a covenant with them and gave them, on Mount Sinai, a law by which to rule their lives.

Jesus was the new Moses. He was destined to set his people free from a bondage more terrible than Egypt's and to create a new people. He gave them, in Matthew's editing of his material, a new law to live by on the mountain top: a new law that surpassed the old in its emphasis on interior worship and love. And he forged the new and everlasting covenant between God and men in his own blood.

The new Moses was also depicted by Matthew as pursued and persecuted by a tyrant king, Herod, who feared for his throne. Jesus escapes the slaughter of the male children of Bethlehem and flies with Mary and Joseph to Egypt. When Herod dies and the family can return home, Matthew sees fulfilled an Old Testament text (Hos. 11:1): 'Out of Egypt I called my son.'

The construction of Matthew's story is splendid but in some respects, it must be admitted, rather complex. The author, as is his custom, sees many apparently irrelevant texts of the Jewish Bible fulfilled in Jesus the Saviour. One example is Rachel weeping in Rama for her lost children. Rachel was the wife of Jacob, the father of Israel, and the mother of Joseph and Benjamin. Those tears of hers were already symbolic when they are referred to in Jeremiah. The prophet (31:15) conjured Rachel out of her tomb to mourn the exile of some of her children in Babylon centuries afterwards. It has been suggested that the road to exile led past the traditional site of Rachel's tomb. Exegetes wonder whether Matthew, with his vivid imagination, stage-managed Jesus' departure to Egypt in order

that the text of Hosea 11:1 could be 'fulfilled' to the delight
of his Jewish-Christian readers. There is almost verbal identity
between Matthew's words and the Exodus text.

Matthew's use of the Old Testament is conditioned by his
knowledge of what Jesus became. He is certainly not romanticizing about Jesus' birth as we sometimes do at Christmas
time. He cannot forget for a moment that liberators of peoples
are born to suffer. And the Saviour of Israel was no exception.

10. LUKE'S USE OF I SAMUEL

Luke, like Matthew, turned to the Old Testament for passages
which would give a structure to his story. He chose the First
Book of Samuel.

Samuel's mother Hannah was for a long time barren, for 'the
Lord had closed her womb'. In Jewish eyes, it was a disgrace
for a woman to be childless, so much were children considered
a blessing from the Lord and the reason for a husband's
pride.

> Truly sons are a gift from the Lord,
> a blessing the fruit of the womb.
> Indeed the sons of youth
> are like arrows in the hand of a warrior.
> O the happiness of the man
> who has filled his quiver with these arrows!
> (Ps. 127:3-5)

The just man is given this marvellous promise of domestic bliss:

> You will be happy and prosper;
> your wife like a fruitful vine
> in the heart of your house;
> your children like shoots of the olive
> around your table (Ps. 128:2-3).

The priest Eli one day discovered Hannah in the temple and
learned of her distress. His prayer for her was: 'Go in peace
and the God of Israel grant your petition which you have

made to him.' She replied: 'Let your handmaid find favour in your eyes' (1 Sam. 1:18).

In due time, Hannah conceived and bore a son whom she named Samuel because she had asked God for him. As soon as Samuel was weaned she took him to the Lord's house at Shiloh where the ark of the covenant was, and there dedicated him to the Lord. Then Hannah sang her Magnificat:

> My heart exults in the Lord;
>> my strength is exalted in the Lord.
> My mouth derides my enemies,
>> because I rejoice in my salvation . . .
> The bows of the mighty are broken
>> but the feeble gird on strength . . .
> The Lord kills and brings life;
>> he brings down to Sheol, and raises up.
> The Lord makes poor and makes rich;
>> he brings low, he also exalts.
> He raises up the poor from the dust;
>> he lifts the needy from the ash heap,
> to make them sit with princes
>> and inherit a seat of honour (2:1, 4, 6–8).

Samuel ministered to the Lord in the presence of Eli the priest. There in the Lord's house, 'the boy Samuel continued to grow both in stature and in favour with the Lord and with men' (2:26). He was destined to be the faithful priest who would fulfil God's purposes. The word of the Lord came to Samuel and confirmed him as the great prophet (or spokesman) of God.

There are countless allusions to the Jewish Bible in Luke's account of the infancy, but this story in 1 Samuel provides him with a general scheme by which to depict the birth of the Baptist and of Jesus.

Elizabeth, the Baptist's mother, was barren and, like her husband, advanced in years. Zechariah, her husband, did not believe Gabriel's words spoken to him as he was exercising his priesthood in the temple; and for his unbelief he was struck dumb. But Elizabeth conceived and, as the months drew on, she hid herself saying: 'Thus the Lord has done to me in the days when he looked on me, to take away my reproach among men' (1:25).

When Mary conceives and goes to visit Elizabeth, her cousin, her greeting causes the babe to leap for joy in Elizabeth's womb. This is a superb symbol of the prophetic herald, in the presence of Mary, the ark of the Lord, acknowledging his master.

The birth of Jesus is more portentous than the Baptist's. In Luke's story he is conceived and born of a virgin. The word of God came personally to her and she, in contrast to Zechariah, receives it humbly and with faith as the handmaiden of the Lord. Her son is to be called holy, the Son of God (1:35).

When Elizabeth calls her blessed among women, Mary replies with her Magnificat. (The 'similarity' with Hannah's needs no elaborating.) Her child was born at Bethlehem and afterwards dedicated in the temple where Simeon, taking him in his arms, declares him to be God's salvation for all peoples and the glory of God's people, Israel (2:32).

After Jesus was lost and found in the temple, Luke writes: 'Jesus increased in wisdom and in stature and in favour with God and man' (2:52). Here is the new Samuel in the temple of God, his Father.

II. JESUS AND THE ROMAN EMPIRE

The traditions on which Luke relied when he compiled his story were not those used by Matthew. In view of the evangelists' theological purposes, we ought not to try to set out the incidents, presented by both as vehicles for faith, in some kind of historical sequence. For instance, it makes no sense, since it violates the literary form of the infancy narratives, to ask: Did the Magi visit Jesus (Matthew's gospel) before or after he was presented in the temple (Luke's gospel)? Luke knew nothing of the tradition which spoke of the Magi, and, in view of the literary form, there was never a question, anyway, of making his story harmonize with Matthew's. The aim of both was to bring out as best they could the meaning of Jesus' presence among men.

Luke says that Caesar Augustus decreed there should be a universal census and this census was carried out when Quirinius was governor of Syria. Certainly, Quirinius did carry out a census, but in AD 6–7. The governor of Syria at the time of Jesus' birth was called Saturninus. Luke (or his sources) was mistaken on a point of fact.

Other problems arise from Luke's telling of the story. He twice implies that Mary was a virgin (1:34; 3:23). Presumably he wanted his readers to understand that Jesus is from God, is the Son of God. At the same time he says that Jesus is of David's line because Joseph was. But if Jesus was really virginally born, how would this legal fiction provide an adequate basis for Jesus' royal birth and Davidic sonship?

All this overlooks the fact that Luke is interested not in genealogical details but entirely in Jesus and his importance for mankind. He is content to depict at this time a census for all the world (that is, the Roman Empire), so that he can find a literary way to get Jesus, known to be an inhabitant of Galilee, to Bethlehem, David's city, where he was born.[16] The pagan Emperor Augustus is to play his part in carrying out God's designs for Israel just as Cyrus, the Persian king, was once instrumental in ending Israel's exile in Babylon.

Luke is so skilful a story-teller even his asides are worth pondering.

For instance, Jesus is set down as an insignificant individual in a census of the world. When the world through its great Emperor was supposedly getting its accounts right, Jesus the carpenter's son, born at Bethlehem, figured three quarters of the way down the fourth column of scroll 2053, Palestinian division. In a word, he figured nowhere. It was the same when he died. His name, no doubt, was entered in the Roman book of executions, lost among innumerable other crucified malefactors.

There is, on Luke's part, an unconscious irony here. The world would one day count its years no longer *ab urbe condita*, from the time of the foundation of the imperial city. It would speak of *anno Domini* (even though scholars got their calculations wrong by a handful of years, for Jesus was born in the days of Herod the Great who died in 4 BC).

Famous events, the rise and fall of empires would be historically situated by their relation to the birth of that Lord who received a brief entry in the census and execution book of the world's most powerful nation. Jesus, from start to finish, pushed around by the Master-race, a depressed person, a nobody. Always obedient to the powers that be, always humble, he who was *Kyrios*, the Lord of heaven and earth, bowed his head and was victorious.

Chesterton has caught the spirit of Luke's aside in his Christmas song:

> There fared a mother driven forth
> Out of an inn to roam;
> In the place where she was homeless
> All men are at home.
> The crazy stable close at hand,
> With shaking timber and shifting sand,
> Grew a stronger thing to abide and stand
> Than the square stones of Rome.[17]

Not that Luke, a Roman citizen, had actually contemplated the decline and fall of the Roman Empire! He could just as easily have envisaged the extinction of the sun. All he knew was that Jesus, the Son of God, in his humility was stronger than Rome.

12. NO ROOM IN THE INN

Luke says that when Mary had given birth to her first-born she wrapped him in swaddling clothes and laid him in a manger, because there was no room in the inn (2:7). Here, as was usual in biblical tradition, the profoundest theological themes are expressed in story form and almost with nonchalance.

The child born of Mary is God's Son. Mary's first-born is

God's first-born as Israel, whose Messiah Jesus is, became God's first-born at the Exodus.

'First-born' was the technical term in Israel for the first male child opening the womb. This child was to be offered to the Lord and then 'redeemed', 'bought back' instead of being slaughtered as had been the primitive, barbaric custom. This child also received his father's special blessing – the significance of the blessing is illustrated in the story of Jacob and Esau in Genesis 27.

Jesus is wrapped up like any other baby newly born. His title is Son of God but he is not some supernatural being. He is not a god who has for a time assumed the form of a human being as in some religious fables. Nor is he made of plaster. He is a baby. Angels sing in Luke's story above his head. God's messengers are there – as they figure in the resurrection narratives – to express the divineness of this event; they summarize Christ's own message in terms of glory to God on high and peace to men who are God's friends. But this child is wrapped in swaddling clothes. He needs warmth and attire, tenderness and mother-love. It would be hard to find in the infancy story any basis for the theological opinion once quite common that Jesus was in some way abnormal and constitutionally incapable of pain.

The sign of their Messiah given to the shepherds was a child wrapped in swaddling clothes and laid in a manger. This is David's son, the saviour who is to become Lord and Christ. This is he who was to say, 'Foxes have holes, and birds of the air have nests; but the Son of Man has nowhere to lay his head' (9:58). This is he who was to enter Jerusalem meek and lowly, riding on an ass (19:35). This is the same Jesus, Luke is implying, who later on was to give his followers a still more unconvincing sign of his messiah-ship: the crucifixion. That, too, was to be a hole-in-the-corner affair, an execution to enliven a public holiday. What happened to him then? – for we must never forget the story's ending. A pauper, he was buried in another man's grave, having been helplessly wrapped once more, this time in the swaddling clothes of death (23:53). The story hangs together. It is all of a piece theologically.

Luke explains the stable birth by saying it came about 'because there was no room for them in the inn' (2:7). We have in this perhaps the most superb and ironic aside of all. He slips it in very casually, and yet the meaning of it is breathtaking. There was no room for the Saviour to be born. Like any baby, a fragile, vulnerable, soft-craniumed, red-skinned, black-haired, eye-twitching little mite. Could the world really not find room for one so small?

'No room in the inn.' This is Luke's pictorial comment on John's words, 'He came to his own home, and his own people received him not' (John 1:11). It is not too allegorical to suggest that in Luke's mind the inn stands for mankind. From first to last, Jesus is the outsider, the unwanted and rejected one. The world is far too crowded. He is a nuisance. In the story, we are not to understand he was excluded from the local Hilton but even the primitive hostelry of the day was denied him. Jesus was too much of a liability.

In Luke's story it is Mary who is turned away. She is not simply a pregnant woman who embarrasses the local inhabitants; she is, at a deeper level, the Word-bearer, the Spokeswoman of Israel. She is to utter God's Word in an incarnational way exceeding all the ways in which it came to Israel formerly. And she is turned away. Luke, for whom Mary is 'blessed among women' (1:42), is telling us that Jesus was rejected even in his mother's womb.

The lesson of all this, since Luke is writing a gospel, is: To him who came and is to come, let us say, 'Welcome.' Now is the day of salvation. Is the Saviour still the outcast? Is there still no room for him?

13. THE SHEPHERDS

We miss the meaning of the shepherds if we think of them only as nice, old gentlemen with pious, weather-beaten faces and white beards. Like the Magi in Matthew's gospel, Luke's shepherds are integral to the preaching of the good news.

They were keeping watch over their flock by night. Therefore, it can hardly have been winter-time, although it is a legitimate extension of Luke's story to think of snow being on the ground. After all, he is trying to tell us that Jesus, in general, had a cold, inhospitable reception.

The Church elaborated further on Luke's story but in complete fidelity to his mood and intentions. The date of the Christmas festival was chosen to coincide with the pagan festival of the Birth of the Sun which it eventually replaced. The ox and the ass were permitted to creep into the stable in the East in the fourth century as a kind of commentary on Isaiah's words:

> The ox knows its owner, and the ass its master's crib;
> but Israel does not know, my people does not understand
> (1:3).

I consider it is not a legitimate extension of Luke to depict the shepherds as devout, religious, law-abiding folk. This would seem to be very far from his intentions.

It is true that some aspects of pastoral life are used in the Old Testament to show God's care and concern for his people. Psalm 23 gives this idyllic picture of God's protection:

> The Lord is my shepherd:
> there is nothing I shall want.
> Fresh and green are the pastures
> where he gives me repose.
> Near restful waters he leads me,
> to revive my drooping spirits.

In the time of Exile, when Israel's leaders were faithless, Ezekiel felt called upon to prophesy against the shepherds of Israel who were feeding themselves and not the flock. They had not strengthened the weak or healed the sick or bound up the crippled or brought back the strayed or searched out the lost. The sheep of God's flock had been scattered on every mountain and hill. Yahweh, through the prophet, says: 'I myself will be the shepherd of my sheep, and I will make them

lie down, says the Lord God. I will seek the lost, and I will
bring back the strayed, and I will bind up the crippled, and I
will strengthen the weak' (Ezek. 34:15).

Jesus presented himself as someone who exercised God's
own shepherding and caring love. He came to seek out the
lost. He was willing to travel a long way in God's name to find
one lost sheep.

In the fourth gospel, Jesus declares himself to be the 'Good
Shepherd' (10:11), one who goes before his sheep, calling them
all by name (10:3). He protects them with his own body as the
shepherds did when they sealed up the fold at night, with
their own body as a door (10:7). He is not a hireling, but gives
up his life for his sheep.

Because of all these biblical allusions, there is a temptation
to look upon the shepherds at Christ's birth with appreciative
eyes: shepherds in Israel here recognize the Shepherd of Israel.

But Luke is hinting at something else. He knew that shepherds were outsiders in Israel. Pious people looked on them
askance. Because of their job, they couldn't keep the whole of
the law: the Sabbath rest, the detailed ritual, the washing of
hands and plates and all the other rubrics of purification. They
used, sometimes of necessity, to pasture their sheep in foreign
territory as a result of which trespassing they were considered
'unclean'. Like the tax-collectors, the shepherds *by profession*
were sinners and excommunicate. Luke's message is: It is for
people of this sort that Jesus has come. Indeed, they are the
first to recognize him. Jesus, despite his own unpretentious-
ness, is welcomed by humble 'sinners' of Israel.

Jesus was a remarkably non-institutional figure. He never
seems to have been bent on bringing people back to the
synagogue. His concern was with the heart not with a man's
livelihood. This emerges strongly from the incident in Jesus'
life when he went in to dine with a pharisee. His host was
astonished to see that Jesus did not wash before dinner. Jesus
said to him: 'Now you pharisees cleanse the outside of the cup
and of the dish, but inside you are full of extortion and
wickedness' (Luke 11:39). Jesus dares to say that the im-
peccable are unholier than sinners.

The shepherds stand for the sinners who continuously surrounded Jesus in his ministry. They didn't wash their hands or tithe sprigs of flowers; but inside them was love and the thirst for real justice. Jesus will eat with them, walk with them, love them, choose from among them his closest disciples. One of them, Magdalen, a woman of the streets, will wash his feet with her tears. One day, in the middle of two outlaws he will die.

The central role in the gospel of the outcasts, the lawless ones, the sinners, the excommunicates, is represented by the shepherds at the crib. They testify that Jesus exalts the humble and searches out all lost sheep even when they come before him in the guise of shepherds.

14. MOTHER AND CHILD

With God, before the world began,
The uncreated Word in whom we move and are
Was there when sun and moon from darkness sprang;
He watched the kindling of each star.
With man, when darkness conquered light,
The humbled Word made flesh, so small like us, so weak,
Is all the world in his proud mother's sight,
And from her lips learns how to speak.

Mary is the archetypal mother of Western tradition. Any artistic representation of a mother and child is likely to remind us of The Mother and Child, The Madonna with the Saviour in her arms.

When, in the imagery of the fourth gospel, God's eternal Word comes down to earth, he is Mary's child. She it was who taught Jesus to walk, to speak, to pray. She gave him the assurances that he was loved; this means that she was the condition, humanly speaking, of his capacity to love others.

Catholics and Orthodox stress more than the Protestant traditions that Mary is important. She is not a mere tool of God by means of which God's Son was to be born; she is thought of rather as the initial sign of the gospel – far more important, therefore, than the Magi and the shepherds. In the words of Karl Barth, one of the most eminent Protestant theologians of our time: 'In the person of Mary, mankind does then have a part in the incarnation. Not merely passively does mankind play this part, nor triumphantly, but by virtue of its freedom – even that of the weaker creature, of a servant: "Behold, I am the handmaid of the Lord" ' (Luke 1:38).[18]

The early fathers said Mary was far more blessed through believing in Christ than through conceiving the flesh of Christ. She became holy not by bearing and giving birth to Jesus but through faith, hope and charity.

Modern biblical studies reinforce the fathers' testimony. In Luke's story, Mary is the virgin daughter of Zion, the ideal image of Israel. Israel represented all peoples in God's sight, and Mary became at the annunciation the representative of that representative race. She said yes for everyone when she consented to be the mother of the Lord. Mary was full of grace, or, better, the 'highly favoured' daughter of Zion, the embodiment of Zephaniah's Israel: 'the king of Israel, the Lord, is in your midst' (Zeph. 3:15).

We must remember that Luke is writing theology rather than history. Throughout his account he is showing in pictorial fashion the break between the old world and the new as well as the divineness of what is done in Mary.

The holy Spirit will come upon you,
and the power of the Most High will overshadow you;
therefore the child to be born will be called holy,
the Son of God (1:35).

Mary was overshadowed, or 'over-clouded' by the divine presence. Over her at this moment of new creation, the Spirit hovers. This justified the fathers in calling Mary 'the new Eve', for she was truly the Mother of all the living. The cloud that in Israel's saga guided God's people to the promised land came to rest in her. The cloud that filled Solomon's temple filled her; she was, in consequence, more blessed than that sacred spot where God's name dwelt and towards which no prayer was offered in vain. The cloud out of which God said, 'This is my beloved Son', the cloud to which Christ ascended and from which he will come in glory, settles in Mary so that her child will be called holy, the Son of God. For the cloud is the divine presence, the '*Shekinah*', the glory of God.

God is really present in Mary's child-bearing, speaking his decisive word, making the final revelation of his glory.

15. ISRAEL'S IDEAS ON VIRGINITY

When wife and husband, both wide-eyed,
Their new-born baby hold,
There's proof that seed is multiplied
More than a hundredfold.

For woman is a fruitful field,
Her breasts are full of grace;
Her womb has never ceased to yield
The future of the race.

When we from nothing came to birth
Eternity began.
What then's most godlike on the earth?
A woman and a man.

A virgin is life's cul-de-sac;
Why should I praise her, why?
We ought for life to give life back,
Increase and multiply.

Remember, virgin, when you die,
Life's stream in you has dried.
To millions will you life deny?
Can this be justified?

But if, despite the gift God gave,
Your field is never sown,
Your womb will be the widest grave
The world has ever known.

Matthew, keen as always to see the Old Testament 'fulfilled' in the New, sees a prophecy of Mary's virgin motherhood in the words of Isaiah 7:14:

> Behold, a virgin shall conceive and bear a son,
> and his name shall be called 'Emmanuel',
> which means, God-with-us.

Scholars have pointed out that *parthenos*, the word for 'virgin' in the Greek Bible, translates the original Hebrew '*almah*' which means simply 'young woman'.

Luke also expresses the mystery of the Son's coming in terms of a virgin birth. Mary says to the angelic messenger who foretells that she will conceive a child, 'How can this be, since I have no husband?' (1:34). And later (3:23), he writes: 'Jesus, when he began his ministry, was about thirty years of age, being the son (as was supposed) of Joseph.'

Luke was far less concerned to stress the miraculous character of this conception and this birth than the theological meaning of it. This meaning merits analysis.

Many Christians have become so accustomed to the notion of consecrated virginity they hardly pause to reflect upon its revolutionary character.

Virginity – and what is said of virginity can be said of its normal accompaniment, celibacy – is not at all loved, admired or even understood by most people. Why should it be?

Remember T. S. Eliot's 'East Coker' with its golden picture of man and woman dancing round the open fire at night. 'Two and two, necessarye coniunction.' (He writes in early English to bring out the sense of perpetuity that the embrace of man and woman evokes in us.) A scene of rustic solemnity is there or rustic laughter.

Somehow – it is because of their association – man and woman belong, yes, they belong to the soil their feet are pounding. Their rhythmic dancing is the sacrament of the deeper rhythm of the seasons and the stars, of milking time and harvest time, and the rhythm of living and dying.

Certainly, matrimony is the loved thing. It binds people to the earth and to all living things that have been and are to come. Men pass, dust into dust; but in marriage they also pass on the gift of life: other dust lives and dances because of them. In their children men express their gratitude for their own existence, they repay their debt to the race.

As with people in general, so it was with Jews. No mention of dedicated and perpetual virginity among them. Childlessness was a curse, a harsh judgement of the Lord, not a blessing. A childless woman had to endure 'a reproach among men'. This is why Jeremiah vowed for a time not to marry, not to engender children, as a prophetic symbol of the hard times ahead at the Exile, times of indigence and sorrow.

Israel, keeping in mind the benediction of God, 'Be fruitful, multiply and fill the earth', often simply referred to woman as *rāham*, a womb. One is reminded of Nietzsche's words, 'All in woman is a riddle, and all in woman hath one answer – that is, childbearing.'[19]

It could be that Israel's emphasis on continuance as a race was a factor in her apparent neglect, puzzling to scholars, of any interest in the life to come. This present life meant much to Israel because blessings here – and childbearing was obviously the greatest – were sometimes hard to come by. Persecuted often, and for the most part beset by the problem of racial survival, Israel was more interested in life after life than in life after death.

With this background of love, joy, marriage, we see why virginity was not extolled or prized in Israel any more than was sterility: it was hard, empirical fact, not a condition a person might have a preference for. Jewish people no more lauded the barren womb than the barren soil or fields found empty at harvest time. If God saw fit to close the womb or the skies – and it was his prerogative to do either – so be it, but neither in the one case nor the other did they pretend to be glad: they went into mourning. In an otherwise obscure verse in the Book of Proverbs, three Insatiables are bracketed together, the grave, the barren womb and the earth ever thirsty for water (30:16). That a Jew should want to close a woman's womb was as unimaginable as that he should willingly step into the grave or withhold water from the land.

Virginity was the lowly condition of one who had, as yet at least, contributed nothing to the progress of life; it was a condition of poverty. The virgin had not yet 'delivered the goods', so to speak. The references in the Jewish Bible to the Virgin Israel are not to be taken as commendations of Israel's purity but rather as pity for her plight and her misery. She too may pass away in her distress without enduring issue like pagan nations around her, the whole race cut off from the land of the living. We need only instance the Lamentations:

> The Lord has trodden as in a wine press
>   the virgin daughter of Judah.
> For these things I weep;
>   my eyes flow with tears;
> for a comforter is far from me,
>   one to revive my courage;
> my children are desolate,
>   for the enemy has prevailed (1:15–16).

These ideas, current in Judaism in the time of Christ, are still held by Jews who retain a wonderful thirst for the enjoyment of life, freed from any sense of world-denial. Dr Samuel Sandmel, in an excellent study of Jewish–Christian relations, writes: 'Overwhelmingly we Jews subscribe to the view that this world is a place which we enjoy. Vows of poverty and celibacy which characterize Catholic clergy are totally unknown to us.'[20]

After the Second World War, a gallant Englishwoman was sent to Nazi Germany to make provisions for any Jews who had survived the terror. In one of the camps she came across a group of Jews among whom the women, due to complete lack of nourishment, had ceased to menstruate. When, with careful diet, their health began to improve, a young girl began her periods again. An old Jew, hearing of it, cried aloud with joy: 'Rachel is as she should be. Now we have a future.'

Mary, according to Luke, was a virgin consecrated to God. God looked upon her humiliation, her poverty, her abasement – that is what Luke 1:45 means. God took hold of a Jewish maiden *without a future*.

16. THE MEANING OF THE VIRGIN BIRTH FOR FAITH

My field is desolate, unsown,
My maiden-body quiet as a tomb.
No seeds of life will now be blown
By breath of man into my womb.

But should this dry and fallow field
By a much greater Breath be blown upon
To hallow it, then will it yield
Fruits that will last when yours are gone.

I know that God will richly bless
This hitherto unlovely thing and wild.
My poverty, my emptiness,
Are for God's and a Virgin's Child.

Mary, like any Jewess, knew what childlessness was: not a condition of esteem but of deprivation and emptiness. God took this and made it rich, abundant, fruitful. For Luke, Mary the empty woman contains the world's future.

Mary was not the only woman in Israel whose childlessness was turned to joy. Think of Sarah, smiling, incredulous Sarah who, according to playful Jewish tradition, had, centuries earlier, grown exceedingly old before conceiving Isaac. This marked out Isaac as the fruit not simply of natural forces but of God's promise. Luke was expressly thinking, as we saw, of Hannah to whom Samuel the prophet was given as a gift to take away her reproach among men. Samuel prefigured the last and greatest of the prophets, John the Baptist, whose old father became speechless at the prospect of paternity.

Each time, in Israel's great saga, the finger of God was there.

The same may be said in Mary's case. In Luke's account, her virginal motherhood is a privilege. So completely and marvellously had God removed her humiliation from her that not only the rejoicing neighbours but all generations are to call her blessed. In addition, Mary's childbearing is one of those decisive events in the history of salvation which is continuous, in Israel's traditions, with Sarah's conceiving Isaac, Abraham's son.

For Luke, the virginal manner of Mary's conception sets it aside as a sign. The Christ was conceived by the power of the holy Spirit without the intervention of man. What is the significance of this sign?

In Luke's story, the Spirit descended to where humanity is weakest, a lifeless womb; and out of this dead flesh he brings to birth the one who is the life and joy of the world. Once more, Luke expresses pictorially what John puts in these direct terms: He who is the Son of God in a unique sense is the pattern of all who are born 'not of blood nor of the will of the flesh nor of the will of man, but of God' (John 1:13). He is 'from above'. This is John's way of saying that, from the beginning, he is the Son of God, and it corresponds to Luke's phrase 'overshadowing by the Spirit'. For both evangelists, the world's redemption begins with an act of graciousness on God's part.

Nothing could express better than the virgin birth the nature of the Christian faith, a religion of grace and of the Spirit who breathes where he wants to. No more than a virgin can conceive the Christ can man receive the Christ except by the power of God which is the Spirit.

The symbol of the divine child coming from a virgin expresses with superb artistry that what is divine in our lives is not merited; justification, the forgiveness of sins, holiness, these cannot be won by men. The loving initiative always belongs to God, even though we, like Mary, must always accept in complete freedom and joy the grace that is offered us. Luke's choice of the symbol of the virgin motherhood corresponds to our Lord's own parable of the pharisee and the publican. How much easier it is to understand Luke's and Jesus' pictorial representations of justification than Paul's abstract analysis of it in his epistles to the Romans and Galatians!

We think sometimes that at least we have a claim on God's *forgiveness*. This, too, is a mistake. Jesus' message is: God will forgive. We are right to expect it, though we have no right to expect it. No right, that is, in the sense of a legal claim. This has its parallel in everyday experience, as Jesus said. For we, like children with a fond father, know for certain that we will be forgiven, though we know with equal certainty that we have no claim to forgiveness. It will be granted because God is good, not because we are good. It is God who loves us first and enables us to be good.

Paul elaborated Christ's teaching with great care: God justifies the sinner not the just. To grasp this is the condition of knowing God and his utter sovereignty as creator and redeemer. No more than a child can cry out to be conceived can a 'dead' sinner cry out to be made alive again. When the child cries, he is already born; when the sinner cries out to God for mercy, God has 'already' shown it to him and he is reborn. We are forgiven not because we are worthy of forgiveness but because, through God's grace, we accept the forgiveness of which we never can be worthy. Were it otherwise, forgiveness would not be an act of grace at all, but something earned. We would have no need of Christ.

As it is, Christ comes to us in our deadness as he came to the Virgin's lifeless and unstirring womb. This is why in Luke's story the Virgin Mary is the great initiatory symbol of the gospel of grace and why, though it is not employed by Mark or John or Paul, it is integral to the message of grace proclaimed by the Bible as a whole. The final symbol of the gospel of grace is, of course, the death and resurrection of Christ. But, in fact, the virgin birth proclaims Christianity as the gift of grace by heralding the death and resurrection of Christ, by being the dawning of the day of salvation.

Once more we see that Christ's life is all of a piece: the womb and the tomb, the crib and the cross, complement each other. Did we not say that the nativity, too, is an Easter story?

17. THE VIRGIN BIRTH, A PASSOVER SIGN

There are more signs of the Lord's passover from death to life within the nativity story.

Jesus was crucified; he died and was laid in the tomb. Such is the Christ who bears our ineffectual flesh (John 6:63); so much is he one with us he condescended to share our death. He lies in the tomb epitomizing our condition before God in a most dramatic way. What is more helpless and hopeless than a corpse? In the dead Jesus we see the figure, the literal embodiment, of the powerlessness of man before God.

To Jesus, as lifeless as the virgin's flesh from which he was taken, the Spirit, the Power of God, comes and raises him to a new, glorious and everlasting life.

Luke makes an exciting use of symbolism here. The death of Jesus was, in God's providence, for the sake of this new life, as the virginity of Mary was, in God's designs, to show forth his sovereignty to all ages in a fatherless birth. Jesus who was conceived by the holy Spirit is 'constituted Son of God in power according to the Spirit of holiness by his resurrection from the dead' (Rom. 1:4). The virgin's womb and the garden tomb each 'challenge' the power of God, and from both he brings life.

There is a close link between Mary's virginity and Christ's death as there is between Mary's motherhood and Christ's resurrection. Both times, we see God's power coming to human weakness and bringing life from death and glory where there was no hope before.

This is not to impose a pattern on scripture. To see this, we have only to examine two hymns, the first from Paul, the second from Paul's close disciple, Luke.

In Philippians 2:5–11, Paul uses an ancient hymn about Christ in which he is said to have taken on the form of a slave. He humiliated himself. This is why God exalted him.

In Luke's hymn, Mary's Magnificat, Mary refers to herself as God's slave. God looked on the humiliation of his slave.

Hence Mary was exalted, since God is like that: he exalts the humiliated.

We are used to a less forceful expression: God regarded 'the humility of his handmaid'. But the words 'humiliation' and 'slave' express more exactly Luke's Greek words whose roots are found in the words which in Paul's hymn refer to Christ. The expression, God has seen 'the humiliation of his slave', has a quite revolutionary ring about it that is absent from the more usual translation.

There is here a close parallelism. Mary's virginity, like Christ's death, is a humiliation. Mary, in her virginal condition, like Christ in his death, is a slave; and because she accepted this condition she had, from the first, the mind of Christ. She held herself in abasement, as Philippians 2:8 puts it. The mother was already like her Son in his willingness to die. Finally, Mary is exalted in her motherhood as Christ is in his resurrection, for both virginal motherhood and resurrection express the sovereignty of God who brings life from death beyond all the potentialities of nature.

Mary calls herself the Lord's 'slave' – an unusual word for Luke to employ. There is no doubt he chose it deliberately so as to correspond to the designation of Christ as a 'slave' in Philippians 2:7. Christ's slavery was shown in the perfect obedience and poverty of his death on the cross. It was in death that Christ's 'self-emptying' – a graphic description of his abasement – was made complete, as in her acceptance of virginity Mary's poverty was completed, too. And, paradoxically, it is in and through the humiliations of the death and the virginity that new life comes.

Mary, to continue the parallel, will be called blessed by all generations (Luke 1:48) as at the name of the risen One every knee shall bow and every tongue confess that he is Lord (Phil. 2:10–11). The reason Luke has connected Mary's virginal motherhood and Christ's exalting death may well have been the new name given by the Christian community to Jesus at his exaltation. At the beginning, Mary was told she was to call her Son 'Jesus' (Luke 1:31). The new name given Jesus at his exaltation is 'Lord'. Jews were accustomed to new names being bestowed on people for some exceptional reason, perhaps a display of prowess or elevation to high office. At the resurrection, Jesus is given a new name because this is his new birth. He is 'the first-born among many brethren' (Rom. 8:29) by his resurrection. He who was, from the beginning, called 'the Son of God' (Luke 1:35) was 'constituted Son of God in power according to the Spirit of holiness by his resurrection from the dead, Jesus Christ our Lord' (Rom. 1:4).

The motherhood of Mary anticipated the resurrection.

> She was a village maid unknown,
> Stranger to joys of motherhood.
> None poorer save for him who's shown
> Hanging in shame upon the wood.
>
> She was an unwooed girl with Child.
> The world has seen none richer save
> For him who, dying undefiled,
> Rises glorious from the grave.

18. MARY, TRUE CHILD OF ABRAHAM

> When Father Abraham, though old, believed,
> His Isaac came whom agèd Sarah bore.
> More numerous, he knew, would be his Seed
> Than heaven's stars or sand upon the shore.
>
> When Mary, child of Abraham, believed
> And said, 'Behold, Lord, here your humbled slave',
> A virgin of the Jewish race conceived
> The world's Life, the Conqueror of the grave.

Luke praises Mary's faith, strongly contrasting it with Zechariah's incredulity. He puts on Elizabeth's lips these words to Mary: 'Blessed are you who believed that those things shall be accomplished that were spoken to you by the Lord' (1:45). In response, Mary recites her Magnificat which ends with the allusion to Abraham, the father of faith, and to his Seed

In his Letter to the Romans, Paul writes that Abraham believed without wavering that from his own body – 'as good as dead because he was about a hundred years old' (4:19) – and from Sarah's barren womb, a child would be born. He believed that God would keep his promise (4:21).

The Letter to the Hebrews completes the picture of Abraham's faith by remarking that Abraham was ready to offer up in sacrifice his own childless son, Isaac, through whom, God had promised, all his descendants were to be named. 'He considered that God was able to raise men even from the dead' (11:19).

If Abraham, in the saga of Israel, is the father of faith it is by reason of his commitment to God who is the master of life and death. We, too, become righteous on the pattern of Abraham when we 'believe in him that raised from the dead Jesus our Lord' (Rom. 4:24).

Luke sees Mary as the true daughter of Abraham: she has excelled in faith by giving herself to God who raises life from the deadness of her body. Through her act of faith, made in the darkness, the Christ in whom we all believe and find life was born of her virginity. Her virginal conception is salvific by being linked to the passover when God raised his Son, the Seed of Abraham, from the tomb to become the life of the world.

In this alone it is easy to grasp the theological significance of Mary's virgin motherhood. As the loamy feet of Eliot's dancers in the flittering firelight catch all the rhythm of nature, so Mary's reply to the angelic messenger catches all the rhythm of grace.

Luke's presentation of Mary's virginity has been, under Christ, the inspiration of consecrated virginity in the Church of Rome, a form of dedication which departs from the tradition of the Old Covenant. Sociologically, the Church could afford to encourage virginity in that the Church, unlike Israel, is not in any sense a race but a brotherhood in faith, a brotherhood that, therefore, surpasses all boundaries. The Church always has a future through the preaching of the word.

Theologically, too, the Church differs from Israel in the kind of messianism she has adopted, as Sandmel has pointed out. Integral to this is her conviction that the new messianic age *has already come*. The Christian virgin tries to live a life that gives dramatic witness to this specifically Christian conviction, so that virginity is meant to express joy more than self-abnegation. This is why it is not sufficient to think of virginity as a 'state of perfection' to be cultivated for its own sake.[21] Like our Jewish brothers today, our Jewish ancestors were surely right in thinking that *of itself* virginity is a non-sense, something irregular and to be shunned. Virginity is only permissible, so to speak, if it retains its revolutionary character, its capacity to change the heart. The virgin can afford to be the unpossessive person, someone who lives not in an ivory tower but in the van of an emerging world. He *can* be an impressive embodiment of the beatitudes: 'O the bliss of the poor',[22] as Christ expressed it.

Only a demonstrably blissful life of fruitfulness for others can justify virginity. It should mirror the childbearing of Mary: each virgin, through faith and love and complete openness to the action of the Spirit, must bring forth Christ in others. What the virgin puts to death is only the 'flesh' in the biblical sense, that is, the old, powerless, self-reliant existence, in order to make room for the new life of God's kingdom with the power and the charity that accompanies it.

Virginity is a terrible cross in that it involves dying. But it can also announce in a dramatic way, like Mary's virginity and Christ's death, that the last things have come upon earth. A new age of life, joy, love, has dawned; the age of the Spirit.

The virgin feels that there is no more time for marrying and giving in marriage. No more time for the conjunction of man and woman in the dance and in the marriage bed. In virgins dedicated to Christ the old world symbolically finishes: they bring doomsday to the world of 'the flesh' through their undivided witness to the new life that Christ brings.

But if virginity is lived selflessly, it becomes a sign not of the end, rather of a better beginning. How else could virginity be approved by the Christian community? For out of virginity comes the Child, and out of death comes resurrection, and after the passing of the old order comes the new heaven and the new earth.

19. MARY IN CHRISTIAN DEVOTION

> First look with care
> On her fair face.
> What thou wilt see
> Will thee prepare
> To see Christ's face
> Most gracefully
> Reflected there.

There have been many excesses in Marian devotion. Equality with Christ has seldom if ever been attributed to her but sometimes she has been treated in practice as the mediator (or go-between) of God and men. This means she has been honoured for fulfilling the role that belongs exclusively to Christ.

This aberration can perhaps be corrected by looking on Mary as a figure of the Church which wants to co-operate with Christ in his work of salvation.

In Newman's words, the glories of Mary are for the sake of her Son. Her goodness and grace are derived from him. And yet, throughout history, Christians have never been able to forget that she was the one to bear and to nurture God's Son.
Besides expressing the nature of the Church, Mary also guarantees that Jesus, the Son of God, is as completely human as we are. This is the significance of her title Mother of God, *Theotokos*.

At the Council of Ephesus (431), it was realized that if Mary were not the Mother of God this could only be because Christ himself was two sons – a man *and* the Son of God – with no substantial identity between them. Mary would then have been the mother of the man, Jesus, but not mother of the Son of God. That in its turn would imply that the incarnation is a sham; that the Son of God is not a man but some pre-existent deity who has simply associated himself with the work done by a man. The Church has always insisted that God did not put on flesh like some of the gods in ancient mythology. Jesus is not a man with a god, or even the one true God, inside him – a view which is, it must be admitted, quite widespread among Christians. Jesus of Nazareth is the one Christ and one Son of God. His birth, his mission, his death, are the birth, mission and death of the Son of God himself. When we look at Jesus, we know he is one with us and one with God. This is why we are sure not only that Jesus knows us intimately as a fellow human being but also that he is Emmanuel, God-with-us. This is made explicit in the confession of faith, Mary's Son *is* God's Son. Mary reminds us constantly of this incarnational principle and this is why she has always been honoured as mother of God.

Dante, in the *Paradiso*, puts the following words on St Bernard's lips just before the Poet is ushered into the vision of God: 'Look now upon the face that most resembles Christ's, for the beauty of that face alone can prepare thee to see the face of Christ.'[23] From the beginning, Mary's face reflects the face of Christ to come and anticipates what we ourselves, in our better moments, would like to be.

I agree with Pannenberg that Mariolatry is the Church's attempt to express its own essence in the figure of Mary. I would add that all the various titles and privileges accorded to Mary, despite occasional excesses, spring from one source. 'The Immaculate Conception', 'The Assumption', etc., are halting theological attempts – of necessity, culturally conditioned – to crystallize the Church's more basic experience of Mary as someone very closely allied to Christ and drawing goodness and holiness from him.

20. MARY IN CHRISTIAN POETRY

It is of great cultural significance that Christian art and poetry have always been attracted by the person of Mary. Artists and poets seized on the fact that Christ would have been incomplete without this deep relationship to the woman who brought him into the world. She was the way to the Way. A great Jewish, Russian author, Isaac Babel, wrote: 'All is mortal. Only the mother is destined to immortality. And when the mother is no longer among the living, she leaves a memory which none yet has dared to sully. The memory of the mother nourishes in us a compassion that is like the ocean, and the measureless ocean feeds the rivers that dissect the universe.'[24]

English poetry has given its witness to Christ's mother. First, fourteenth-century Chaucer in the Prologue to the Prioress's Tale. There is in it an almost incredibly cruel streak of medieval anti-semitism in which reference is made to: 'The serpent, our first foe, who has his nest / Of hornets in Jews' hearts.' Then come these words in praise of Mary, a Jewish maiden:

> Lady, thy bounty and thy regalness,
> Thy virtue and thy great humility
> There is no tongue nor knowledge can express,
> For often, Lady, before men pray to thee
> Thou comest first in thy benignity
> And through thy prayers thou makest the way clear
> To guide us to thy Son to thee so dear.[25]

Then there is a pre-Reformation carol which tries to capture the gentleness of Mary:

> He came all so still
>   Where his mother was
> As dew in April
>   That falleth on the grass.

> He came all so still
>   To his mother's bower
> As dew in April
>   That falleth on the flower.

> He came all so still
>   Where his mother lay
> As dew in April
>   That falleth on the spray.

> Mother and maiden
>> Was never none but she.
> Well may such a lady
>> God's mother be.

Moving to John Donne at the turn of the sixteenth century we come across a poet who thinks of Mary as the one who has given the Son the weakness he needs to save us. The Son's pity to man is so great that he comes to us to be pitied. In his 'Nativity', Donne writes:

> Immensity cloistered in thy dear womb,
> Now leaves his well beloved imprisonment,
> There he hath made himself to his intent
> Weak enough, now into our world to come.

Crashaw, in his seventeenth-century 'Nativity', uses all his charged and concentrated eloquence to express the confluence of apparent contradictions in Jesus' divine birth:

> Welcome all wonders in one sight!
>> Eternity shut in a span,
> Summer in winter, day in night,
>> Heaven in earth and God in man;
> Great little one! whose all embracing birth
>> Lifts earth to heav'n, stoops heav'n to earth.

I was intrigued to find a poem honouring Mary in the collected works of Charles Lamb published in 1818. He wrote it after visiting the National Gallery in London. There he had studied Leonardo's painting, 'The Virgin of the Rocks':

> Maternal lady with the virgin grace,
> Heaven-born thy Jesus seemeth sure,
> And thou a virgin pure.
> Lady most perfect, when thy sinless face
> Men look upon, they wish to be
> A Catholic, Madonna fair, to worship thee.

From this century, there is first Alice Meynell's little verse, so much like Dante's quoted earlier:

None can be like Him, none;
Not she who bore Him. Yet I saw the whole
Eternal, infinite Christ with the one
Small mirror of her soul.

Lastly, these few lines from Eliot's 'The Dry Salvages'.[26] He manages to convey in them the sense of confidence that a shrine of Mary inspires in the believer. Mary, wife as well as mother, stands by the side of all women in the hour of need:

Lady, whose shrine stands on the promontory,
Pray for all those who are in ships, those
Whose business has to do with fish, and
Those concerned with every lawful traffic
And those who conduct them.

Repeat a prayer also on behalf of
Women who have seen their sons or husbands
Setting forth and not returning:
Figlia del tuo figlio,[27]
Queen of Heaven.

Also pray for those who were in ships, and
Ended their voyage on the sand, in the sea's lips
Or in the dark throat which will not reject them
Or wherever cannot reach them the sound of the
sea-bell's
Perpetual angelus.

I like the image of the ship's bell, rocked by the incessant sea, sounding its perpetual angelus.

21. THE WORD MADE FLESH

Give me, some say, the strong staff of the Deed,
As if the Word must be a bruisèd reed.
Why, have they not been battered, broken, stirred,
Maligned, inspired and mended by a word?
Words that are only words are so much breath
Deeds that say nothing impotent as death.

Words *can* be empty. Faulkner writes in *As I Lay Dying*: 'I would think how words go straight up in a thin line, quick and harmless, and how terribly doing goes along the earth, clinging to it, so that after a while the two lines are too far apart for the same person to straddle from one to the other.'[28]

But words are not always as thin and evanescent as smoke; they can be among the most powerful social forces. If it were not so, why should dictators and totalitarian regimes reserve their cruellest punishments for writers? The censoring of authors and the public banning of their books, throughout history, has been invariably associated with bigotry and inhumanity. It indicates, on the part of authority, both a terrible fear of freedom and a lack of confidence in truth.

God's word, in particular, was, for Jews, never empty. It is himself. In their vivid imagery, God is in his word accomplishing mighty deeds. Often this word of his was put upon the prophet's lips. Thereby the prophet became not merely the spokesman but also the workman of God. Between words and doing there was no distance needing to be straddled.

God's creative word drew the good earth out of chaos. God's word incessantly visits the same earth like rain and returns to him full of the fruits it brings to birth.

God's word is constant. In it God has pledged himself and vowed unchanging fidelity. His word, therefore, stands in stark contrast to the frail flesh which is man. God's spokesman, Isaiah, expressed this contrast in unforgettable terms in Chapter 40:

> All flesh is as grass, its beauty will pass
> As in a field the flowers do.
> The grasses grow pale and the flowers fail,
> Frail as the flowers are you.

> Take comfort, my people, take comfort from me,
> Remember my love is so strong.
> Speak to Jerusalem tenderly,
> Tell them I've pardoned their wrong.

A voice in the desert cried, 'Make straight the way,
The hill roads must look like the plain.
The Lord is to come on his chosen day,
You die but his Word will remain.'

A shepherd the Lord is and we are his sheep,
He leads us his flock to be fed.
Weak lambs are picked up when the ground is steep,
Ewes heavy with young, gently led.

All flesh is as grass, its beauty will pass
As in a field the flowers do.
The grasses grow pale and the flowers fail,
Frail as the flowers are you.

The fourth gospel develops the Old Testament imagery: God's creative, constant and unchanging Word became personally the flesh which is grass. What God is, his Word is. And the Word is flesh.

God, Silence, Mystery, the nameless One whom we do not know and yet call 'Father', comes to the earth in the frailty of Jesus whom we call his Son.

We are not meant to conclude from the biblical phrase 'Jesus came into the world' – any more than from 'A new baby came into the world' – that Jesus once existed 'outside' the world or 'up there' above the heavens. Nor are we to think of him as *literally* pre-existing himself, as if he first existed in 'a timeless time before time' known as 'eternity' from where he made an incursion into time. God exists; the world exists in total, barely expressible dependence on God. But we cannot deduce from this that God existed 'before' the world came into being, unless we are prepared to acknowledge the mythological force of the word 'before'. In other words, we are entitled to speak of God existing 'before' the world in order to express pictorially God's sovereignty over the world, his creative action upon it; but we must not take pictorial language as a *description* of reality.

Jesus is God's Word. What God is, Jesus is. There is a oneness between Jesus and God his Father. Jesus is God-with-us and for-us; he is God made near and accessible, and in him the Father is ceaselessly working.

In Jesus, Christians believe, we find the satisfactory focus and the face of the unnameable Mystery, God. The Word of God which, as Justin said, is present in varying degrees of intensity everywhere and in everyone, is present in Jesus with such adequacy that in him we discover the meaning of our existence and the satisfaction of our boundless longings.

Yet, how weak this Word is; how foolish a venture on God's part the incarnation seems. We are called to taste and see whether this weakness is stronger and this folly is wiser than men. If we believe it is – I mean if this is our life-fashioning conviction – we will confess that Jesus is the Son of **God**. We will accept him as the parable of God the Mystery.

Christians cannot forget, however, that when they meet God's Son in the scriptures for the first time, he is a child in the arms of a woman.

22. THE LITERAL CHARACTER OF THE VIRGIN BIRTH?

One problem remains concerning the virgin birth and we should face it squarely. Having acknowledged its theological significance and the impact it has made on Christian devotion and culture, we still need to know whether it is to be understood literally. Did Mary really conceive Jesus without the assistance of man?

An affirmative answer has been presumed by Christians over the ages and understandably so. They had little 'feel' for the literary character of the Old and New Testaments and there were no reasonable grounds for doubting or denying the factualness of this 'mystery of faith'.

However, many other presumptions were made by Christians over the centuries which have been recognized subsequently to be false, for example, that the world was created in six days, that Abraham was a centenarian when he fathered Isaac, that the Magi really came from the East in pursuit of a star. There are, besides exegetical difficulties, other factors at work in our culture making it extremely difficult to accept the literalness of the virgin birth. To these we will return later.

A major biblical problem of which exegetes have become aware only comparatively recently is that, in the Bible, fact and interpretation of fact are very closely interwoven. The believer cannot wait until the experts sort out fact from interpretation before exercising his faith. In many instances, he would have to wait indefinitely. The believer has to accept the *message* of the Bible, more or less adequately comprehended, even though he cannot always be sure that a particular event happened precisely as the Bible relates or even whether there was any such event at all. Jews would not cease to look upon themselves as a people who depend entirely on God just because the story of Abraham begetting Isaac at an advanced age is today understood as theological saga rather than history.

While Christians have by and large accepted this of the Jewish Bible, they show a marked distaste for applying the same principle to the New Testament even though the New Testament is thoroughly Jewish in inspiration. Unless this resistance is overcome, we will not benefit from the findings of modern scriptural research and we may miss the gospel message itself. Instead of facing God's demands, we may pull up short in sheer bewilderment at the mythical wrapping of the message.

The Bible is primarily a library dealing with man's confrontation with God. In the course of the books of the Bible, many literary forms are utilized by various authors to express their belief and confidence in God.

It is a mistake for a Christian who feels convinced that the virgin birth is not to be taken literally to dismiss it with a flourish as 'untrue' or as 'a fable' having no significance for the contemporary world. The virgin birth, while not belonging to the earliest proclamation of Christianity, is nonetheless part of the story of Christianity, which has been recounted over the ages. This story *is* Christianity and that is why it must be retold integrally if we are to have anything on which to exercise faith. The story is the source and foundation of all subsequent Christian teaching.

The first important question to be put to the Bible is not, Did this or that happen exactly as related? To know 'the facts' may seem crucial to Western minds but it was not the primary concern of the authors and first readers of the Bible. If we follow their lead, we will first ask, What is the *meaning* of this story? What does it tell us about God and our relationship to him? Why did the author express himself like this?

I tried to take cognizance of this priority when analysing the virgin birth. I stressed – perhaps I over-stressed – the meaning of the story and what we can learn from it of God's graciousness and sovereignty. We saw why the symbolism of it was so helpful to Luke in his presentation of the Christian message. But the blunt question about the literalness of the virgin birth cannot be avoided.

On the basis of exegesis, even Protestants differ. Karl Barth, for example, accepts the virgin birth as literal fact; Pannenberg treats it as Christological legend which cannot be harmonized with the teaching on Christ found in Paul and John.

In my view, we usually take sides on issues like this, not simply on exegetical grounds, but also on more general ideological grounds, such as the philosophical, the historical, the scientific. I personally do not hold to the literalness of the virgin birth (which is consistent with believing in it as a theologically meaningful doctrine). I do not intend to wage a campaign to win people over to my opinion because such a campaign is not necessary. There is at work a spirit of the age – not in any pejorative sense – that makes some interpretations of scripture untenable to the mass of thinking people. (The same phenomenon occurs in philosophy where certain positions are not taken by frontal assault but are, in time, quietly abandoned.)

Religious authorities, in times of change, try to stop 'the progress of unbelief', as it is called, by carefully drawing the line of orthodoxy they learned when they were young. And not religious authorities alone. We all tend to play an inquisitorial role and draw our own unofficial boundary lines: too far to the right of it merits the epithet 'obscurantist'; one step to the left is heresy. As Bishop Warburton remarked, orthodoxy is my doxy; heterodoxy is your doxy.

The history of theology, especially in recent times, demonstrates that the boundaries of orthodoxy are being repeatedly and sometimes rapidly altered. Since the Vatican Council the heresy-hunters have had to search – with the usual 'easy' successes – for new targets. They seem to have no historical sense nor any memory of the positions they have themselves been forced to abandon only recently. One generation's demarcation line is trampled on by the next generation which sees its own sacred line suffer the same fate in its turn. The original drawing of the boundary line may have been intelligent but adherence to it in the face of fresh evidence and a new outlook may very well be foolish.

Dr John Robinson, the former Bishop of Woolwich and one of the most influential Christian writers today, has dealt with the virgin birth in his popular book, *But That I Can't Believe.*

He first notes that for the men of the Bible, the idea of a heavenly Being 'sending' his Son to this world was perfectly acceptable. 'Up there' was where God, true reality, was to be located. God's Son coming from 'up there' or 'out there' was for them the revelation of God.

This manner of speaking is so alien to people today that there is a danger they may miss the truth of the message altogether. To quote Robinson in full:

If it helps to say that in Jesus reality comes through, rather than comes down, then by all means let's say it.

Then there are all the 'tinselly' bits of the Christmas story – the star, the angels and the celestial choir. These are recognized ways for the men of the Bible of saying 'God is in all this.' As poetry, I believe, they still have a magic power to take us out of our mean selves. They speak of the mystery of Christmas. But if all they succeed in doing for you is banishing Christ to an unreal world of fairy-lights, then cut them out.

Again, the Virgin Birth. If it helps, as it helped millions, to see in Jesus God at work, well and good. But if it merely succeeds in convincing you that he was not 'one of us', then it's much better that you *shouldn't* believe it – for that was never its intention. I'd rather you suspended judgement than let it become a stumbling-block.[29]

It may seem at first as if Dr Robinson is saying: 'If you don't like one of the Christian doctrines or if you feel you can't swallow it, it's far better not to believe it or at least to suspend judgement for a while.' This is not really the case. Dr Robinson is trying to safeguard the true doctrine. He is not speaking for modern sceptics in particular but for modern man in general. He is admitting that he shares modern man's reluctance to accept the world-view in which the Christian message is embedded, but that is no reason for rejecting the Christian message itself.

I will not dwell on the scriptural arguments against the literalness of the virgin birth. Three brief queries must suffice. How could Mary have dedicated herself to virginity in view of Israel's complete lack of feeling for it? Isn't the virgin birth represented by Luke as being in the line of those miraculous Old Testament births which are today reckoned even by conservative scholars to belong to saga and legend? Aren't the nativity narratives in Matthew and Luke simply filled with theological devices for expressing the significance of Jesus as the Son of God without the authors being committed to the literalness of what they relate?

I prefer to spend more space on explaining why the literalness of the virgin birth is opposed to the Zeit-Geist, the spirit of the age.

Karl Barth does not agree that it is so opposed. He writes of Jesus' birth: 'Man is to contribute nothing to what is to begin here by his action and initiative. Man is not simply excluded, for the virgin is there. But the male, as the specific agent of human action and history, with his responsibility for directing the human species, must now retire into the background, as the powerless figure of Joseph.'[30]

I concede that this represents fairly enough Luke's standpoint and it explains how he came to use the imagery he did.

But, if we leave aside the male-superiority syndrome, Barth does not appear to ask himself whether Luke's standpoint is at all permissible in the light of modern embryology. There is nothing wrong with Luke's theological vision, but is it possible *to ground it* in an outdated scientific hypothesis?

The ancients, for whom a woman's inside was more remote than the source of the Amazon, were of the opinion that the male only initiated the process of generation. In the middle ages, St Thomas Aquinas, following Aristotle, agreed with this. It was reasonable for him to hold, therefore, that in Mary's case the holy Spirit was the agent of change while Mary supplied all the matter for a human body.

But what if the male is required in human generation not only to initiate the process but to provide part of the enduring structural composition of the child? The provision by a 'foster-father' of a genealogical tree is no substitute for the genes that only a father can supply. It is through the genes and chromosomes inherited *jointly* from father and mother that any human being is integrally related to all the physical and evolutionary processes that are and ever have been in the universe. Through father and mother the child becomes part of 'the whole world' and its history; he belongs to everything that has been, is and is to come. Without a human father, would Jesus have been really human? It may once have been sufficient guarantee of his humanness to point to his virgin mother. Today we know that every child requires father and mother to possess the correct hereditary patterns. To assert that Jesus had a father as well as a mother is as necessary to us as a pledge of Jesus' humanness as was the title *Theotokos* given to Mary at the Council of Ephesus.

Dr Robinson has drawn an interesting parallel between the problem of the virgin birth and that of Genesis in the nineteenth century. In Darwin's time, Christians, presuming the chronology of Genesis was accurate, asserted that the world came into being in 4004 BC. Then the empirical sciences revealed that various strata with fossils in them proved conclusively that the world and life itself existed hundreds of millions of years ago. One solution embraced by some

Christians – an Orthodox Jew explained it to me only a few years ago in Haifa – was that when God created the world in 4004 BC he made it so it *looked old*.

If the virgin birth were literally true, Jesus would not be a human being whose origin is traceable ultimately to the beginnings of things as ours is; he would have been created by God so he *looked* as human as the rest of us.

In view of arguments like this, is it necessary to make the literal interpretation of the virgin birth a precondition of Christian orthodoxy? To insist that it is may well prevent countless people from facing the real challenge of Christianity. The teaching on the virgin birth in the gospels is not scientific but literary. It refers not to a gynaecological miracle but to a theological mystery in the proper sense. It is an image, as Matthew Arnold put it, 'thrown out at an immense reality'; and, understood as such, it can still speak to us today.

Part 2
LIFE AND MINISTRY

1. BEHOLD THE MAN

A few years ago, Jacob Epstein's sculpture of *Ecce Homo* (Behold the Man) was in an open-air exhibition in a London park. It had a powerful, primitive quality about it, a quality one finds in the highest forms of African art or the art of the North American Indians.

In his autobiography, Epstein tells how he would visit a stone yard and notice a tremendous block of marble ready to be sliced up and used for interior decoration. Seeing these monoliths awaiting the butcher's hand, he says, there comes over him a kind of sentimental pity for them. They could contain so many works of art; so he purchases one, not having as yet any definite plan for it.

The stone may be a subiacco block of marble, a really hard material. He tries tool after tool on it, and each of them breaks one after the other. At length he finds the right point that resists and begins to make an impression on the stone.

On this occasion he wants to create an *Ecce Homo*, 'a symbol of man, bound, crowned with thorns and facing, with a relentless and overmastering gaze of pity and prescience, our unhappy world'.[1] This sculpture which I picked out from the exhibition as being the most moving, the most beautiful, was not at all liked by many of the critics when it first appeared. Questions were asked about it in the British Parliament; even G. K. Chesterton referred to it as the greatest insult to religion he had ever seen. Epstein, for his part, remarks with the assuredness of the true artist: 'I look at the work and feel that it confronts time and eternity.'

On another occasion, Epstein possessed a huge block of alabaster. For a whole year it rests in his studio. While he works on other projects, he casts a glance at the alabaster block from time to time. It lies prone. Should he raise it up, he wonders. No, better leave it where it is; it is comfortable there.

This is how he describes his feelings: 'I can conceive any number of works in it . . . a single figure or a group of figures. I have been listening to Bach's *B Minor Mass*. In the section, Crucifixus, I have a feeling of tremendous quiet, of awe. The music comes from a great distance, and in this mood I conceive my *Consummatum Est*. I see the figure complete as a whole. I see immediately the upturned hands with the wounds in the feet, stark, crude with the stigmata.'

Epstein maps out the sculpture on the block. The work begins that will captivate his mind all day and at night when he is forced to retire. It is there as an inescapable presence. 'I would say', he writes, 'that on a work like this, one lives in it until it is finally finished.'

The *Consummatum Est* is finished. And the critics move in again to gobble him up. Epstein, with resignation and magnanimity, only remarks: 'Instead of writing about it, and people standing about talking, arguing, disputing over the prone Son of Man with protesting palms upturned, there should be music, the solemn music of Bach.'[2]

I find this description of Epstein's artistry a very satisfying image of Christian discipleship. Our experience of Christ – like an uncut block of marble – is a single piece. We must not allow it to be cut up by butchers for decoration – not even for theological decoration. It is so easy to dissect the faith into treatises on the Trinity, the sacraments, the Church, and so on endlessly. What we ought to do is to seek in our Christian experience the form, the figure, the features of Christ. He must captivate the mind, for he is God's word to us. Day and night, his is the inescapable presence that haunts us.

There is a place for disputations and arguments. Theology *is* necessary and, when good, it is only faith brought up to date, made relevant. Nevertheless, the top priority is the Spirit of peace. Christ should fill us like the swell of music so that we attend to him, the Son of Man, who has consummated everything in himself.

St Ignatius of Antioch, who was martyred at the end of the first century, was a man completely absorbed in personal communion with Christ, even if his desire for death in a good cause may strike us as being a trifle immoderate. Paul, in his letters, used the phrase 'in Christ Jesus' or its equivalent over a hundred times. Ignatius, in his few brief letters to the churches on the road to Rome, exceeded this number easily. 'All happiness to you in God the Father and in Jesus Christ. I want to address a few words to you in the faith of Jesus Christ. . . . We must continue simply loving each other consistently in the Spirit of Jesus Christ. . . . He who died for us is all that I seek; he who rose again for us is my whole desire. . . . Farewell. See that there is a godly unity among you and a spirit that is above all divisions; for this is Jesus Christ.'[3]

When a Christian is walking towards the lions' jaws as Ignatius was, his faith becomes nothing but a communion with God in the person of Jesus Christ. It is Christ whom he wishes to know and to serve.

But which Christ are we referring to? The Church's Christ. The Christ of the community of faith. The Christ of the gospels in which fact and interpretation of fact have become almost inextricably intertwined. We are the disciples of the Jesus of history who became the Lord of glory.

2. THE QUIET MAN OF NAZARETH

A quiet man was he,
In a quiet country place.
He lived so very quietly,
The Saviour of the race.

A quiet man with wood,
His town had a quiet air.
It was well known that nothing good
Had ever come from there.

A quiet man he died,
Breathed a last, deep, quiet breath.
He should have stayed at home, they sighed,
In quiet Nazareth.

Beyond our garden fence, there stood until recently a clump
of trees. Then all the trees were removed to make way for
houses. One morning I watched with fascination a young
carpenter working in a ground-floor room on the doors and
window-frames. At first, he wore a shirt, but removed it when
the sun grew warmer. I saw the muscles rippling on his brown
arms and chest. His hair was black; behind his ear a pencil.
From the back pocket of his jeans a rule protruded.

Sometimes he used a wooden mallet which emitted a rich
hollow sound. At other times he would pick out nails from a
leather pouch he wore around his waist and hammer them in
with an admirable dexterity. I noticed how he held the hammer
at the end for full leverage and how clear and metallic was the
noise of it.

What gripped me most was the sheer absorption of the man
in his work. He became one with his instruments. Circling
ceaselessly like a boxer around his workbench, seeking new
angles of approach, puffing out his cheeks to clear the lingering
sawdust from the wood, he was a picture of pure harmony and
peace.

I shall not see him any more. The planks have been removed.
The ringlets of wood shavings have been cleared away. His
work is finished.

I do not know his name.

What if someone were to insist that his name is Bill and
he's the saviour of the world?

'Jesus' or 'Joshua' was, among Jews, as common a name as
'Bill' is to us.

I have already said more about the nameless carpenter I
watched at work than the evangelists said or anybody knows
about the first thirty years of Jesus' life. But some conjecture
is in order.

That Jesus, like Joseph, was a carpenter is stated in Mark

6:3. Then, Jesus most likely spent the major part of his life doing woodwork in a backyard. No wonder, when he returned to Nazareth after a brief interval away, he was not greeted with wild acclaim.

Charles Péguy, in his idiosyncratic way, says of Jesus' quiet years:

> Thirty years of carpentry and three years of the spoken
> word . . .
> For he worked as a carpenter, he carpentered.
> In carpentry.
> He was a woodworker . . .
> His father was a boss with a very small business . . .
> How he liked that trade.
> He was made for that trade.[4]

Isaac Babel tells the delightful Cossack fable in which Christ on his cross was so worried by the midges that he lost heart. A bee was also flying around Christ and the midges cried out to it to strike Christ, too. ' "Strike at him, and we'll be responsible." "Can't", says the bee, and raises its wings above Christ's head. "Can't. He's a carpenter like us." '[5]

Jesus' preaching showed how observant he was. His professional eye, in particular, noticed that houses constructed on rock, however poorly made, were better than palaces built on marshland. He was probably thinking back to earlier days when he told people to take the planks out of their own eyes before looking for splinters in the eyes of others. Planks he had fallen over many a time but splinters were not always so easy to find! Take my yoke upon you, he tells the crowds, it is a sweet yoke and it's well made; your shoulders won't be scraped or bruised by it.

Even so, a doubt recurs: Couldn't Jesus have made more use of his life? Couldn't those thirty quiet years have been better employed? The young Alexander had a more urgent sense of worlds waiting to be conquered.

Ivan Turgenev, having watched the greatest novelist in Russia, Leo Tolstoy, working in the fields among the peasants, mourned the loss to literature. But Tolstoy thrived on physical exertion. He rose at four and joined the muzhiks in the heaviest chores. His comment was: 'After sweating blood and tears, everything seemed beautiful to me, I began to love mankind.'[6]

By the time Jesus began his ministry, he was completely in love with mankind. In his quietness, he had accomplished what Gandhi, in his autobiography, called 'an experiment with truth'. 'The seeker after truth should so humble himself that even the dust could crush him. Only then, will he have a glimpse of truth.'[7]

Jesus the carpenter was probably proud of his trade and the assignments it brought him. He liked the sense of achievement at the end of a job well done and the healthy tiredness when night came and it was too dark to go on. He knew the feel and grain of every kind of wood. The casual visitor to the Ginkgo forest on the Columbia river perhaps discovers for the first time what the craftsman knew all along: that the grain of wood differs as much from tree to tree as the leaves do and as petals differ from flower to flower.

Among his followers – mostly fishermen – Jesus must have seemed no better or worse equipped for life than they. He probably couldn't tell a turtle from a tortoise but he was most likely something of an expert when it came to mending boats. When he laid his hands on the sick, on the ears of the deaf, on crippled limbs and sightless eyes, no doubt, those hands felt good on the skin, comfortably rough like their own, not at all like the hands of scholars.

At the end, when he was given his cross to carry, Jesus must have known the sort of timber it was made from and whether it was well made or not. He might have thought he could have made a better job of it himself – but that was perhaps only a craftsman's pride. With a helping hand, he bore that cross to Calvary as he had borne many planks before. He was used to carting wood around for long distances. Then the instruments of his own trade were used against him to fix him to the tree. And he hung on gnarled, strong hands with splinters in them for three hours. In life and death he was supported by those hands.

It had been for the most part a quiet life and only lately

turbulent. He was just further proof that nothing good ever came out of Nazareth.

3. GROWING UP

> If only hills could speak and stones
> And the quiet village well,
> What stories of that quiet man
> Would they not have to tell?
>
> But if the Word was silent there,
> There is nothing to unfold.
> The silent hills and well and stones
> Tell all that can be told.

I admitted in advance that everything I wrote about Jesus' hidden life is guesswork. We really know nothing about how he spent those quiet years in Nazareth and presumably we were not meant to know. He was only growing up.

In the early years of Christianity a number of stories were in circulation about Jesus' boyhood. It was related, for instance, that as a child he had made clay birds which flew away when he released them from his hands. However dearly Jesus' disciples would have treasured any recollection of that large, backwater period of his life, the Christian community did not accept these stories as containing authentic memories.

Nor did the Church accept such legends as having any theological value. This is because they failed to represent truly the Jesus whom the community knew in faith. The gospel is in no way like *The Little Flowers of St Francis* in which Francis is depicted as making friends with wolves and birds. The Church thought it better to leave Jesus' years in Nazareth in total obscurity than to represent him as being other than a normal child. He wasn't one to work miracles nonchalantly – perhaps as an alternative to playing children's games. Everything that was written about Jesus had to be part of the gospel in the sense of involving and challenging the reader at this and every moment.

There have been more academic attempts to guess how Jesus spent those thirty years in Nazareth. According to St Thomas Aquinas, Jesus at his very conception must have been endowed as the Son with special knowledge of God his Father and a holiness befitting his divine nature.

In Aquinas' view, Jesus, through the beatific vision,[8] saw all actual things – the words, thoughts, deeds – of everybody at all times. Through his infused (angelic) knowledge, Jesus was able to 'take a look at' whatever can be known by the mind of man, even current advances in science and technology, without any previous acquaintance on the level of experience. As to experimental knowledge, Jesus knew everything that was, is and will be by means of his surpassing intelligence, even though his empirical contact with reality was, in the nature of things, extremely limited.

St Thomas argues further that Jesus was perfect, at conception, in love and holiness. He was able to grow in the *effects* of wisdom and grace but not in holiness itself. As Jesus advanced in years he manifested the wisdom and virtue appropriate to his age 'in order to show himself to be a true man'.[9]

Aquinas' attempt to safeguard Jesus' humanity, however impressive it may have appeared in his time, does not strike us as being wholly successful. We are tempted to characterize it as a 'theology of pretence'. We do not take to some of Aquinas' ideas, for example, that Jesus never learned anything from anyone, not even from Joseph and Mary; that even in the crib he could really tie up the thong of his sandals and speak Greek, though he humbly refrained from demonstrating his expertise; that he was not subject to corporal defects such as come 'from within the body' like rheumatism or, in St Thomas' view, mumps or measles; that Jesus had it in his power to do anything he wanted, every kind of miracle included, *quidquid voluit, potuit*; that all his self-sacrificing deeds did nothing to increase his love and goodness; that he foresaw every detail of his life in advance, a gift that in no way impaired his free will; that he was tempted only so as to help *us*, to afford us an example of how we should react in times of temptation; that he *permitted* his soul to suffer in his passion, despite the overwhelming joy of the beatific vision, by means of a miracle; that he laid down his life willingly, in the sense that he didn't prevent it when he could, just as a man is said to make himself wet when he chooses not to close a window through which the rain comes.[10]

It required great mental agility on the part of Aquinas to deal with those biblical texts in which Jesus is spoken of as growing in wisdom, stature and grace; as being subject like ourselves to temptation; as not knowing certain things and needing, on occasions, to make inquiry, as when at the age of twelve, he asked questions of priests in the temple. St Thomas' problem was difficult enough: there are other passages in the New Testament which seem to contradict these texts. Assuming the biographical character and accuracy of the four gospels, he concentrated very much on John's gospel in which the divineness of Jesus figures most prominently.[11] It is from John's theological statements about Christ, often placed in the text on Jesus' lips, that Aquinas infers the kind of humanity that Jesus of Nazareth *must* have had. The state of scripture studies in his day left him no alternative in the matter.

What has been the effect of the Thomistic teaching? It has been virtually impossible to look on Jesus as a normal human being. His growing up seemed but a matter of biological increase. All his days from infancy, some Thomists have argued, must have been spent in quiet contemplation of his Father in heaven and meditation on his passion by which he was to save the world. He didn't have to learn to be a carpenter, even though it was admitted that his hands and eyes and muscles had to become acquainted with, and adept at his job. My sympathies were very much with a teacher friend who told me that a child once asked him, 'When Jesus was a little boy did he have a grown-up mind?' Blushingly, he admitted his reply had been affirmative. On the Thomistic view, it is even necessary to ask without facetiousness whether Jesus, being by nature exempt from sickness, emitted baby cries and manufactured tears as part of his campaign to feign normality.

St Thomas died seven hundred years ago, before the researches that fashioned the thinking of our time. His view of Jesus is even less acceptable than that implicit in the legend of the boy Jesus making and then quickening clay pigeons.

Luke says of the boy Jesus: 'He went down with them and came to Nazareth, and was obedient to them . . . And Jesus increased in wisdom and in stature, and in favour with God and man' (2:51-2). The evangelist is content to describe Jesus' youth in words which once had described the youth of Samuel.

If we need to speculate, we would have to say that Jesus was an exceptional child because he was an exceptional man. After all, life is a long process of change and development; at any moment we are the product of everything we have done and endured, of every action and reaction. What we must not do is ascribe to Jesus anything that would make him seem an abnormal child, a god in the guise of a child.

When we see Jesus in his public life, we see a man of authority, someone who knew that he stood among his people in a unique relationship to God and had the task of preaching the kingdom. But we don't have to imagine he was conceived or born with this tremendous sense of authority and nearness to God. With the advent of modern embryology, it is no longer possible to give any intelligible meaning to such a hypothesis.

A child is a human being at the very beginning of a process of growth. If this Jewish child is related to God in a special way – a relationship which he was to designate in Jewish terms as being the Son (of God) – presumably his consciousness of this will become an integral part of his spiritual development.[12] As to knowledge of the future, it is hard to see how this is compatible with spontaneity and free choice in a person's life. Aquinas was inconsistent with his own principles when he argued that Jesus could have retained free will while possessing the beatific vision in his lifetime. He tries to make out that though Jesus' will was confirmed in good, he was still able to choose for himself this good rather than that good. But, surely, in the beatific vision, Jesus would have known already what was *best* for him; and this means he would not even have enjoyed the limited freedom Aquinas attributes to him, namely, of judging for himself that any one course of action is better than another.

The Jesus of the Thomists would never have had any sense of wonder, discovery or enjoyment in his life. His would have been a life without risk. In his ageless, divine vision, he would have seen, with piercing clarity, his followers grown in number to a massive 800 millions in the twentieth century out of his little flock of simple, cowardly, good-hearted fishermen, publicans, prostitutes and zealots. The truth is that Jesus needed to trust in God as no one else has ever done. He believed, despite the hazards of his life and the unpromising beginnings, that the harvest would follow this strange sowing of God's word, the mustard tree would shoot up from the tiniest seed.

The whole supposition of the New Testament is that Jesus lived as precariously, as much in the dark, as we do. He is as human as, indeed more human than anyone else. It is in and through his sheer humanness that God is with us – not on account of something added to his humanity or working behind the scenes of his humanity.

The danger – and the source of much confusion – is, we may think in terms of Jesus living a double life, as though he is someone who functions on two engines. When he works miracles, the human engine cuts out; when he dies, the divine engine is disengaged. But, as the Council of Ephesus said, Jesus is not two sons but one son. He is the one Son of God. His whole human activity *is* his divine activity in the only way in which both he and we can appreciate and experience it. Jesus is not someone who leads a completely human life and *as well* a shadow divine life which from time to time intrudes and manifests itself; this is an interpretation springing from the days when exegesis was in its infancy. The incarnation does not mean that God is behind or added to or over-and-above the human: it means the human *is* the very expression (the Word) of God. Jesus' human life is the manifestation of the divine life. If the divine were present in any way other than the human, we would not be able to recognize it because we ourselves are only human. In the superb theological exposition of the fourth gospel, Philip says to Jesus, 'Lord, show us the Father, and we shall be satisfied.' Jesus replies: 'He who has

seen me has seen the Father' (John 14:8–9). It is enough to see
Jesus, for that is to see God.

Jesus' manhood is the form in which God appears among
us. Or to put it more simply and not so misleadingly, Jesus is
the form in which God appears among us. He is God-with-us.
If it were otherwise, why should we say the Son is, by identity,
the man from Nazareth?

4. A JEWISH CHILD

He was a Jewish child,
He had a Jewish nose,
He read the Jewish Bible
And wore all Jewish clothes.

He kept the Jewish law
With Jewish thoroughness.
His Jewish mamma wouldn't let
Her Jewish boy do less.

He loved the Jewish feasts,
The Jewish temple too.
He prayed the Jewish psalter,
A proud and Jewish Jew.

Can we say anything more about Jesus' boyhood in Nazareth?
I think so. It was the time when he became acquainted with
the scriptures, the life and religion of his people.

Since Jesus grew up normally, he must have developed in
his understanding of what it was to be a Jew. As Blake tersely
put it:

Was Jesus gentle, or did he
Give any marks of Gentility?[13]

For too many Christians, the 'divinity' of Jesus is the only
important thing about him. They fail to see that his divinity is
not even intelligible apart from his Jewish life and background.
For them, the fact that Jesus was a Jew is of no consequence;

the statement 'Jesus is God' is a sufficient and specifying account of the Christian faith.

Forgetfulness of Jesus' Jewishness, together with an exclusive concentration on his divinity, has had disastrous effects upon the people from whom Jesus came. They have been accused of 'deicide' - though it is hard to know why they were never accused of 'Jewicide'. To 'the Jews' collectively has been attributed sole blame for the crucifixion of God's Son when, apart from the fact that an infinitesimal number of Jesus' own race opposed him, the Christian faith is: All men by their sins have put, and continue to put the Christ of God to death.

Forgetfulness of Jesus' Jewishness has played a major part in fostering anti-Semitism. Who can dispute that 'the Jewish problem is in essence a Gentile problem'?[14] Christians created and perpetuated the Jewish problem, as Adolf Hitler well understood. In an interview with Bishop Berning in 1933, the Führer pointed out 'that the Church had always regarded the Jews as parasites and had banished them into the ghetto. He was merely going to do what the Church had done for 1,500 years.'[15]

Browning, in one of his fiercest, most passionate poems, recalls the enforced obligation of Jews to attend an annual Christian sermon in Rome. 'Compel them to come in', the gospel had said! Rome was making amends for Calvary! Then Browning writes of the Jewish boast that they are on Jesus' side against the Devil's disciples:

> By the torture, prolonged from age to age,
> By the infamy, Israel's heritage,
> By the Ghetto's plague, by the garb's disgrace,
> By the badge of shame, by the felon's place,
> By the branding-tool, the bloody whip
> And the summons to Christian fellowship.[16]

It was in a pogrom heralded by a procession bearing the cross that Isaac Babel, at the age of ten, lost his grandfather. He returned from buying a dovecot and came across the old man. 'Two pike perch had been stuck into grandfather: one into the rent in his trousers, the other into his mouth. And while grandfather was dead, one of the fish was still alive and struggling.'[17]

It is not from purely academic interest that I want to emphasize Jesus' Jewishness. It is one of history's tragedies that our Jewish brothers should have developed their traditions in isolation from ours and mostly in ghettoes of our making.

It is not a parody of a widely held view to suggest that Jesus' connection with the Jewish race is a nuisance. His Jewishness only confuses the vital issue of *God's* incarnation and complicates Christianity by saddling it with the Jewish Bible. It was someone of this school who once referred to the Old Testament as a millstone around the neck of Christianity.

I suppose it might have been more convenient had Jesus been born an Etruscan; a member of an extinct race whose history is forgotten and whose language and literature are undecipherable; someone of whom we can but tell, by an examination of wall-drawings in a cave, the shape of his nose. The Son of God had to become a man, true, but it would have been less confusing had he been a kind of man-in-general, a neutral man, a man of whom we know nothing except that he was born of a virgin, worked miracles, died and rose again. Information about the shape of his divine nose would have been a bonus.

The fact is: Jesus' nose was an unmistakably Jewish nose. His thoughts were thoroughly Jewish thoughts. His God was Yahweh, the God of Abraham, Isaac and Jacob. It was of crucial significance to Jesus that he was a Jew; and if he was the Son of God it was in strict continuity with the line of Semitic thought according to which Jews were the people of God and the king was, in a special sense, God's son.

We can be sure that Jesus' years in Nazareth were years of assimilation into the human race by way of Judaism. The Jewish religion was his religion – he had no other – and he was a pious, law-abiding Jew. The history of his race, the patriarchs, the glory, were as much his as they were Paul's and they seem to have engendered in him still more pride. By everything he did and said, by the way he acted and the prophetic manner of his speech, Jesus proved that his roots were entirely Jewish. Jewish, too, must have been his thoughts about himself and his mission.

If Jesus had been other than Jewish, our Christian faith would now be completely different. In fact, there would be no such thing as the 'Christ-ian' faith. From Judaism, we inherited the belief that the world is set free by one event in which God's action is especially discernible. The Son of God did not come from outside the world but from within Judaism. He came from God within Israel, the people of God. This is the significance of the Johannine phrase, Jesus 'came into the world'. It is neither geographical nor chronological but theological. It means that through this exemplary Jewish life God is manifest in the world. As C. H. Dodd put it: 'No great religion was ever a wholly new religion. Christianity could hardly have made its universal appeal if it had not taken up into itself so much of the deepest religious experience of past generations. . . . It found the continuity of tradition which a great religion requires in Judaism; and this continuity it could never abandon without essential loss.'[18]

If this is so, Jesus' years in Nazareth were the formative period of his life. Then it was he acquired his taste for rural beauty, noticed the onset of summer when the fig trees came to leaf, watched the spring flowers bloom and the careless flight of birds. But then, too, he read and reflected on the sacred literature and experiences of his people. The Old Testament was his Bible; it was God's word to him. The Word of God was fed on the words of God and not on revelations out of the blue. Had Jesus been endowed with 'the beatific vision', the whole revelation-disclosure of the Old Testament would have been instantly nullified; it need never have taken place. The Christ of Israel would not have consummated but simply have bypassed the history and experience of his people. It is more reasonable to assume that revelation was disclosed to Jesus as it is to any man, slowly, within the processes of living and becoming one with his people.

An excellent way to read the Bible is with the kind of ardour the young Jesus showed when he sought in it the face of Yahweh, his God. For the Bible incorporated an experience that was to be completed but not forgotten. He was to absorb all those tumultuous centuries of growth in the Jewish consciousness of God and the divine will – and to interpret it all in his own way. The Old Testament did not provide a blueprint which Jesus had to abide by. Jesus creatively brought the Jewish Bible up to date. Without his interpretation, the Christian meaning does not exist in the Jewish Bible, and this is why Jews today cannot find it there. Jews would agree at least with Matthew Arnold's opening remark when he wrote: 'Jesus is not the Messiah to whom the hopes of his nation pointed; and yet Christendom with perfect justice has made him the Messiah, because he alone took . . . a way obscurely indicated in the Old Testament, and the one possible and successful way, for the accomplishment of the Messiah's function: *to bring in everlasting righteousness.*'[19]

Jesus is not the Messiah his nation looked forward to. It is fallacious to say his nation *should* have looked forward to him. This is to disparage Jewish people and to minimize the daringly creative contribution of Jesus as a religious genius. Of course, the New Testament is in the Jewish Bible, but more in the way that Epstein's *Consummatum Est* is in the alabaster block than an intelligible word is in an anagram. Jesus became the Christ he had determined he should be by his daringly new reading of the Bible, a reading to which the disciples were fundamentally faithful after he was crucified.

Jesus must have delighted in the festivals of passover, pentecost and tabernacles. These fed his soul. And what must he have felt when he read scriptural passages like these in Isaiah?

> My beloved had a vineyard
>   on a very fertile hill . . .
> What more was there to do for my vineyard,
>   that I have not done in it? (5 : 1, 4)

> And he said to me, 'You are my servant,
>   Israel, in whom I will be glorified.'
> But I said, 'I have laboured in vain,
>   I have spent my strength for nothing and vanity'
>   (49:3–4).

He was despised and rejected by men;
  a man of sorrows, and acquainted with grief (53:3).

The spirit of the Lord God is upon me,
  because the Lord has anointed me
to bring good tidings to the afflicted;
  he has sent me to bind up the brokenhearted,
to proclaim liberty to the captives (61:1).

These passages and others no less tremendous in Jeremiah, the Psalms, the Book of Job, must have been Jesus' inspiration. The Christian way to read the Old Testament is on the pattern of Jesus who found there the life he felt called upon to embrace in order to become the Christ and Saviour of his people.

In a real sense, we do know a great deal about the childhood of Jesus. The Jewish Bible was his childhood.

Great joy must have filled Jesus' heart when he participated in the Jewish festivals. Once more, Luke the artist hints at this. He tells the story of Jesus at the age of twelve going up to the holy city for the passover and entering for the first time his Father's house. He was so overwhelmed by the splendour of it all, he got lost. Here is a Jew so passionate for the faith of his fathers, he forgets, at least momentarily, the obedience which the law demanded of a son.

5. WAS JESUS EVER NAUGHTY? THE DILEMMA

He learned as other children learn
That knives are sharp and fire will burn,
He learned to talk then sing a song,
Learned right from left and right from wrong.
One day he would be wise and good,
But this took time, as well it should.
He did not want it sooner than
The time it takes to make a man.

Theological speculation about Jesus' consciousness and knowledge of the future has led many to conclude that his 'humanity' is a kind of façade behind which 'divinity' operates and through which it sometimes explodes in glory. Statements about the sinlessness of Jesus have also been interpreted in such a way as to raise doubts about his human personality.

'He committed no sin,' says Peter (1 Pet. 2:22). Of many conclusions derived from this verse some have been to the detriment of Jesus' normality as a child. An American theologian, Norman Pittenger, tells of a worried teacher referring to him one day a question that had been put by a young pupil: 'Was Jesus naughty when he was a little boy?' The teacher was under the impression that to reply 'Yes' would amount to a denial of Jesus' divinity; to reply 'No' would undermine Jesus' humanity.

This dilemma highlights the problem of what is strangely called 'reconciling the divine and the human in Christ'. This dilemma is almost as perplexing and longstanding as Zeno's famous paradox of Achilles and the tortoise. Zeno maintains that though Achilles runs ten times faster than this (I suggest) rather fleet-footed tortoise, he will never catch him up. When Achilles has completed ten metres, the tortoise has completed one; when Achilles traverses that one metre, the tortoise has progressed a decimetre; when Achilles comes to the end of that decimetre, the tortoise is a centimetre ahead. And so on *ad infinitum*. Zeno's patently absurd conclusion is that Achilles can never catch the tortoise up. A refinement of the paradox is to say that neither Achilles nor the tortoise can begin to move because neither could cover the first centimetre, but only go half-way, then another half of the next half-centimetre, and so on. In other words, all movement is impossible and it cannot even begin. The absurdity of the conclusion does not seem to have worried Zeno unduly.[20]

Much of the thinking about Jesus has had the same kind of lunatic quality about it. How do we reconcile infinity and finiteness in Jesus, omniscience and nescience, impassibility and the capacity for pain? In their search for a solution, many theologians virtually denied that Jesus was a human being.

The impression was given that divinity and humanity in Jesus constitute two realities. The characteristics of both are so infinitely diverse that great feats of intelligence are required to harmonize them! Such mental acrobatics are no more justified, in fact, than the efforts of some philosophers to prove that the world cannot be distinct from God, only a kind of *emanation* from God. The basis of this philosophical position is that a perfect God cannot co-exist with an imperfect world. Now, there is a vital truth contained in their argument, namely, that God and the world do not co-exist as two apples co-exist. The world is an expression of God; it is not identified with God nor is it *added to God* as if God and the world can be bracketed together as two.

The phrase dating from Christian antiquity that Jesus had two minds and two wills is a curious and, today, an exceedingly misleading way of saying that Jesus' mind is the expression of God's mind, his will the expression of God's will. It is theologically simplest to bracket together, as if they co-existed as two classifiable realities, the divine and human 'minds and wills'. Once that false step is made, there is endless conjuring with two minds and two wills, with infinity and finiteness, with the eternal and the changeable. Jesus himself must have been the greatest juggler of all! As Schleiermacher put it: 'How can divine and human be brought together under any single conception, as if they could both be more exact determinations, co-ordinated to each other, of one and the same universal?'[21] The problem of reconciling two irreconcilables is a pseudo-problem. It needs not to be met but side-stepped, not to be solved but dissolved.

It is not good enough to say that scholastic theologians have never fallen into the trap I have mentioned and that this is proven from their careful doctrine of analogy. It is true that this doctrine has saved them from looking on the divine mind as simply an infinite version of a human mind. Nonetheless, feeling themselves constrained by the formula 'two minds in Christ' – likewise, 'two natures in Christ' – they undoubtedly dealt with Jesus *in terms of a duality*. This duality is detectable in their whole approach to the relationship between the divine and the human, a duality not at all dispelled by their realization, gained from their insights into analogy, that God is not a superman. My point is that the assumption of any duality in the God-man relationship distorts the uniqueness of this relationship. I want to affirm: (i) God is not identified with the world; (ii) God and the world do not make two; (iii) Jesus must *in no way* be thought of on the model of God and the world making two; (iv) Phrases like 'Jesus is God and man', 'Jesus had two natures, two minds, two wills', etc., inevitably raise insoluble dilemmas and lead to the implicit disavowal of Jesus being an integral human being; (v) Even to speak of 'Jesus' humanity' or 'Jesus' humanity *and* divinity' can encourage this duality, but I'm aware that we cannot eliminate 'beguilement' from our language altogether! (vi) The biblical phrase, 'Jesus is God's Word', is splendid precisely because it gives the impression not that he is God's Word *and* man but that he is God's Word by being the man he is.

There can be no doubt that past attempts to solve the problem of Jesus' alleged duality ended in attributing to him characteristics incompatible with being human. This should have alerted theologians to the probability that something was fundamentally wrong with their procedures. It is of the very nature of a human being to be limited and subject to the processes of becoming. Too often these traits have been eliminated in Jesus' case. His head has frequently been thought of as a kind of machine for decoding messages fed into it from eternity or from his 'other infinite mind'.

I have deliberately used the word 'machine' because Jesus is so often represented as being, humanly speaking, quite impersonal. Aquinas was led to hold that though Jesus had a human nature he is not rightly termed a 'human being' since his 'being' is divine. Even an authority like Cardinal Newman once asserted that we should not refer to Jesus as '*a* man' but only as 'man'. These are a few of the frightening results of theologians' refusal to speak until recently of Jesus' human personality and their insistence that Jesus is 'a divine and not a human person'.

This last classical phrase, intended, as we noted, to stress that Jesus is the one Son of God and therefore entirely human, has been popularly taken to mean that Jesus was lacking in what is essential to being human, namely, person-hood. His manhood seemed in consequence to be only an 'it' assumed by the person of the Word. When Jesus said 'I', it was concluded, the divine, infinite Self was speaking through an impersonal manhood. As if there was no human self or reference centre of consciousness in Jesus! As if the word 'I' employed by Jesus came from an infinite, eternal 'distance' instead of exclusively from that human experience which he, Jesus of Nazareth, was undergoing at that very moment!

We must not diminish Jesus' manhood in this way. John Knox is worth quoting extensively here because no modern theologian has spoken more clearly or more eloquently on this theme. In *The Death of Christ*, he wrote:

> The authentic marks of Jesus' humanity are not found in his physical appearance or in his susceptibility to hunger, thirst, or weariness . . . [but] in his consciousness. Unless he had a human consciousness, he was not a man. If he did not think and feel, about himself and others, as a man does; if he did not take man's lot for granted as being intimately, entirely, and irrevocably his own; if he did not share, at the very deepest levels of his conscious and subconscious life, in our human anxieties, perplexities, and loneliness; if his joys were not characteristic human joys and his hopes, human hopes; if his knowledge of God was not in every part and under every aspect the kind of knowledge which it is given to man, the creature, to have – then he was not a true human being, he was not made man, and the Docetists were essentially right.[22]

Knox returned to this subject in another exemplary study:

> Can we imagine Jesus saying to himself, 'I am not a man', or asking himself, 'Am I a man?' any more than we can imagine our entertaining such thoughts about ourselves? . . . He must have learned as we learn and have grown as we grow. His joys must have been human joys and his sorrows the immemorial sorrows of men like ourselves. He must have known loneliness, frustration, anxiety, just as we do. He

must have felt temptations to doubt and fear. He would have loved others in the way men love their fellows – more, we shall say, but not differently. He, too, would have shrunk from death, the breaking of familiar ties with beloved things. His knowledge of God, for all its sureness and its peculiar intimacy, would have been the kind of knowledge it is given men to have of their Creator and Father. If all this were not true, would we be able to say that he was truly man? For the real marks of a man are not his shape and appearance, or the way he walks, but the way he feels and thinks in his heart, the way he knows himself, others and God.[23]

Knox refuses 'to define Jesus' being "man" in any way that prevents him belonging, integrally belonging, to the whole process of man's evolutionary history, or his sharing, fully sharing, in the self-conscious existence which all other men have known, or his being subject, really subject, to all the limitations of power, knowledge, and virtue which constitute our human finitude or belong inescapably to our existential or "fallen" estate.'[24]

The 'sinlessness' of Jesus raises the problem of the limitation of his virtue. Having set aside the Thomistic view that Jesus was perfectly holy from his conception, how far are we entitled, even obligated, to think of him as a morally perfectible human being?

6. WAS JESUS EVER NAUGHTY? A REPLY TO THE DILEMMA

To the simple question, 'Was Jesus naughty when he was a little boy?' we are in a position to give an equally direct and simple reply, 'I presume so. How else is it possible to think of a little boy?' We can hardly look on Jesus as the paragon of Nazareth, never disobedient or mischievous, always saying his prayers and completely disinterested in his immature peers as playmates.[25] A child who is never naughty is a contradiction in terms. We have no reason to imagine Jesus as the little Lord Fauntleroy of Palestine. Had the infant Jesus never told untruths, indulged in temper tantrums, taken things behind his parents' backs, been spiteful and greedy – this would have illustrated his abnormality quite as much as making real birds out of clay. The normal child is, by nature, difficult.

Life is a process of discovery. Mischief is an integral part of this process. To become human involves coming up against the limits of permitted human behaviour and realizing that it is possible to wound people who are not objects but other selves.[26] This takes time to learn; to say that there is a necessary failure here is simply to say that it *can* only be learned by trial and error.

An example may clarify this. No one has ever gone through life without being hurt, however slightly, by fire. We do not know what fire is until we have experienced one of its main characteristics: it burns. And being burnt is painful. Somewhat similar is learning to live the moral life. At the beginning, we overreach ourselves. We say to ourselves, 'I have gone too far this time, I have done wrong.' This failure is, it would seem, part of the process of becoming moral beings. Morality is like language, indeed it is a form of language. A child makes 'moral' mistakes as he makes linguistic errors, as did my three-year-old niece, who said to me recently in response to my teasing, 'My mummy's not old, she's new.'

Jesus' uninterrupted progress in holiness, while not self-contradictory as is the Thomistic idea of his instant holiness in his mother's womb, is scarcely less difficult to accept as a factor in a genuine human life. Can it be doubted that Jesus went through life as we all do, regretting that he blurted out this or that; kicking himself, as we would say, at his insensitivity, his unconcern; worrying that he did not do his best to make himself understood, and so on?

What are we to say, then, of the biblical affirmations of the sinlessness of Christ. The first point to make is that they are not twentieth-century reflections on the psychology of Jesus' development. We have to put these affirmations in their context.

Peter is speaking in 1 Peter 2 about Christ being an example to us in suffering. He instances the manner in which Christ behaved in his passion. 'Christ also suffered for you. . . . He committed no sin; no guile was found on his lips. When he was reviled, he did not revile. . . . He himself bore our sins in his body on the tree.' The reference is clearly to the generosity, the meekness, the courage of Christ when he was surrounded at the end of his life by injustice and iniquity. There are allusions in the text to Isaiah's Suffering Servant (Isa. 53) who went like a lamb to the slaughter without opening his mouth. To say Jesus was without sin is equivalent to saying he was not a criminal, he committed no crime for which he merited a slave's death.

In Hebrews 4:15 and 7:26 the context is the same. The author is contemplating Jesus as our high priest whose sacrifice was completed on Calvary. 'We have not a high priest who is unable to sympathize with our weakness, but one who in every respect has been tempted as we are, yet without sinning.' We have a high priest, 'holy, blameless, unstained, separated from sinners, exalted above the heavens'.

The biblical authors are not making abstract statements about Jesus from which conclusions can be drawn about his earliest, hidden years when he must have done everything he was told – or was so naturally good he never needed to be told to behave himself. Nor are they suggesting that Jesus was never sorry, never had any remorse or regrets about his intentions, actions, omissions. They are making concrete claims about Jesus: in the time of trial, he did not fail as others fail. He was in no way loveless but a pattern of generosity and forbearance. Furthermore, this was not due to some kind of metaphysical necessity; it was not the inevitable consequence of him being the Son of God, as though his courageous response was in every way painless and, as it were, natural to him. His goodness was something he had to fight for. He was tried and tempted as any man. He suffered not simply because he was already good but to prove his goodness as we all need to do.

This was the overwhelming impression Jesus made on his followers: he went about doing good. When they first came into contact with him, they met a completely mature, loving, selfless human being, someone who was empty of vanity and full of God, someone whom it made sense to follow when he preached the kingdom because the kingdom had taken possession of him. He was a worthy spokesman (or prophet) of God's word. In John's phrase, no one could convict him of sin. He did not belong to the world of darkness: he was all light.

To say, in the biblical context, that Jesus was sinless is equivalent to saying that when Jesus was manifest in Israel he came as a real man determined to do God's will and that alone. And he carried out his intent right up to the moment of dying on a cross. Indeed, it was that unforgettable picture of Jesus on the cross, sacrificing himself humbly and lovingly, that determined all subsequent claims about his sinlessness.

The child is father to the man. That Jesus reached in early manhood such devotion to God and his fellows proves he must, throughout his life, have given them splendid service. But G. W. H. Lampe is surely correct in saying that Jesus' sinlessness 'is hardly to be evaluated by reference to the question whether every action and saying attributed to him bears the stamp of moral perfection. Sin is essentially a religious concept. It refers to the personal relationship of man to God. It represents a deep-rooted and fundamental attitude rather than the particular moral lapses, offences and transgressions which are the external symptoms of it.'[27] Jesus proved conclusively that there was in him no 'basic estrangement', no barrier to complete trust in God.

'Was Jesus ever naughty as a child?' I hope the question now looks ludicrous to everyone. Only a very foolish adult, projecting his own developed moral consciousness on to a child, would identify naughtiness with transgression – let alone with the basic estrangement of sin – in a little one who has only begun the enormous and exhilarating experiment of life. When did any sane and sensible mother say of a mischievous child, 'He is guilty of sin'?

Interestingly, the only story Luke tells about Jesus' boyhood, taken at its face value, shows a youngster of twelve not yet able to appreciate the sentiments and anxiety of his parents. He was so busy asking questions that he was quite 'lost' in the clouds of his own thoughts. Luke does not scruple to tell a story about Jesus in which he is shown as capable of hurting those he loved most without even realizing it.

It is after relating this painful incident that Luke applies to Jesus the scriptures' words. '[He] *increased* in wisdom and in stature, and in favour with God and man.'

7. JOHN THE BAPTIST

At the beginning of the preaching of the good news towers the figure of John the Baptist. Christians of earlier ages had a deep appreciation of his importance in the scheme of things. They honoured him as the one who, in Christian devotion, continues to prepare the way of the Lord. They knew that no one can say of himself, 'In me the old aeon is completely over and the new has taken its place.'

All four evangelists witness solemnly to the inauguration of the Baptist's ministry. Luke, it is true, had pictorially anticipated this testimony. He recalled that Isaiah, the prophet whose words the Baptist used, had proclaimed: 'The Lord . . . formed me from the womb to be his servant' in order to be 'a light to the nations' (49:5,6). Jeremiah, too, believed he heard the Lord speaking to him of his prophetic vocation:

> Before I formed you in the womb I knew you,
> and before you were born I consecrated you;
> I appointed you a prophet to the nations (Jer. 1:4).

These texts explain why Luke has the Baptist jumping for joy in his mother's womb when Mary, the new ark of the covenant, comes near.

The Baptist's preaching marked the final preparation for the Lord who was to come. The time was one of intense messianic expectation. The hatred of the Roman occupation – it led eventually to the zealots' slaughter of the Roman garrison in Jerusalem prior to the sacking of the city in AD 70 – had never been more bitter. In such a climate, the Baptist's heralding of the imminence of the last times found an eager audience among people deprived of political and so, according to their creed, of religious independence, too. The Baptist was a voice crying in the wilderness for crooked paths to be made straight, and valleys to be filled and mountains to be levelled into plains.

The Baptist was recognizably prophetic in countenance and appearance. The people who swarmed out from Jerusalem and Judea into the desolation of the desert south of the Jordan believed they saw the new Elijah. He was clothed in camel's hair; he abstained from wine, and ate locust beans and wild honey. This was a man of whom anything could be imagined and *was*. Later on, some people supposed that he had come back from the dead in the person of Jesus.

John preached repentance. He warned those who put all their trust in being sons of Abraham that without repentance their election was worthless and that God could raise up the desert stones, if he so wished, to be Abraham's children. The publicans heeded him, the pharisees and lawyers did not.

Those who repented John baptized in the Jordan. He worked no miracles. Baptism was his only sign, a messianic sign of purification to make the heart ready for the advent of God's kingdom which only the pure could enter.

Jesus came to the Baptist to be baptized in the Jordan. And John witnessed to him. There seems little doubt that Jesus saw in John a sign from God that his own time of peaceful preparation was over. It has been conjectured that Jesus had once been one of the Baptist's disciples. It is possible that John was the first to recognize Jesus' outstanding qualities and, by designating him, inspired Jesus to begin his own public ministry. However, the evidence for this is scanty.

The Baptist had a privilege granted to no other prophet in Israel: others had pointed to a glorious future; the Baptist raised his finger and said, 'He is here.' There was one in their midst who was to baptize with fire and the holy Spirit.

John feared no one. He spoke openly against the tetrarch, Herod, for marrying his brother's wife, Herodias. For this he was imprisoned. Jesus, ever eager to read the signs of the times, saw in this a warning. It was at this time he withdrew into Galilee and began preaching the good news there.

Like his predecessors in the prophetic line, John understood
that the word of God comes to a man not always as a soft
breeze but often as a raging storm. The prophet is a judgement
upon his fellows, and sometimes, as in Jeremiah's case, it
makes him curse the day his mother bore him:

Curséd be the morn when I was born,
Soft stranger to the earth.
No benediction on the day of that affliction
Called my birth.

Curséd be the man who quickly ran
To my father and thus cried:
'Your wife's had a boy, my tale is of nothing but joy.'
For he lied.

No joy did he bring, that nurseling thing,
My wretched father's son.
Curséd be the mite who should have brought only delight.
He brought none.

Great God, tell me why I did not die
When they severed my birth-cord?
Why make me survive, in my sorrows more dead than
alive?
Tell me, Lord.

The Lord God replied, 'If you had died,
My own word had died, too.
My word is your child. To mother it, gentle or wild,
I chose you.'

The word had come wild to John the Baptist. But he had
mothered it; and now his days were drawing to a close. I
imagine him in his cell at Machaerus like a caged eagle, the
kind of captured, wounded steppe eagle that Dostoevsky refers
to in *The House of the Dead*. Even the prisoners wanted to
release it. 'Let him die, but let him die in freedom', they said.[28]
John's freedom was in his heart. He went from his cell to
execution; his head on a dish was a birthday gift from a vain
and cowardly king to a dancing girl.

John's greatness is never questioned by the evangelists. This was no reed shaken by the desert wind. This was no em-purpled, soft-living courtier. He was even more than a prophet. The Baptist was God's messenger or angel who proclaimed: 'Here is the awaited One who is to bring in the kingdom.'

The evangelists were careful to point out John's humility. They do this because even after Jesus' resurrection some disciples of John were still baptizing as their master had done. To counter this aberrant activity, John is made to say that he was only the groom's friend waiting on the groom and rejoicing in his joy. John had declared that he was not worthy to tie up the lace of Jesus' shoe and that, despite the acclaim of the people, his task was to become little so that Jesus could become great.

It is likely that the Baptist bestowed on Jesus his most treasured possessions: the first disciples, John and Andrew. It was Andrew who brought his brother Simon to the Lord.

Great, then, was the Baptist, the Elijah who had come again to prepare for the Christ and who sealed his personal witness by martyrdom. Greater still is the least in the kingdom of God which Jesus was soon to bring in with his baptism of fire.

8. THE BAPTISM OF JESUS

Jesus was first baptized with water. When, after centuries of silence, a prophet, John the Baptist, appeared, Jesus followed him. He took his place humbly among sinners. He was 'num-bered among the transgressors' on the banks of the Jordan.

Through that river, the Israelites had passed centuries before. The Promised Land was journey's end after their Exodus, their passover from slavery in Egypt to freedom. There in Canaan, according to their most famous saga, they had consolidated and brought to fruition the new life they had nurtured in their desert wanderings.

In the fast-flowing river Jordan, Jesus insisted on being baptized by John. This fact we know for certain about him but we can be sure of little else. The evangelists nowhere speculate on the reasons why Jesus offered himself as a candidate for 'the baptism of repentance'. The story, as now told, has been brought up to date by early Christian tradition. It has become a deep, theological meditation on what Jesus eventually proved himself to be: the Christ, the Son of God.

Jesus stepped into the waters, was buried in them and came out on to the Promised Land. It was as though he wanted to identify himself completely with his wayward people and their history; to bear their sin away and bury it for ever in the waters. Love entails identification with the sinner in his sins if the sinner is to be converted and live. No theologian has expressed this better than Martin Luther:

> Faith, therefore, must be purely taught; namely, that thou art so entirely and nearly joined unto Christ, that he and thou art made as it were one person: so that thou mayest boldly say, I am now one with Christ, that is to say, Christ's resurrection, victory and life are mine. And again, Christ may say, I am that sinner, that is, his sins and death are mine, because he is united and joined unto me, and I unto him. For by faith we are so joined together, 'that we are become one flesh and one bone' (Eph. 5); we are the members of the body of Christ, flesh of his flesh, and bone of his bones: so that this faith doth couple Christ and me more near together than the husband is coupled to his wife.[29]

Jesus went so far as to identify himself, the Saviour, with the whole world order of sin as a system of relationships antagonistic to God who is love.

The baptism is presented in the gospels as the triumphal, public inauguration of Jesus as the Messiah. 'This is my beloved Son', the Father's voice said afterwards from the cloud, as though Jesus had just been born for a new task. In the context of the gospels, these words are reminiscent of those of Isaiah about the Servant of God, 'Behold my servant [or son], whom I uphold, my chosen, in whom my soul delights' (42:1). According to Christian reflection, while Jesus was praying, the Spirit anointed him in power for his mission as

Messiah and then drove him into the desert. This is seen as a time of personal decision for Jesus. He who is soon to preach the kingdom in crisis terms must first be sure his own heart has accepted all the kingdom's demands.

He fasted for forty days and nights in the wilderness. This was looked on as a kind of painful sacrament of Israel's forty years wandering in the desert. When he was weakest he was tempted. The leader and saviour Moses had also 'fasted forty days and forty nights eating and drinking nothing' (Exod. 34:28), so had Elijah. Moses had worked wonders in the desert. Elijah, after eating, 'went in the strength of that food forty days and forty nights to Horeb the mount of God' (1 Kgs 19:8). Was Jesus to be a lesser figure than these? Jesus, the new Moses, the new prophet of 'the last times', was tempted to liberate his people through glory and renown; tempted to change the desert stones into contemporary manna so that everyone would think of him as a great and glorious king; tempted to work wonders in order to impress an incredulous multitude.

Jesus, using Mosaic texts, will have none of it. Israel had sometimes failed but he will not fail. In this desert story, under the guiding and promptings of the Spirit, he faces up to the vocation his Father had given him as the representative of Israel, and, through Israel, of all mankind. The theology is: he will redeem not *from* suffering, as Jews expected, but *by* suffering. Satan, the tempter, is answered from the sacred text.

Perhaps the fourth gospel means us to understand that it was when Jesus returned from the desert, at once triumphant and haggard with exposure and fasting, that the Baptist pointed him out to some of his future disciples with the words, 'Behold, the Lamb of God'. He was Isaiah's servant in whom there is no beauty or comeliness, the Lamb who is to be slain in atonement for the sins of many.

The story of Jesus' baptism, no less than the story of his birth, is part of the gospel; it is integral to the theme of passover and is seen to anticipate it. Here we are supposed to see that the Jesus who emerged from the desert is the same who, some little while afterwards, was to be baptized a second time. 'I have a baptism with which I must be baptized' (Luke 12:50), said Jesus, referring to his purifying and atoning death on the cross. He felt himself in his prophetic way to be unclean and soiled by sin. On the cross he was to bear the sin of the world, the sin which could only be washed away when he went through the waters of death and passed over, alive and immortal, to the Promised Land of heaven.

The theology underlying the account of Jesus' baptism is highly developed. His baptism is seen essentially as his messianic inauguration; and yet Jesus himself never allowed, indeed, discouraged messianic titles such as Son of David and Son of God. This was not because he was without a properly messianic consciousness, as is evidenced in his preaching of the kingdom and in some of his dramatic acts as when, entering Jerusalem as king of peace, he cleansed the temple. But he was otherwise silent on the theme of messianism, presumably because of the political hopes surrounding Jewish expectation of the Christ with which he disagreed.

Jesus spoke of himself as 'son of man', which is a Hebraism for 'man'. In so far as the term 'Son of Man' was the designation of some divine, pre-existent, celestial figure found in Daniel and the Jewish apocalypses, Jesus seems to have distinguished himself from such a one. This Son of Man, he believed, would vindicate him whatever his own fate, provided he remained faithful to his Father unto the end. It was only after Jesus' death and resurrection, when the disciples grasped that Jesus' suffering was not incompatible with messiahship, rather, in God's providence, was the expression of his messiahship – only then was it possible for the disciples to redeem the title 'Messiah' or 'Christ' and apply it unreservedly to Jesus. The ironic description blazened above the cross, 'Jesus of Nazareth, King of the Jews', turned out to be the highest theology. Now, too, Jesus, the risen and exalted Lord, could be identified with the heavenly Son of Man who would come from heaven to judge the living and the dead.

As usual, the passover determines the evangelists' narration of events. The baptism is made to prefigure the passover. It is seen to be not only Jesus' way of summing up and taking on himself the whole of Israel's history, it is, in addition, a symbolic rehearsal of his baptism of death, the final Exodus, when sin and death were left behind in death's waters. The remembrance of Jesus on his cross determines the story of the baptism. H. S. Coffin writes:

> The sinless sufferer on the cross, in his oneness with his brethren, felt their wrong-doing as his own, confessed in his forsakenness that God would have nothing to do with it save destroy it, felt that it separated between men and God, and that he was actually away from God . . . That he with his recoil and quiver should still have loved us so intensely that, when he felt the gulf fixed between God and sinners, he thought himself on our side of the breach and numbered himself with the transgressors – that is the marvel.[30]

This is the essential significance of Jesus undergoing the baptism of repentance. He is one with sinners. It is because he is so good and loving that he is strong enough to stand *on our side* of the divide.

When Jesus emerged from the desert, his main task in life loomed ahead of him: to preach the kingdom of God, with what results he was not immediately able to see. One thing he was determined on: he would be God's servant, his true obedient Son, even if, at the end of the road, suffering and death awaited him.

9. PREACHING THE KINGDOM

The Baptist had gone like a hermit into the wilderness where crowds followed him. Jesus went into the towns and villages where the crowds already were.

The Baptist had preached the proximity of the kingdom; this is why he pointed away from himself. Jesus claims that the kingdom is presenting itself now in his own words and deeds. 'Blessed are the eyes which see what you see! For I tell you that many prophets and kings desired to see what you see, and did not see it, and to hear what you hear, and did not hear it' (Luke 10:23-4).

The kingdom is focused on Jesus. Jesus' conviction is that in him God is beginning to rule. This explains the sense of imminent crisis that characterizes Jesus' ministry. Be on the watch, he repeats constantly, be ready.[31] The kingdom is in process of coming; it is as inevitable as the harvest after the sowing. But people have to decide: will they accept God's rule as it breaks in *through Jesus' words and deeds*?

The kingdom, in Jesus' preaching, does not entail a restructuring of the physical world. It consists in a comprehensively new relationship now made possible between God and man, a relationship which brings with it immeasurable joy. This is why Jesus offers no apocalyptic omens by which the kingdom is recognizable. He himself is an adequate sign of the kingdom. For the kingdom is characterized by meekness, mercy, poverty, purity of heart, forgiveness of enemies; and Jesus is the embodiment of these characteristics by which the new relationship with God is attested. He is a sign only in the sense that Jonah's warning to Nineveh was a sign: he preaches God's message of forgiveness bestowed even on enemies provided they repent.

Indeed, those entering the kingdom may have enemies but they are enemies to no one. The question, 'Who is my neighbour?' is reversed by Jesus' declaration, 'You must not ask who is my neighbour, but rather, to whom am I neighbour? You must be neighbour to everyone, even to your enemies.'

Those people are subject to the rule of God who dispossess themselves, who are anxious not about this world's goods but only about doing God's will. God's will comes first and everything else follows from that. To do God's will requires in principle a fearful renunciation: leaving father and mother, plucking out the right eye if it scandalizes us. A man must abandon his systems of piety. The kingdom takes priority over the rigorous keeping of the law. This is why the child is the image of one who enters the kingdom. The child knows he has earned nothing: he accepts what is offered him with simple gratitude. The child is the opposite of the pietistic person.

Everything is summed up in the Father prayer. God's name must be hallowed; his rule must hold sway over the heart, and his will be done; all anxiety must be laid aside and absolute trust be put in God who will provide for us; we must be forgiving as God is, and trust him in all adversity. The demands of God's kingdom are absolute.

'Seeing the crowds, [Jesus] went up on the mountain, and when he sat down his disciples came to him. And he opened his mouth and taught them, saying: "Blessed are the poor in spirit, for theirs is the kingdom of heaven. . . . You are the salt of the earth . . . You are the light of the world. . . . You, therefore, must be perfect, as your heavenly Father is perfect" ' (Matt. 5 : 1–3, 13, 14, 48).

Jesus teaches that whoever wants to enter the kingdom must make a dramatic and far-reaching decision. The new law for the imminent kingdom is a law of love. Only the gospel of love and not a series of enactments and prohibitions can lead to the fulfilling of the law. Jesus aims to bring about a complete reformation of the inner man, a renewal of the heart.

It is a denial of 'the gospel to every creature' to suggest that in Christ's name only 'moderate' demands should be made of some of his disciples. It may seem elementary good sense to say that asking everything of all Christians is asking too much. We must surely be careful not to break the bruised reed or quench the smoking flax. We must temper the wind to the shorn lamb, proffer milk not meat to babes. But what does this mean: that we should preach a kind of common denominator of Christian behaviour, mostly termed 'natural law', a high minimum level of decent, God-fearing living?

The truth is, the whole gospel must be preached to everyone, including the Christian ethic at its most radical. We must not hide the Christian ethic on the plea that the gospel's demands are too difficult or unrealistic.

Jesus demands of *everyone* who wishes to be his disciple and to enter the kingdom a radical conversion or change of heart. 'The kingdom of heaven is like treasure hidden in a field, which a man found and covered up; then in his joy he goes and sells all that he has and buys that field. Again, the kingdom of heaven is like a merchant in search of fine pearls, who, on finding one pearl of great value, went and sold all that he had and bought it' (Matt. 13:44–5). Entrance into the kingdom depends upon a man renouncing everything for its sake. So great is the joy he experiences on finding it that he gives up everything to make the purchase.

Jesus was trying to evoke this radical decision in all his hearers all through his ministry and he was satisfied with nothing less. The kingdom of God was already in process of coming, and a person had to respond to him by becoming absolutely poor and chaste and meek. Any disciple of his had to show an absolute generosity, self-denial and willingness to forgive, a love which embraces everyone, even enemies, and especially the despised and the outcasts. Christ's disciples must be like their master and take up their cross; they must be prepared to endure every form of contumely and insult on the way to crucifixion.

Luther was perhaps right in his intention at least when he left his monastery to campaign for this gospel truth: everyone is called to be *a Christian*. Bonhoeffer wrote: 'Luther's return from the cloister to the world was the worst blow the world has suffered since the days of early Christianity . . . Hitherto the Christian life had been the achievement of a few choice spirits under the exceptionally favourable conditions of monasticism; now it is a duty laid on every Christian living in the world.'[32] It would be inexcusable if religious – monks, friars, nuns – instead of highlighting the gospel's demands as they fall on everyone, were held to be the only people called to live up to those demands. In the gospels, there are not two standards but one: the ideal standard of the kingdom. There are no first- and second-class travellers on the journey to God: all of us must strive to be perfect as our heavenly Father is perfect if we are to be faithful to the new age that breaks into the world with the coming and consummating death of Christ.

Who can deny that in long stretches of Christian tradition, the layman was not expected to reach a very high degree of sanctity? If married, he was already judged to be making un-Christian concessions to the flesh.

How did this unevangelical notion become widespread? Doubtless, the reasons are complex. Perhaps the main one was an unbalanced attitude to sex and marriage which led eventually to the restriction of office in the Church to the 'eunuch' class (Matt. 19:12) of celibates. When, in the patristic period, heretics affirmed 'procreation is evil', theologians like Augustine responded by saying, 'procreation is the *only* good of marriage'. Procreation and not love became the only justification for marriage. For a millennium and more, there is no single instance of a pope or theologian saying that the act of sex is an act of love. The act of sex was always presumed to be at least venially sinful and only justifiable by the prospect of procreation. This is why intercourse between husband and wife during pregnancy was considered evil: even animals don't do such a thing. Besides, it is a form of profligacy to sow seed when the field is sufficiently sown already. Pope Gregory the Great went so far as to assert that all pleasure *even in lawful intercourse* is necessarily sinful.

The Christian community accepts today that sexual intercourse is permissible in marriage even when the intention is expressly *not to procreate*. We have to admit that the encouragement of the safe-period method of controlling birth, with its deliberate dissociation of intercourse and procreation, is contrary to more than fourteen hundred years of constant teaching.

With the earlier outlook on Christian marriage, it is not surprising that the Christian layman – not being a celibate – was held to be ineligible for the higher echelons of holiness. He was only expected to keep the Mosaic law, interpreted as an explicit clarification of the precepts of natural law inherently accessible to the pagan human mind. The religious, on the other hand, was expected to keep the 'counsels' which, as commonly explained, were nothing but the gospel of Jesus Christ! The 'high' standards of the gospel were considered particularly suitable for cloistered monks and nuns as well as for priests who, by their sacred calling, had a special standard to maintain.

The gospel is not open to this interpretation. The ideal of

absolute poverty, chastity and obedience is proposed to everyone. The gospel insists that we should all leave everything, sell everything, give everything, obey in everything for the sake of the kingdom. Any lesser standard is a refusal of Christ, a refusal to be like God.

10. THE DEMANDS OF THE GOSPEL

The plain gospel is that everyone, in whatever condition of life he chooses, must strive to be as perfect in love, generosity and forgiveness as God himself. The great refusal of a person's life may not be a contravention of the natural law or a precept of the decalogue but the refusal to be a saint. For the absolute demands of the gospel fall upon us all differently – and sometimes more heavily in particular crises of our lives.

A person may become radically sinful by refusing to do what no law could order him to do, namely, the heroic, the humanly 'impossible'. Jesus teaches that we can still be sinful after having broken none of the commandments, but he goes further: we can be sinful, too, by turning our backs on a task that requires heroism for its accomplishment. In other words, Jesus has no immediate interest in law as such.[33] A law-keeper who keeps the law for the law's sake is precluded from any vision of greatness. Only the 'lover' is capable of heroism, of deriving otherwise inconceivable strength from the force of love itself. Jesus asks for perfect love which regulates and supersedes law and does so effortlessly.

According to Jesus, no law can fulfil the demands of love but love can fulfil the demands of law unthinkingly and with relish because the lover is essentially free. This is the force of Augustine's often quoted remark: 'Love, and do what you like.' What love wants is good because the lover has an affinity towards the good. And love can reach the heights and the depths where law cannot gain a foothold.

An example from daily life will illustrate this. We know that ultimately it is impossible to legislate for motherhood. Local or government authorities may insist on certain legally approved

accurate when he wrote: 'Christian teaching doe
wn laws for everybody, and does not say to people
, for fear of punishment, must obey such and suc
then you will be happy"; but it explains to ever
his position in relation to the world, and allows hir
results, for him individually, flow inevitably fror
n.'[35]

can cope with the individual demands that Goc
hrist, makes on us *because he loves us*. He wants us a
ct as he is perfect, to love him as his Son loved hir
is asking of us the 'impossible'. The source of ou
that we construct an ethic of the possible and fe
ur capacity to live up to it. But in the process v
ed in making ourself *homo religiosus*, the contente
g pharisee.

. THE ASSAULT ON HOMO RELIGIOSUS

osus resorts to reasonable rules and regulations. T
ce is that in both personal and social life there
liferation of religious rules that the Book of Levitic
is, in comparison, as simple as the highway coc
nden, sj, in a book of rare moral insight, writ
Church authorities can check the rabbinical prolife
clesiastical legislation, inherited from the count
on, and bring it back to decent proportions.'[36]
igious' man above all aims at safety and security.
y wants to be able to gauge how he stands in
he Almighty. This amounts to saying that basica
n his own deeds but he does not trust God.
igiosus is to be found in all religious groups. Beca
litions, we are most familiar with him in Judaism a
y.
im has amused us with the Talmudic teaching on
aw. 'Cold water might be poured on warm but
e, nor was it lawful to prepare either cold or wa
s. Nay, a Rabbi went so far as to forbid throwing

standards of babycare, hygiene, clothing, schooling and so on. But even when these standards are exactly conformed to, there may still be no real mothering of the child at all.

Jesus knew that all 'God's rules' may be kept while God and man are not in the least loved or served. It is not possible, Jesus realized, to save mankind by forcing them to keep laws, whether out of tidiness or fear or the desire to amass merits (to become 'holy') or anything else. By stressing law, the law is probably not kept or, if it is, it is kept to the harm of the law-keeper. I mean, a man may so pride himself on abiding by the law and so disparage someone else who does not that he is worse by far in God's sight than a sinner who acknowledges he is a sinner. It is by emphasizing not law but love that we receive the strength from God to keep the law.

This is the paradox that Paul, too, is continually playing with. The emphasis on law – whether in the area of commands or prohibitions – leads people to be ultimately powerless in its regard. Why is this? Because law makes them depend on themselves and their own achievements instead of on God; it makes them self-regarding and not God-regarding. And this is the root of all sin. The rule-keeper can become so absorbed in his own struggle for perfection he is oblivious of anybody else.

Jesus knew how easy it is to have a religion of nothing more than comfortable and, in the end, senseless conformity. A strict legal code may be just another way of stifling the request God makes for a person's heart. This is why Jesus, 'a troubler of the peace', expressly aimed at engendering a perpetual disquiet in his disciples. They were never to say, 'I have fulfilled God's will, I have done enough.' The kingdom asks for all they have to give all the time. However much they have done, they stand before God as 'unprofitable servants' (Luke 17:10). Hence Christ's continual demand, the tiresome tension his word sets up in us, the unpredictable incursions he is continually making in our lives. He is the representative of a God who is Father, perfect and all-holy, a God who wants all his children to be like him.

Still, how can we account for these inexorable precepts of Christ: 'Go, sell all thou hast, Take neither staff nor scrip,

Have no thought for tomorrow, Turn the other cheek'? What does it all mean? To interpret it as a new series of laws is to treat Jesus as a legislator of minute and astonishing enactments. Keeping them becomes the condition of salvation!

'Turn the other cheek.' Are we forbidden to telephone the police when a thief breaks in or to charge him if and when he's caught?

'Take no thought for tomorrow.' Perhaps we are to keep no savings under the mattress or in the piggy bank, to give up property and possessions, to tear up all pension books and insurance policies?

'Leave the dead to bury their dead.' What a scandal to the Jewish listener who held the interment of their dead to be a sacred duty! Was Jesus really trying to put undertakers out of business?

'Do not have two tunics.' Do we have to clear out the wardrobe, sell the arsenal of shoes, take spare clothing to the Oxfam shop? Does it mean that the divine wrath hangs over Carnaby Street and the Paris fashion shows, over Wall Street and the Bank of England, over the Yen, the Dollar and the Deutschmark?

Some people have tried to interpret such statements as new laws and become in consequence absolute pacifists or hermits or freaks. Most common-sense Christians say it's ridiculous to take all this literally. Jesus couldn't have meant that; he was far too sensible a fellow for that. Not at all an extremist. Perhaps he was just in one of his 'poetical' moods.

Some Christians think that Jesus is proposing an absolute ethic on the basis of his conviction that the end of the world was imminent. Since his conviction was false, the emergency (or interim) ethic, they argue, has no further relevance.[34]

Some think that Jesus was laying down an ethic that was practicable for Middle-Eastern peoples dwelling where the climate is temperate all the year round. In Palestine, it was possible to make do with loin-cloths for covering, with water and beans for nourishment.

Some (mainly Catholics) think that Jesus had in mind a few cloistered Carthusians, the only folk who can justifiably be called Christ's followers. Tough and sile[nt] cells, they are what Christ wanted his di[sciples]

Jesus, I suggest, is saying none of the[se] is: If any one is to be a child of God, he [must know] that he is called to do his Father's will, [and that] God requires that we sell everything [at any] price and not once but every day and e[very] day. Christ is speaking not to monks [but in]cluding monks. He is saying: 'Because I [love you] I demand everything of all of you; all [your] whole heart. No vow of yours can acc[ount for] sion. A vow of poverty may prevent [being] radically poor. Such a one may not hea[r me] any more because he thinks he has no[thing,] such a one, poverty has only meant s[urrender of] chattels to the community, when I wa[nt a naked] and emptied heart so as to fill it with [my] kingdom.'

As far as Christ is concerned, there [is no] way of perfection. Certainly, Christ said [to one:] 'If you would be perfect, go, sell what [you have, give to] the poor, and you will have treasure [in heaven and] follow me' (Matt. 19:21). But it runs c[ontrary to all we] know of Christ's teaching to suggest [that this is a] general prescription for perfection, as i[f the way] to become perfect is to hand over all [one has.] Jesus is addressing an individual, thi[s man.] Seeing that *his* heart was 'possessed by [his goods', he told] *him* that, as the condition of disciples[hip, he sell] his goods and follow him, the only [way he could.] faces individual rich young men and [tells] them that they make a similar sacrifi[ce whether they be] believers or unbelievers, religious or l[ay, kings or] beggars.

Each of us in the circumstances of [our own life must ask, what] would the Lord have *me* do?' That [question honestly put] and faithfully responded to leads to [his kingdom in] spite of his extreme pronouncemen[ts] water over one's self for fear of spreading the vapour, or of cleaning the floor thereby.' 'Women are forbidden to look into the glass on the Sabbath, because they might discover a white hair and attempt to pull it out, which would be a grievous sin.' 'A person might go about with wadding in his ear but not with false teeth nor with a gold plug in the tooth. False teeth might fall out, and the wearer might lift and carry them, which would be sinful on the Sabbath.' 'A radish may be dipped into salt, but not left in it too long, since this would be to make pickle.'[37]

Many centuries later, Blaise Pascal was inveighing against the hypocrisy of contemporary Christian moral theologians. The gospel says we should give in alms of our superfluities, but the moralists so conveniently defined superfluities that the richest classes in society didn't have any. To give money for a benefice is obviously simony, but to give money to induce the incumbent to resign his benefice is not. The Church condemns duelling, but to preserve his honour a man may chance to be at the right spot at the right time, not with any intention of fighting a duel, God forbid, but only to defend himself against unjust attack. To fulfil the Sunday obligation, we can hear half of one priest's mass and then half of another; it is even lawful to hear two halves of mass at the same time when mass is being said simultaneously by two different priests. By this method, Pascal comments, mass in Notre Dame in Paris would only take a minute.[38]

Unfortunately, these forms of religious duplicity are perennial. Not even Edersheim can match the case reported very recently in *The Jewish Chronicle*. According to Jewish law on marriage and divorce in Israel, a man, whether he be already married or not, is bound to wed his widowed sister-in-law if her husband (i.e., his brother) has died without leaving any children. Usually, the man refuses this obligation, which the law entitles him to do. But first he has to participate in the chalitza ceremony. Part of this ceremony is the pronouncing of a special Hebrew formula in the presence of a rabbi, after which the widow is free to remarry any one else she pleases.

The difficulty in the case reported in *The Jewish Chronicle* was that the surviving brother was deaf and dumb. This meant he was unable to pronounce the formula of renunciation in the chalitza ceremony. The two chief rabbis of Israel, Rabbi Itzhak Nissim (Sephardi) and Rabbi Isser Unterman (Ashkenazi) were called in to resolve the dilemma. They decided that the widow and her brother-in-law should marry for twenty-four hours, consummate the marriage, and then be granted a divorce. To quote the newspaper:

> The 'groom', already married with a ten-month-old baby, and his 'bride' were married before two Ashdod rabbis. The couple were then taken direct to a hotel where a room had been reserved for them by the rabbinate. The next morning, the couple having performed mitzvat hahityachdut (the mitzva of the act of union), they were taken to the Rehovot rabbinate, where the divorce was pronounced.

It seems that divorce does not require the actual pronouncing of words.

This immoral pantomime, whose plot would not discredit a Molière farce, disgraces religion. As the editor of *The Jewish Chronicle* remarks, it requires no halachic expertise to know that this incredible tale 'is opposed to some of Judaism's most distinctive values'; he might have added, 'it is opposed to common decency, as well'. The decision of the chief rabbis was legalistic in the worst sense of the word, that is, it is an example of law for law's sake. It is completely loveless; it showed no concern for the people involved. The rabbis' fear of breaking the law overwhelmed their fear of hurting and desecrating people.

If only one could honestly say that these same symptoms were not present in Christianity. After two thousand years of the gospel teaching, we read passages in books of moral theology quite up to the standard of Talmudic excess. It is kindest to quote without comment from the work on which many English-speaking Catholic priests were brought up until recently, Davis' *Moral Theology*.

'It is certainly sufficient to be in a place from which the ceremonies of the mass can be substantially apprehended . . . not, however, more than about forty paces clear from the rest of the worshippers.' It is absurd 'to say it would be sufficient to observe mass through a telescope from a considerable distance'. 'Servile work may not be done, without necessity, for pleasure or recreation . . . It is usually held servile work to plough, dig, sow, grind corn, reap, load, print, knit, sew, make rosaries, scapulars, artificial flowers, to plaster, whitewash, wash, iron. It is not servile work to study, write, do artistic work in sculpture, painting, design, embroidery, nor to typewrite, photograph, even if these things are done for pay. Crochet-work is perhaps artistic; and fly-fishing is considered skilful, but not rogging with nets for salmon . . . Servile work of a fairly arduous nature – such as ploughing and digging – done for a space of between two and three hours would be a serious violation of the precept, but . . . lighter work, such as weeding or light gardening, done for the same space of time, would not be serious sin.' 'The one full meal that is allowed on fast days may not, according to common opinion, be extended beyond two hours . . . The extraordinary length of three to four hours for dinner was stated by Elbel and Gobat as an occasional custom in Germany. Some authors maintain that in such extreme cases of very protracted dinner, the evening collation should be omitted. The view may be probable. Furthermore, the one full meal may not be so interrupted as to develop into two meals. An interruption of little more than half an hour would be contrary to the spirit of the law.'[39]

In 1960, the Catholic Truth Society of London printed a pamphlet by a moral theologian called *Attending Non-Catholic Services*. The author maintained it is absolutely forbidden for any Catholic 'to take part in or even merely be present at the religious rites of non-Catholics whilst at the same time giving internal voluntary approval to such rites'. A father, converted to Catholicism, is forbidden to give away his Anglican daughter at an Anglican wedding. This would 'be taking an active part in the service as well as recognizing the authority of the minister to conduct it by presenting the bride to him and placing her hand in his so that he in turn may place it in the hand of the groom'. 'The death of a non-Catholic relative or friend is an occasion for exercising Christian charity by showing sympathy towards the bereaved and paying respect to the deceased. A Catholic may, therefore, be present at the funeral of a non-Catholic relative or friend provided the conditions for passive presence are fulfilled.'[40]

A Catholic, on this view, is permitted to attend a non-Catholic wedding or funeral in the capacity of a corpse.[41]

Far worse than all this has been the unevangelical atmosphere that has pervaded some of our sacred institutions. For example, men and women religious were given as an 'infallible' guide to holiness this dictum: 'Keep the rules and the rules will keep you.' But the gospel says the contrary: Keep all the rules and as many pious additions to them as you care to devise, and still you may be unpleasing in God's sight. 'Keep the rules and the rules will keep you' is as opposed to the gospel of Christ as 'Love your friends, but don't try too hard to love your enemies; that will only land you in trouble', or, 'Don't be so proud or naïve as to think you should attempt to be perfect as God is perfect.'

The basic gospel *ideal* has often been converted into further legislation. Jesus said, 'Love your enemies, and pray for those who persecute you' (Matt. 5:44). The demand is uncon-ditional; it is made of everyone all the time. And yet it is possible to read in some sad books of moral theology that we have to behave a little more generously towards those who take away our money than towards those who filch from us our good name. Rules were drawn up to help us decide whether we had to go out of our way to speak to those who had unjustly offended us or only to speak to them when they address us first.

That may be a reasonably generous pagan ethic; it is cer-tainly not Christ's gospel. His message is: When you are slighted, dishonoured, maligned, maltreated, persecuted, un-justly put to death, you must love unconditionally as I love you. You must forgive from the heart everything all the time because God is as generous as that towards you.

The texts I have quoted – they span the centuries – prove that *homo religiosus* is ubiquitous. Isaiah did his best to convert Israel to religion 'pure and undefiled'.

When you come to appear before me,
     who requires of you
     this trampling of my courts?
Bring no more vain offerings;
     incense is an abomination to me. . . .
Your new moons and your appointed feasts
     my soul hates;
they have become a burden to me,
     I am weary of bearing them.
When you spread forth your hands,
     I will hide my eyes from you;
even though you make many prayers,
     I will not listen (Isa. 1:12–15).

Jesus continued Isaiah's work with his onslaught on those who used religious practices to cover up the uncleanness of their hearts. His denunciation of the Jewish leaders and priests – he was himself a layman without any official voice – was long and vehement. This was because they were totally opposed to the gospel of grace. They rejected the image of God as love and forgiveness to which Jesus committed himself when he offered pardon to the poor and the despised.

The scribes and pharisees, so scrupulous in their religious observances, sedulously tithed their herbs; and neglected justice and mercy and faith. They strained out gnats and swallowed camels; they spotted the splinter in their neighbour's eye and could not see the plank in their own. It was to such people that the outcast Christ said: 'The tax-collectors and the harlots go into the kingdom before you.'

However, his parable of the pharisee and the publican (Luke 18) contains the severest comment ever made upon the 'religious' man. According to Luke, Jesus told this story against those who trusted in their own righteousness and despised others.

It should be emphasized that, by the criteria then in force, the pharisee in the parable was a very respectable and honourable man. He was no grasping, sanctimonious, insidious, lecherous Tartuffe. His brand of hypocrisy cannot be dismissed so easily. He did not try to get round the law; he added considerably to its prescriptions. He was generous to a degree; he fasted more than the law demanded; he was overscrupulous in that he tithed everything he bought though, most probably, it had already been tithed before he purchased it. He kept all the commandments. He asks for nothing for himself and seems to thank God only for making him good and holy. Here is the supreme example of the 'religious' man, someone who excels in virtue.

The publican, by contrast, is out-lawed and contaminated by his profession. His prayer is one of despair, for he is unable to leave his work or make restitution for his crimes as the law insists. He says: 'God, be merciful to me a sinner!' He prays God to be merciful to him even though he cannot change the very calling that constitutes him as a sinner. This is why he lowered his eyes, and beat his breast for mercy.

To his self-righteous audience, Jesus' final remark was astounding. 'This man went home justified; the other did not.'

Never did Jesus show a surer touch than in this parable. It is his supreme defence of the gospel of forgiveness in the new age dawning. In it he tells of God's judgement on the hearts of men, a judgement which is very much the reversal of purely ethical considerations. By normal ethical criteria, the pharisee would have been given very high marks with a warning that he should try and purify his motives further. Jesus gives him no marks at all. The pharisee was an idolater: he worshipped the image of himself.

This story contains the core of the gospel. It is wrong to think it concerns only a few scribes and pharisees who lived and died two thousand years ago or some zany moral theologians whose heyday is over. This is the gospel. Christ addresses it directly to each of us today. It is meant as a judgement on our lives and ways of thinking.

Translated into modern terms, the parable might read: Two women, one a virtuous wife, the other a city prostitute who spent her nights on the streets, stepped into a church one day to pray.

The virtuous wife thanked God for giving her eight lovely

children. She had not resorted to artificial methods of birth control like some of her acquaintances whom she could mention. She had been faithful to one man, her husband, unlike this hussy who was praying – ineffectually, as was evident - before the statue of the Virgin.

Her own children she had brought up in the Catholic faith and sent, not without sacrifices, to Catholic schools. She had given two sons to the Church as priests – one was a missionary in Africa – and her only daughter was a nun. The harlot merely beat her breast and said . . .

Two monks, in a spare moment, dropped into the chapel to pray before the blessed sacrament. One was a very respected religious, indeed. He spent all available time in front of the tabernacle upon his knees. He had kept all the rules from his novitiate days onwards. He answered every bell like an English butler; he kept the Great Silence of the night hours with unswerving fidelity; he interpreted his superior's will before it was ever spoken, which St Thomas Aquinas said is the sign of a very obedient person. He thanked God for the manifest advantages he had been given over his poor confrère in the chapel.

The latter was certainly not everything he was vowed to be, nor everything his founder had in mind when he drew up the rule. In fact, he had been struggling, poor fellow, to keep his head above water from the day he entered. When he didn't actually break the rule, he bent it beyond all recognition.

His laughter was louder and more raucous than was seemly in a monk; and many a pious visitor to the guest-house was mildly surprised to discover just how many cigarettes he managed to cadge from them in any single day. His one (literally) redeeming feature was that under the folds of his nicotine-stained habit he kept a fist ready to pound his breast while he said . . .

These stories, like Christ's original parables, are calculated to hurt and incense. For there is pharisaism in all of us; a great deal of it passes unnoticed because it is cultivated and sanctioned by the institutions in which we live. We must take into account the possibility that to the daily mass-goer, to the strictest of seminarians and monks, to the most prim, proper and dutiful of wives, the Lord will say: 'The tax-collectors and the harlots go into the kingdom before you.'

Jesus, far from guaranteeing the legal systems of Christians as systems of holiness, is as opposed to them as he was to the scribal legalism of his day and as he would have been to parts of the Talmud of a later period. The attempts of Jews and Christians to domesticate the Bible, as Ebeling puts it, so that it no longer threatens our institutions are fortunately never wholly successful.

Jesus' gospel remains the great threat to all forms of legal piety. He is the first critic of false religious insurance schemes like the Nine First Fridays and the *system* of gaining indulgences against which Luther fought so nobly. As if the cross of Christ were not enough! As if, should the gospel fail, there is any other hope for us! As if canonists and moralists can add to the assurances of God's comforting word!

Christ is still vitriolic in his denunciation of today's scribes and pharisees who try to fool us into thinking that if we keep all the laws they or their society or Church prescribe we can consider ourselves automatically good, wise, honest members of the kingdom. Such scribes cannot contemplate the possibility that God might countermand their orders because, in their view, their orders are God's own. This is why they are fearfully impregnable and impervious to grace. They spend their whole lives shutting the doors of the kingdom in people's faces and blaspheming the name of Jesus Christ who opposed such legalism all through his ministry and died outlawed upon the cross. Should Jesus or any other great religious founder return to earth today, who is to say he would not reject and, in turn, be rejected by the institution that bears his name?

All the time, dear reader, I have been condemning myself. And you.

12. THE FATHER WHO CARES

Chirrupping birds God feeds,
    He sees their needs.
He watches when they fall,
    He knows them all.
Lilies more beauty don
    Than Solomon.
Men good and bad obtain
    Bright sun, sweet rain.

Jesus' foundation image of God is as 'the Father who cares'. In Matthew's gospel, in particular, we are told that this world – notwithstanding its many apparently contrary features – is the home given us by God our Father. This is a tremendous, domestic idea around which Christ's followers are to shape their whole existence.

God cares for the birds of the air and the lilies of the field. He feeds the birds: not one farthing sparrow falls except our Father knows it. He clothes the lilies of the field with more beauty than ever Solomon put on. How much more, says Jesus, will God care for you, his children, who were not made for tomorrow's fires?

Keeping in mind God's care for us, we ought to live blissfully and without anxiety. The person who is anxious about tomorrow loses the joy of living today. The solicitous man does not trust in God who is our real, final (eschatological) future made present to us already in the joy of the kingdom. Instead, he lives in the chronological future, which is to say, he is not living at all. We are forbidden by Jesus to live in tomorrow, even if we understand by that the eternal tomorrow. We must live now; always and only now. Tomorrow will take care of itself.

Of course, we must plan for tomorrow, but only on condition that we don't stop living today. The danger is we may be like a man building, in imagination, tomorrow's barns when tomorrow never comes.

If we seek first of all the kingdom of God our Father, everything else will be ours as well; we will be really rich. We must pray for everything we need in secret to our Father who sees in secret. We must pray unceasingly but without anxiety. He will take care of us, knowing as he does all our needs. After all, any father knows what his child requires and answers his requests. When the child asks for bread, his father doesn't hand him a stone. If the child wants fish, he doesn't put a snake in his hand.

The secret Father-God is always there. He rewards us secretly with his love. If we ask him, he gives us the holy Spirit to speak through us.

This secret Father-God reveals to his little ones, the humble and child-like of the earth, a secret wisdom which the 'wise and understanding' do not even suspect. And it is his will that not one of his children should perish.

Such is the serenity of the teaching of Christ, the God-filled man. The world has found it too soul-searing and too revolutionary, which is perhaps why it has seldom been tried.

God is a *forgiving Father*. He is that ground of forgivingness in which our sinful and faulty reality finds strength and comfort.

> Never a change in the grain
> Wherever the axe cleaves the wood.
> And God is always the same,
> He is merciful, he is good.

We must not be afraid of God. He is love, and love must never be feared. The biblical term 'the wrath of God' in no way refers to a quality of God but to our own godless situation when we fail to respond to love. Jesus teaches us to have a legitimate suspicion of our own frail and unreliable selves, but there is no hope for us if we project this understandable fear of self upon God. He is the answer to our fear of self; we can truly love ourselves because he loves us. This is the self-love that is the precondition of both sanity and sanctity alike. Jesus recognized this when he told us to love others as we love *ourselves*. True self-love is not narcissistic or selfish but the

condition of altruism: the other becomes one with us in love.
Erich Fromm has shown that the selfish person really hates
himself. He does not love himself too much but too little.
There is even such a thing as a neurotically unselfish person
incapable of genuine love or joy, whose unselfishness is a
façade behind which he hides in an exclusive concentration on
self. Fromm quotes Eckhart's dictum: 'If you love yourself,
you love everybody else as you do yourself. As long as you
love another person less than you love yourself, you will not
really succeed in loving yourself.'[42]

God is love. When a person's fear becomes projected on to
God, there is no escape from self; for only Love, Forgiveness,
our Father in heaven, can provide us with an escape from self
that is not a delusion.

Another way of saying God's fatherly forgiveness is at the
heart of Jesus' message is to say the sinner is at the centre of
the gospel. The sinner needs to be convinced that besides his
own capricious, variable, unloving self there is Reality that is
all love. This is one way of formulating belief in God: accepting
that ultimate reality, distinct though not separable from the
world, is all and only love. This was Jesus' conviction. Forgiveness, consequently, is accessible even to the most hardened
sinner. People who despair of being pardoned might well be
asked: 'If you were God, would you forgive yourself?' Should
they reply 'Yes' they prove that their basic problem is thinking
that God is less loving than themselves! God, the Mystery, is,
in fact, what we would like to be and cannot be: essential love.

John Donne wrote a famous epigram on his marriage: 'John
Donne, Anne Donne – Undone.' The same pun on his name
appeared in a more amusing and tender way in his 'Hymn to
God the Father' (1633):

> Wilt thou forgive that sin where I begun,
>   Which is my sin, though it were done before?
> Wilt thou forgive those sins through which I run,
>   And do them still: though still I do deplore?
>   When thou hast done, thou hast not done,
>   For I have more.

Wilt thou forgive that sin by which I won
   Others to sin? and made my sin their door?
Wilt thou forgive that sin which I did shun
   A year or two, but wallowed in a score?
     When thou hast done, thou hast not done,
      For I have more.

I have a sin of fear, that when I have spun
   My last thread I shall perish on the shore;
Swear by thy Self, that at my death thy Sun
   Shall shine as it shines now, and heretofore;
     And having done that, thou hast done,
      I have no more.[43]

Be merciful, says Jesus, because you have received mercy.
Forgive because you have been forgiven by God your Father.

Jesus adds what looks like a threat: 'If you do not forgive,
then neither will God forgive you.' It is a threat but only in
the sense that we threaten ourselves. We will be our own
judges; we will be treated as we treat others. We will be
examined – sentenced or acquitted – by the same criteria we
have applied to our fellows. The Great Judgement, in the last
analysis, is a self-judgement.

There is a difficulty here. If God is more loving than we are,
will he not judge us more mercifully than we would judge
others or even ourselves? How can it happen that God will
not forgive us if we do not forgive others? Friedrich Nietzsche,
the great critic of Christianity, was quick to fasten on to those
passages in the New Testament in which God does not seem
to emerge with credit. 'With the judgement you pronounce
you will be judged' (Matt. 7:2). 'What a conception of justice,
of a "just" judge!' comments Nietzsche. 'If you do not forgive
men their trespasses, neither will your Father forgive your
trespasses' (Matt. 6:15). Nietzsche adds: 'Very compromising
for the said Father.'[44] (Certainly, there is a great deal in
Nietzsche's criticism of those Christians who, while repeating
Jesus' admonition, 'Judge not', are prepared to consign to hell
in God's name all those of whom they disapprove.[45])

I think that Jesus is saying, If we don't forgive, God *cannot* forgive us. It's not that he will be vindictive and retributive if *we* are, that he will punish our unforgivingness by being unforgiving to us in his turn. God is not disposed to copy our worst faults. He is our Father; he is always loving and forgiving towards us. The person who does not forgive has closed his heart to the changeless, forgiving heart of God.

> Out of love God bids the sinner turn and live,
>   But he must play his part.
> Even God all merciful cannot forgive
>   The unforgiving heart.

13. THE FATHER'S NEARNESS

A Muslim does not call God (Allah) by the name of Father. God is too far removed from man to be given such a familiar name. I once asked a learned Muslim, 'What is the biggest difference between Islam and Christianity?' He replied instantly: 'Islam has never brought God to earth.'

As Christians we live so close to God, we hardly pause to reflect how daring it is to address him as 'Father'.

Not even the greatest genius can comprehend a single grain of sand or the tiniest drop of water. Yet we call out with childlike confidence to the incomprehensible Creator, 'Father', 'my Father', 'our Father'. How did it happen that this ambiguous, enigmatic, sorrow-ridden world should be considered the home of a good Father who never ceases to care for us?

Until we feel the force of that question we will never appreciate the liberation that Christ accomplished – in his own life first of all. It was from his own experience of love, joy, frustration, rejection, crucifixion, that the man of Nazareth first cried out to the Mystery, 'Abba, my Father'.

Jesus must have experienced a uniquely intimate relationship with Yahweh, the God of Israel, to address him as 'Abba'.

In the Jewish Bible, Israel is named God's first-born. Through the experience of its Exodus from Egyptian bondage, Israel thought of itself as God's beloved, his son.

> When Israel was a child, I loved him,
>> and out of Egypt I called my son (Hos. 11:1).

A son, but by no means always an obedient son:

> The more I called them,
>> the more they went from me . . .
> Yet it was I who taught Ephraim to walk,
>> I took them up in my arms;
>> but they did not know that I healed them (Hos. 11:2–3).

The prophet Hosea represents God as a father pained at his son's refusal to return him love for love, yet determined never to revoke his covenant however disloyal his son might be.

In Israel, the king as the representative of this royal people became God's son in an official sense. But the kings, too, with only rare exceptions, were themselves disloyal.

Nonetheless, there was some foundation in the Old Testament, Jesus' Bible, for Jesus describing his relationship with the nameless Mystery of Israel as that of son to Father and proclaiming that his Father's kingdom was in process of being realized.

But Jesus superseded all that went before. He turns to God and addresses him in prayer in Aramaic, the language of everyday which had supplanted Hebrew from the third century BC, and he says, 'Abba, my Father'.

Scholars say that this has no precedent in Israel's history; nor is there any parallel in a thousand years of rabbinic writing afterwards.[46] An individual Jew has arrived who, not in the formal prayer-language of Hebrew, but in daily Aramaic speaks with God as a son – whether young or adult – speaks with his father, quietly, peacefully, trustingly.

There is a phrase in the synoptic gospels which surprises scholars in that there is nothing like it outside the theological commentary of the fourth gospel. Jesus declares his intimacy with God in the following terms: 'All things have been delivered to me by my Father; and no one knows the Son except the Father, and no one knows the Father except the Son and any one to whom the Son chooses to reveal him'

(Matt. 11:27). It is difficult to know whether the second half of the sentence expresses anything more than the general observation that fathers and sons are intimately related. Nonetheless, Jesus' whole conduct towards, and respect for God as his Father justifies the elaboration of John's gospel.

A father sometimes says of his boy whose worth has been tested, perhaps by some feat of courage, generosity or endurance, 'Now he is really my son.' Jesus, too, had to prove his sonship by a loyalty so often lacking in Israel, God's first-born. In this sense, Jesus' sonship grew in stature throughout his life.

In Mark, the earliest gospel, Jesus says to God in the hour of his agony: 'Abba, Father, all things are possible to thee; remove this cup from me; yet not what I will, but what thou wilt' (14:36). Almost all we know about Jesus is summed up in this moment. So close is he to God he says, 'Abba, Father'. His confidence in God is absolute. He feels that if he appeals to God, he will send him twelve legions of angels – enough to conquer empires. But a son must be obedient to his Father's will and Jesus had a profound awareness of God as holy and good. He came to share with us the relationship in which he stood to God, the relationship of Son to Father.

14. A WONDERWORKER FROM COUNTY CAVAN

> If I ask, 'Is this house sound?'
> It is for me no proof
> To hear that a sparrow
> Perches safely on its roof.
>
> If I ask, 'Is Jesus God?'
> Is it enough for me
> That you exultant, say,
> Look, the lame walk, the blind see?

In the remote village of Arva in Ireland's County Cavan lives a lad called Finbar Nolan. In appearance, he is no different from any other Irish youngster of his age. He goes to dances; he takes out girl-friends for rides in his sports car.

But Finbar happens to be the seventh son of a seventh son. This is why many people attribute to him wonderworking powers. Finbar earns his living by curing the sick. Thousands of people flock to him each year hoping that, at the touch of his hand, their ailments will leave them.

His rate of success is strikingly high. He is especially proficient in curing arthritis and ringworm. Many people, educated and uneducated, are willing to come forward and testify that Finbar has cured them. The quiet discouragement of the local doctors and clergy seems not to deter the crowds that encircle the wonderworker of the neighbourhood. They come by car and pony trek and, assembled in serried ranks in the village hall, they eagerly await his ministrations.

Finbar, like any labourer, is worthy of his hire. The highest fee he has been paid for a cure is £500. But that is his average weekly wage. Everyone pays a stipend – whether it be £1 or £5 – according to his means or his ambitions.

Many have asked, 'What harm is there in this?' Perhaps little enough. After all, we live in the age of advertising witchcraft. Today, anything from a jar of cream to a specially processed loaf of bread is guaranteed to have magical properties capable of transforming any plain-looking girl into a beauty-queen. Finbar may be a superstition, for even if it is God who cures through him, why should God be so partial to the seventh son of a seventh son? Still, Finbar appears to be a fairly helpful superstition. People, for reasons unknown to religion and medical science, do go away cured. They seem to trust more in Finbar's powers than in prayers and prescriptions.

Finbar knows that, in the case of many people with certain kinds of ailment, sickness is a habit they get into. Once ill, they seem to accept illness as their normal condition. When they are in Finbar's presence, he inspires them with a confidence which enables them to break the habit, to overcome the inertia of thinking themselves permanently ill, and to mobilize all the recuperative and life-giving forces within them. The word that covers this as yet unknown is 'faith'. Finbar attributes his relatively few failures to lack of faith both on his part and on the part of his patients.

Turning from Finbar to Jesus, we see a surface similarity between the wonders ascribed to each of them. Mark paints a vivid picture of Jesus who, early in his ministry, became the centre of mass pilgrimages. 'That evening, at sundown, they brought to him all who were sick or possessed with demons. And the whole city was gathered together about the door. And he healed many who were sick with various diseases, and cast out many demons' (1:32–4). This must have been the earliest and most enduring memory of Jesus. He was a man surrounded by crowds of people suffering from many kinds of ailments. He healed them. He had power from God. But his continual plea is for faith. 'Have you no faith?' he asks. 'Daughter,' he says, 'your faith has made you well.' The thing he marvels at most is unbelief. When he came to his own country, Nazareth and the towns about, people took offence at him. No doubt, the local rabbis and physicians were the first to point out that they knew this so-called wonderworker well: he was Jesus, the carpenter's son. Jesus experienced the truth of the old saying: A prophet finds honour anywhere except at home. Mark, in his blunt way, says: 'He *could* do no mighty work there, except that he laid his hands upon a few sick people and healed them' (6:5). The really sick are usually desperate for a cure.

No one could fail to see striking similarities between Jesus' healing activities and Finbar Nolan's.

15. THE WONDERWORKER FROM NAZARETH

Even among radical scripture scholars, few question today that Jesus did the kind of wonderful works attributed to him by Mark, such as healing the sick and casting out demons. Expunge the miracles from the gospel story and the whole picture of Jesus and his ministry would alter.[47]

Of course, these statements need careful qualification. Jesus' deeds came down to us, as they did to the evangelists in the first place, by popular report. A great deal of rumour, generalization, ornamentation, had affected them by the time Mark came across them. Still, Jesus' influence upon people, at least as to the sort of thing he did, is guaranteed. R. H. Fuller adds modestly: 'We would not rule out the possibility that occasionally a *specific* memory of an actual incident has been preserved.' But 'we can never be certain of the authenticity of any actual miracle story in the gospels'.[48]

Another kind of qualification has to be made: even when the reports are accurate, they necessarily reflect the interpretation put upon them by the eye-witnesses or the hearers. Miracles usually happen as and when they are expected to happen. They are not absolute, 'objective' events which overturn or suspend laws of nature, nor are they completely open to impartial investigation; they are culturally conditioned phenomena. As with hypnosis, people have to be susceptible to miracles for them to occur.

When, for example, Papa Doc was buried in Haiti, he 'organized' in advance his own miracle. He had forecast that at his funeral there would be an earthquake and the ground would open up to allow him safe passage to his trans-terrestrial abode. It only needed the word to be passed among the crowds at the cemetery that such an event was going to happen and it happened. At the crowd's stampede, the earthquake unmistakably took place and Papa Doc was vindicated. Not that there is any record of his enemies being 'converted' by this phenomenon.

Returning to the New Testament, we read there that Jesus often 'cast out demons'. Many take these statements at their face value as 'objective' descriptions of what Jesus actually did. It is much more likely, though, that Jesus' casting out of demons is an *interpretation* of what Jesus did, an interpretation in which Jesus himself as a first-century Jew most probably concurred. What actually happened was that someone who was sick became well through something Jesus said or did.

The process of interpreting Jesus' miracles has continued down until the present time. Today many take these demons to be 'devils' and give them a place in the hierarchy of devils understood to be spiritual – real, 'bodiless' – entities.

The fact is, the demons did not come out of hell. They required bodies to exist and human bodies provided them with a habitation. They paid for their accommodation by making those in whom they dwelt ill. The 'demons' can be satisfactorily accounted for by certain well-known physical symptoms and the absence of medical science in first-century Palestine. Anyone who has ever seen someone undergoing an attack of epilepsy will readily appreciate this. The epileptic, at one moment perfectly normal, suddenly stops in his tracks; a glazed look comes over his eyes as if he is in a trance. Next, unless supported, he will fall; the eyes may then roll, the lips foam and ugly contortions of the body follow. To a primitive onlooker, ignorant of medicine, demons have taken over an otherwise healthy organism and need to be cast out, perhaps by some religious rite or magical incantation. Medicine, in its infancy, also had its amusing metaphors to 'explain' various ailments and, some would say, it still has plenty.

In some parts of Africa today, evil spirits are thought to be at enmity with humans. In *The African Child*, Camara Laye, who was brought up in French Guinea, tells how everybody he knew had esoteric methods to ward off the evil spirits. In his father's private hut, pride of place was given to mysterious pots with metal lids. 'They contained the magic charms, those mysterious liquids that keep evil spirits at bay, and, smeared on the body, make it invulnerable to black magic, to all kinds of black magic.'[49] As Camara Laye remarks, the medicine men are not charlatans.[50] They fulfil a very useful function, often performing genuine cures in ways which cannot yet be explained. The modern equivalent of demonology is perhaps something on the lines of neurology or microbiology.

The suggestion that Jesus could not have done wonderful works because such works are 'against the laws of nature' is not heard as frequently as once it was. Jesus and his contemporaries lived in the pre-scientific age, before Galileo, Newton, Pasteur, before anyone had ever heard of 'laws of nature'. At such a period, it was assumed that God and Satan and demons often acted directly upon creatures as and when it pleased them. Many occurrences were attributed to 'supernatural' intervention which we would attempt to explain differently. Science has so restricted the areas of these 'interventions' that, while it is impossible to prove a negative, few scientific people today believe there have ever been such happenings.

Even were we to agree with this philosophy, would we have to concede that Jesus did nothing extraordinary? To say this without looking at the evidence would be really unscientific. Further, a Christian, believing that Jesus is the supremely forgiving presence of God among us, the man for all men, expects, as it were, the divine presence to manifest itself in him in some special way. This is not necessarily because Jesus had the power to act contrary to the laws of nature but because those who saw God in him were most likely to experience such a revolution in their inmost being that even their sick bodies responded and found a 'wholeness'.

Returning to Finbar Nolan. On the one hand, he silences the sceptics who say the sick cannot be cured by the laying on of hands; on the other, he seems to suggest that Jesus is far from being unique in his activities, because Finbar, working among the same kind of people as surrounded Jesus, also gets astonishing results.

One way of overcoming the difficulty is for the believer to affirm that Jesus did more extraordinary cures than other wonderworkers. Certainly, Finbar does not make the claim that he can cure lepers or give sight to the blind. But other wonderworkers at about the time of Jesus were said to have done these and more marvellous things. There were, for instance, the legends of Elijah and Elisha, taken all too literally in Jesus' day, in which the prophets were reported to have raised the dead.

It is a mistake to enter Jesus' miracles in a competition for wonderworkers. Such rivalry would have no specifically religious character. There would be endless discussions among the 'faithful' as to whose founder or leader had performed most prodigiously!

Having cleared the decks a little, we come back to the basic question: How did Jesus' miracles differ from those of others?

16. WHY JESUS WORKED MIRACLES

There is one further difficulty to examine first. After Jesus had emerged from the desert, in the power of the Spirit he went through Galilee like a storm. Reports of his wonders circulated everywhere. People were looking for him on all sides. It was then, according to Luke, that Jesus came to Nazareth, the home of his boyhood, which he had but lately left. The local hero returned was asked at the synagogue to read the Sabbath lesson. Jesus seems to have deliberately selected this passage in Isaiah:

> The Spirit of the Lord is upon me,
> because he has anointed me to preach good news to the
>   poor.
> He has sent me to proclaim release to the captives
> and recovering of sight to the blind,
> to set at liberty those who are oppressed,
> to proclaim the acceptable year of the Lord
>   (Luke 4:18–19; Isa. 61:1–2).

The difficulty is this: the reason the evangelists told of Jesus' temptation in the desert was to make it plain that Jesus was not going to work miracles in the pursuit of worldly ambition. Why, then, as soon as he leaves the desert, does he set Galilee alight with his wonders?

This is not so much a difficulty as the beginning of an answer to all the difficulties concerning Jesus' miracles. We cannot imagine Jesus working wonders – or even being able to work them – except in the context of faith. Miracles were certainly neither a means of pursuing worldly ambition nor a substitute for the personal response of faith.

But doesn't Finbar ask for faith? Yes, but only the word 'faith' is common to his and Jesus' requirements.

What distinguishes Jesus' works from any others is . . . Jesus. When he works wonders, he inevitably points to himself as the focal point of God's action. In Jesus, in his proclaiming of God's kingdom through word and deed, God is presenting himself in a decisive way. The evidence that the new age is dawning is that blindness, deafness, leprosy, unwholeness of every sort, death itself, are ended. Bereaved people in their loneliness and sick people in their humility, their desire for wholeness, their inability, particularly in a society without scientific medicine, to heal themselves – these all exhibited the kind of attitude demanded of the searchers after the kingdom: utter poverty. The miracles Jesus works for them come about through their response as believers to the God who is manifestly in him changing the human situation from hopelessness to hope.[51] Jesus always showed an unshakeable confidence that God was with him. Only, people would not always accept him as God's word and deed among them.

· There is no need to claim that Jesus did more *spectacular* things than other wonderworkers. But the meaning of what he did was different. Everything was decisive and God-centred. His deeds were sacraments of a divine action not restricted to the surface level of a physical cure but reaching down into the heart. The curing of sickness stood for, indeed, *proceeded from* the deeper cure of spiritual maladies which he alone was able to effect. This is why he is able to ask for faith in himself: he has become identified with God in his forgiving and saving work.

Jesus could not perform wonders where there was no faith, not simply because the desire for health was lacking in those who came to him, but because there was not that deeper desire for spiritual regeneration. Their refusal of God's fatherly rule in their lives incapacitated Jesus. Not even the Saviour can save people unless they feel a need for salvation and make a humble request for it. In this sense, Jesus depended on the faith of his followers. He had to ask for faith as a commitment to a new life through obedience to him and his message. He was at the opposite pole from those wonderworkers who leave their beneficiaries spiritually unaltered.

Jesus was convincing because he was so obviously in possession of everything he offered to his disciples. He is the one who sees, who is clean, who is close to God. It's hard to imagine Jesus taking money for his cures. He is a completely disinterested man, poor, meek, pure of heart, the embodiment of the kingdom. It makes sense to follow him with complete abandonment because he is utterly transparent to God.

Jesus' wonders, it would seem, are only comparable with the wonders others do at the superficial level. In his case, they are part of the process whereby he, in God's name, is already remaking the world.

17. INACCURACY IN THE REPORTING OF JESUS' MIRACLES

Questions about inaccuracy in the gospels' reporting of Jesus' miracles need to be dealt with. This alleged lack of accuracy, I believe, is integral to their meaning and influence on our lives.

Our viewpoint has been: in the gospels we are dealing with the proclaiming of God's good news to us today. The gospels were written in the light of the resurrection faith, in the conviction that Jesus is not one of 'the dear departed' but is with his disciples in a living way. He is here in his word summoning the hearers or readers to be his disciples.

But faith in the context of the proclamation of the gospel has a richer meaning than it had in the days of Jesus' own preaching of the kingdom. Jesus showed the kingdom was already in the process of coming through his preaching and miracles. But that same kingdom has come fully and finally in his death and resurrection. Christian faith is a giving of oneself to Jesus crucified and living. It entails commitment to Jesus not simply as the one who preached the kingdom but as the one in whom the kingdom has come.

We have already seen some of the differences between Jesus' wonders and those of other wonderworkers. A profounder difference needs to be emphasized: Jesus' wonders continue. The primary confession of Christian faith is: Jesus is not dead but the living Lord.

When we read about Finbar Nolan's wonders, we are not able to participate in them. He needs people to go to him to feel the touch of his hands. Some faith-healers may communicate by letter. But Jesus' wonders were proclaimed and then written down so that they may heal perpetually and everywhere.

The evangelists are convinced that the man healed of his blindness is more than a first-century figure who saw again: he is every Christian believer who is in touch with Christ. The vision restored is the vision of the heart by which a man sees God and his will for him. In this light, he is able to find his way in this ambiguous and often frightening world.

The miracles of the gospels are addressed, then, to us. This is why they are part of the gospel preaching. Alan Richardson writes: 'Our earliest gospel [of Mark] tells us nothing of a time when the miracles of the Lord were regarded as simple events devoid of theological interpretation.'[52] They are the believer's means of entering the kingdom. We must not ask scholars, as top priority, to test their historical reliability for us and so rebut the sceptics' arguments. We want to know first, why did the earliest missionaries preach the miracle stories? We find the answer to this when we test the truth of them for ourselves by being cured of our blindness, deafness and lameness. Like the blind man in John 9:25, each must give his personal testimony: 'One thing I know, that though I was blind, now I see.' Unless we can say that, there is no point in bemoaning the inexactness of the evangelists' reporting: we have not heard the gospel. We will still be demanding proofs of what Jesus is supposed to have said and done in order to believe on the basis of these proofs. As if a blind man ever saw because another blind man recovered his sight! Only when we commit ourselves to Christ, do we find his word is true and his power to heal is a power *over us*. By his word, we come alive today; by his power that reaches into the heart, we undergo a lasting, spiritual reformation.

My contention has been: if we do not understand the unique and exciting literary form of the gospels we shall hardly understand anything in them according to the authors' intentions.

In the first place, we may contradict the explicit teaching of Christ about miracles. We may try to make miracles a condition of, and a way to faith, whereas the gospels constantly show Jesus refusing to give a sign to the incredulous; indeed, he was unable to work miracles for them. A miracle is not a condition of faith; faith is the condition of experiencing a miracle. Bultmann writes: 'Jesus did not, like the later apologists, think of miracles as a proof for the existence and rule of God; for he knew no doubt of God. Miracle indeed presupposes belief in God. Therefore Jesus puts no special stress on his miracles, and at any rate is never greedy for miracles and does not, like other ancient and modern Messiahs, revel in his power of performing them.'[53]

In the second place, if the miracles are described in the gospels, they are there as part of the proclamation of the conquering death and resurrection of Jesus. They tell us in a powerful, pictorial way that he is the Lord, and allow us today to enter into his triumph. To focus only upon the past, I repeat, is to lose the gospel as gospel. What Christ has done and will do is drawn, by preaching, into an ever accessible present. The miracles of the gospels point to the cross. They illumine God's decisive work of saving men in the cross of Jesus Christ. God had been working in him from the beginning, but his disciples could not see it clearly at the time. In the wonderful deeds he had performed, Jesus was heralding the kingdom, in fact was bringing in the kingdom. Jesus gave sight to the blind, hearing to the deaf, healing to the possessed, as signs that God's kingdom was in process of coming. The meek and humble of heart were able to read the signs correctly.

Miracles are not 'proofs' in any scientific sense, but they are proofs in the sense that they are signs and expressions of God's love and saving concern. They are there as part of the gospel in which God's glory is manifest, a glory which we can share today. They are written down so that we can test for ourselves that what they say is true: Jesus crucified and living is the life, the light, the health, the joy of all the world.

18. THE RESURRECTION IS NOT A
MIRACULOUS PROOF

Jesus is alive. This was the basic confession of the early Christian community. Christian faith is a resurrection faith. Further, the gospel from beginning to end is a proclamation of the resurrection of the Crucified.

However, the resurrection must not be thought of as a kind of unique or extraordinary phenomenon which leads, worse, impels us to faith in Christ. The resurrection would then become the last great trick in Jesus' repertoire, the outstanding miracle which proves that all the rest, too, differed substantially from those of other wonderworkers.

It is true that the resurrection 'vindicates' Jesus and his message, but this must not be understood in a way that flatly contradicts the gospel teaching.

Consider Jesus' story of Dives and Lazarus (Luke 16:19–31). In this story, Dives, tormented in Hades, asks Abraham to send someone to his father's house to warn his five brothers lest they come to the same fate. Abraham says, 'They have Moses and the prophets.' That should be enough. Dives replies: 'No, father Abraham; but if some one goes to them from the dead, they will repent.' He said to him, 'If they do not hear Moses and the prophets, neither will they be convinced if some one should rise from the dead.'

In the story of Jesus' temptation in the desert, his stance was made very plain. He was not a Messiah who would change stones into bread or jump off the pinnacle of the temple to be borne up on angels' wings for the sake of earthly renown. He was to be the ministering, and, in the event, the suffering servant of God.

The evangelists testify that this pledge was kept even after Jesus had been nailed to the cross. Strung up there, the onlookers mocked him, saying: 'Come down from that cross and we will believe. Work a miracle for us, Jesus, a really impressive one and we, too, will be your disciples.' This was a temptation no different from the one he underwent in the desert. But, according to the tradition, Jesus never worked miracles to prove he was the Messiah or the Son of God. If he did work miracles for such a purpose he failed lamentably! The cross is proof that there never was any Christian discipleship based on miracles understood as mind-dazzling phenomena.

This principle of discipleship applies to the resurrection, above all. It would be strange to argue, at least implicitly, as follows: On the cross, Jesus was asked in mockery to come down from the cross. On these terms, the bystanders promised him faith and loyalty. Jesus knew such a miraculous descent would convert them but he had a better plan in reserve. His intention was to go one step further and let them kill him. Afterwards, he would raise himself from the dead on Easter morning to provide them with an unassailable proof that all the claims he had made were true.

This is not in the least a caricature. In apologetics, the resurrection of Jesus has often been utilized as a miraculous proof of a type Jesus expressly rejected in the desert.

The Jesus of the nineteenth-century apologists should perhaps have come down from the cross, saying: 'Now you can go on your knees in adoration. You have your proof at last.' Then we might have had plaster statues of Jesus clambering or floating down from the cross. Had such a thing occurred, it would only have demonstrated that Jesus was not a human being as we are and that God cannot ultimately be revealed in this man's life and death but only by means of an abnormal intervention in which man had no part to play. The incarnational principle would have been annulled at source. God's salvation would not come *through man* but through a 'supernatural' phenomenon that bypassed man.

There were no wonders on Calvary. This was not because Jesus was employing delaying tactics so that his power should stand out in a better light on the third day. That would mean the cross has ceased to be the centre, the absurd centre of Christian faith.

The cross, despite all appearances, is God's answer to sin

unbelief; and there is no other. We hold without any recourse to miracles – for on Calvary there weren't any – that the cross is the climax of Israel's history. It is the decisive showing of God's love and power, his only answer to man's wickedness, a triumphant answer. To believe this is to believe that Jesus is really alive now. Only if Jesus remains dead did God fail. But we trust in the God whom Jesus preached and trusted in; and we believe God did not fail.

To try to use the New Testament stories as scientific proofs that Jesus is risen is to shy away from an essential aspect of the cross: its scandal. The resurrection does not reverse or annul or dispense with the cross: it simply gives to it or, better, exhibits its meaning. It is only through the cross's scandal that we can come to the light.

Ultimately, no one can take from each of us the burden of believing in Jesus risen. Jesus is alive. His resurrection is witnessed to by the apostles. But each must verify for himself that what the gospels say is true.

Jesus is alive and I know it because he gives *me* life today, because *I* live in him. Jesus is a wonderworker because he cures *my* heart of blindness, deafness, leprosy. He is my Lord because he really exercises sovereignty over *my* life. I hold him to be the Son of God because in seeing him I am satisfied I know what God is like, what God is doing to save me and what existence, at its roots, is, namely, love. Jesus is God-with-me and God-for-me because I acknowledge that in him God is reconciling the world, myself included, to himself.

If I do not meet Jesus now and if he does not heal me now, all the scholarship in the world will not help me. My faith does not rest on scholarship; it rests on the Lord Jesus who is alive and present to me in my life and in all its undertakings.

19. FAITH IN JESUS CHRIST

We have seen that the gospel miracles should be thought of in the context of a living faith and not as extraordinary phenomena in which the workings of nature are overturned or superseded.

Miracles are integral to the message and person of Christ who was the prophet and Son of God whose message was vindicated at the resurrection.

Had Jesus not been the kind of person he was, had he not died out of love and been exalted by God his Father, whatever wonders he performed would soon have been forgotten. A trace of them might have remained for a brief while in local folklore. In that case, they would have been written up in a manner quite unlike that of the evangelists. The evangelists grasped that, through the cross, the sacramental and saving character of Christ's miracles is highlighted and preserved for us in the preaching of the gospel.

The real and, in a sense, only miracle of the New Testament is Jesus himself. He never asked for faith in his miracles. In apologetics, on the contrary, it is often argued: 'If you can first be persuaded to believe in Jesus' miracles, you will afterwards accept Jesus for what he is, Messiah and Son of God.' The fact is, even Christ's enemies among the scribes and pharisees had little difficulty in believing he worked miracles. Only, they ascribed them to Beelzebub, the prince of demons. This illustrates an interesting feature of the times: Jesus was expected even by his opponents to do extraordinary things. In their view, the 'extraordinary' was quite normal for those with pretensions to be prophets. As Martin Dibelius explained, whatever was not instantly explicable was miraculous or 'supernatural'. It was not necessarily the authentic deed of God because it was miraculous. It was a case for either adoration or condemnation, for seeing either God's hand or Beelzebub's at work.[54] This is why Jesus looked on his own casting out of demons as his most telling sign that he came from God and brought God's kingdom with him (Luke 11:20). Beelzebub would not be so foolish as to divide his own kingdom by expelling his supporters.

Jesus asked not for faith in his miracles but for faith in God working through him. Faith is always in someone. (I may believe *that* Christ worked miracles, but I can only believe *in* Christ and *in* God.) What Jesus demanded was faith in himself as the agent of God's kingdom, as the one who would transform the world order by bringing in the decisive, eschatological age. He was not someone proficient at instant cures: he claimed to bring lasting, indeed, everlasting salvation by ushering in God's kingdom.

Looked at merely as biological wonders, Jesus' miracles have been surpassed by those of Sir Alexander Fleming, the inventor of penicillin, and by other great scientists. We are constantly besieged today by the latest 'miracles' of the medical market. The belief we have in them is not theologically significant. If we want 'to believe in a miracle' that miracle must be Jesus himself.

Other wonderworkers – like Finbar Nolan – ask for faith as a way to a cure; in the gospels, faith *is* the cure. Faith is not a means to anything, even though, as the gospels show, it often resulted in healing and wholeness which were interpreted as 'the expulsion of demons'. Faith is the true light, the true life, the true healing. The perceptible cure is but the outward sign of the inner transformation.

This explains why only those who believed were cured, and how it is that, in the deepest sense, what Christ offered to his disciples in his lifetime is offered to us still. In fact, more is offered to us, since we believe in his resurrection. Our faith in him brings him closer to us than he was to those on whom he laid his healing hands by the roadsides of Galilee.

20. THE PROCLAIMER BECOMES THE PROCLAIMED

To adopt a flamboyant, Cecil B. de Mille approach to the miracles of Jesus is to forget they have come down to us in the form of gospel. Having committed ourselves to Jesus the risen Lord within the world-wide community that lives by him, we are tempted to gloss over the fact that he was an obscure Galilean, a quiet man from Nazareth. In him, God's glory was hidden and yet revealed through its hiddenness. He was but a seed growing secretly in the dark earth. He did not die a hero's death; he made no gallant death-bed speech like Socrates or Thomas More. He was butchered by Roman soldiers as part of their day's work; and he needed all his strength for dying.

The gospel is about the unknown who *became* the Lord and the Christ, about a man who, once crucified in weakness, is with us still in the power of his Spirit.

The special character of the gospel as the presentation of this person to the believer enables us to understand the astonishing tension and ambiguity which characterize the gospels: Jesus is at once weak *and* strong. If the gospel were precise, factual reporting of what the mortal Jesus said and did, it would not have this tension; nor would it have much present relevance. It would not be a document of faith in Jesus as the Christ.

Failure to recognize the gospels as gospels runs the risk of underplaying the real lowliness and ordinariness of Jesus' life. It may even be assumed that the Proclaimed One, Jesus Christ of the gospels as we read them, was in every way identical with the Proclaimer, Jesus, the lowly one of Nazareth. This cannot be right. Bultmann says that after the resurrection the Church proclaimed Jesus as the Messiah to come; they do not simply repeat Jesus' original message. 'He who formerly had been the *bearer* of the message was drawn into it and became its essential content. The proclaimer became the proclaimed.'[55] In substance, of course, there is strict continuity between the lowly Jesus of Nazareth and the Christ of Easter, great, glorious and immortal.[56] But, evidently, traits attributable to the Christ of glory are not attributable to Jesus in the days of his flesh, nor vice versa. Yet in the gospels we have *Jesus Christ*, at once lowly *and* glorious. *The presentation of the lowly-exalted one is precisely what a gospel is.* The evangelists are *not* biographers, it's worth repeating, but skilful theologians working, in the medium of 'story', on the meaning of Jesus Christ for today.

Certainly, the gospels give many indications of the lowliness of Jesus and of his kinship with us in our weakness. Nonetheless, because he is being proclaimed as the exalted one, his presence is always suffused, in faith, with the 'glory', the divine radiance. John's gospel only differs from the others in degree: the process of earthly exaltation has reached its culmination. It is very difficult to know how the Jesus of the fourth gospel could die at all. The truth is, he could not have died. This is because the Jesus of John is already, in his lifetime, as it were, the Christ which in reality he had yet to become.

This insight, however, does not take account of all the complexities and subtlety of the fourth gospel, for while no other evangelist compares with John in stressing the divineness and lifetime glory of Jesus, he emphasizes as much as, perhaps more than the others that Jesus still had to be glorified. John's Jesus is as weak and vulnerable as any man.

If we play down the gospel as proclamation, as the fusion of past and future in the ever-present now, we will approach the gospels with a literalistic, pedantic mind and not with the mind of faith. We will treat the transfiguration as a literal account of what happened on the mountain-side, with astonishing results. For instance, St Thomas Aquinas deals with this gospel story as a real incident and then requires several miracles to explain it.[57] Elijah, who had gone up to heaven in a chariot, came down again to put in a special appearance. Moses, who had died, couldn't be permitted to anticipate the general resurrection at the last day: his soul must, therefore, have materialized on the mountain through a body which he put on, as, according to scripture, angels sometimes do. (Once more, we notice the literal interpretation is never consistently literal.) Jesus, though mortal, showed the 'clarity' of the risen body to his three disciples – and so on. If only the medievals had grasped the form of the gospels, how many pains would they and subsequent generations have been spared. The transfiguration is the early Christian community's way of saying pictorially that Jesus *was* the Christ, that the Christ could suffer and *still be* the Christ.

If we are mistaken about the gospel form, the history of theology shows it is not possible to appreciate the real difficulties and dilemmas facing Jesus: his struggle to understand, the terrifying effort he, above all, had to make in order to discover and fulfil God's will. All these things are essential to being a man. That Jesus is completely and integrally a man is the very supposition on which the New Testament preaching rests. He stands among us, a man among men.

Before modern scriptural studies, theologians were unable to appreciate what a gospel is. This meant they were doomed to think of Jesus as working miracles to boggle the mind or prove some point or other of doctrine. For the same reason, they ascribed to Jesus of Nazareth, as we saw, a detailed knowledge of past, present and future incompatible with him being a real man who must walk into the future as we walk into the dark: groping, moving one step at a time, searching for a secure foothold. The gospel was presumed to be exact, biographical report down to the last detail; the theological reflections of the fourth evangelist on Jesus as the Christ, the Son of God, were read as an accurate description of Jesus' mind when he walked the earth.

Jesus said: 'Before Abraham was, I am' (John 8:58). This was taken as proof that Jesus pre-existed the world and was conscious of this. Today a biblical theologian would say, this is another way John has of stressing that Jesus Christ is God's Word to men.

Jesus proclaimed: 'I lay down my life, that I may take it again. No one takes it from me, but I lay it down of my own accord' (John 10:17-18). This – together with statements in the synoptics in which Jesus predicts his passion and resurrection in all their details – was taken to mean that Jesus knew in advance everything that was going to happen to him. Today, scripture scholars suggest this is John's theological way of saying that the death of Jesus was not an accident outside the providence of God, not an unmitigated disaster, but part of God's plan for the world's salvation.

In his book, *The Passover Plot*, Hugh J. Schonfield treated Jesus' resurrection as part of a scheme that went wrong. According to Schonfield, Jesus deliberately undertook to fulfil the Old Testament messianic prophecies. He planned to get himself crucified, drugged by vinegar and hyssop, taken down before he was really dead; finally, he was to reappear as though he had risen from the dead. (Schleiermacher, long before Schonfield, had interpreted Jesus' death as a swoon and his resurrection as his recovery from fainting.) Unfortunately for Jesus, continues Schonfield, Jesus was removed from the cross too late. He had sustained more damage then he had bargained for. He was unable to say very much to his disciples 'after his death' before he really expired.

This book is more than far-fetched. The strange thing is: most scholastic theologians hold almost the same view of Jesus' life as Schonfield. For them, too, Jesus was playing a prearranged part; he *did* know everything in advance; he deliberately set out to fulfil all the Old Testament prophecies; he even gave maximum details of his end to his closest disciples. Almost the only crucial point on which these theologians disagree with Schonfield is the finale: they insist Jesus *did* intend to die on the cross and he succeeded there and then, so that his resurrection, also planned and predicted, was genuine, too.

However widespread this approach may be, it is a disastrous way of coping with the tensions and apparent contradictions in the New Testament presentation of Jesus. These tensions can only be resolved by accepting the gospel for what it is. Indeed, the resolving of them in the fashion I've suggested seems to me the condition of holding Jesus to be no more or less of a man than any of us.

Jesus was no hybrid. He was not at once a man omniscient *and* ignorant of what the morrow would bring; he was not glorified, beatifically happy by reason of some kind of vision of God *and* still tempted and terrified of dying.

Only the proclaimed Lord, Jesus Christ, can be presented simultaneously as weak and strong, mortal and immortal. The resurrection has coloured the whole story of Jesus. It has guaranteed that everything Jesus did and suffered for us is still relevant. We can sympathize with Jesus in his crucifixion, even though we know that he is glorified. Devotion has always been able, to some extent, to live with the tensions in the gospels which once bemused theology and drew from theologians the most incredible affirmations and hypotheses about Jesus.

21. THE CREATIVE TENSION WITHIN THE GOSPELS

A balanced assessment of the nature of a gospel enables us to hold in a creative tension the weakness and the strength displayed by Jesus Christ.

Prior to the work of scripture scholars over the last hundred years, theologians found themselves in the unenviable position of having to choose between two sets of attributes both of which characterized the central figure of the gospels but which were out of harmony with each other. Much of the literature on Christ, naturally, arose at a time when it was far from clear how the dilemmas could be resolved on elementary scriptural grounds.

Theologians investigating the scriptures came across a Jesus who appeared to be omniscient – especially in John – and, at the same time, humanly ignorant of when the Son of Man was to come; he knew exactly what someone was going to say while showing wonder when that person spoke to him. The solution was to say: at one level of manhood 'fed' by the divine mind, Jesus knew; at another level of manhood, he did not know.

Apart from the unfortunate division of Jesus' mind into different compartments, it is surely an abuse of language and common sense to say a man knows and does not know the same thing at the same time. To the objection, he knows in one way and not in another, I reply that the qualification 'not in another' does not negate the fact that he does know. A man may know something in his professional capacity as a priest-confessor and not in his capacity as a witness in a trial. His knowledge as confessor remains real knowledge; it is simply that he does not allow this knowledge to influence his actions and the answers he gives. But this is recognizably a piece of professional make-believe – his 'not knowing' is not an epistemological term – and it happens rarely in any case. What would it be like if a man's whole life were such that all the time he was having to distinguish knowing something in one capacity and 'not knowing' it in another?

Further, there are some things which if known in any capacity must influence action or inaction. If I know, from whatever source – however pledged I may be to secrecy – that George has died, I can hardly pray with any sincerity that he will be appointed to the executive board tomorrow. If I know that my leg, just broken in three places, is not going to mend for at least three months, I can hardly enter my name for tomorrow's hundred-metre sprint, except as a joke.

St Thomas Aquinas expressly acknowledges this principle when he applies it, with staggering results, to Jesus. He asks whether Jesus' prayer was always heard. The objection is: it seems not, because Jesus prayed that the sin of those who crucified him should be forgiven (Luke 23:34). The proof they were not all forgiven is that the Jews were punished for that sin.

To this objection, St Thomas replies that Jesus did not pray for all his crucifiers, nor even for all those who were to believe in him, but only for those who were predestined to attain eternal life through him.[58]

It is hard to assess which is the most astonishing element in St Thomas' reply because there are so many amazing things to choose from. I would probably select his opinion that Jesus did not pray for all men but only for those who, he knew, were actually going to benefit from his prayers. How could he seriously pray for people when he was *certain in advance* that his prayers for them would be ineffectual?

I consider the logic of Aquinas' argument to be irresistible but it results in such an incredibly un-Christian conclusion, one wonders why he didn't re-examine the truth of his premises. Was it really the case that Jesus had such foreknowledge? If he did, Aquinas must surely be correct: Jesus, availing himself of this prescience, could scarcely have wasted time and energy praying for people who were, with absolute certainty, not going to prove worthy of it or benefit from it at all. That would have been as absurd as praying that the Babylonian Exile had never happened. But isn't it far more reasonable to hold that Jesus did not possess 'foreknowledge',[59] that he prayed hopefully and in the dark as we do, that his prayers were offered for *all* men, not for a select few (or a select many), and were totally sincere whatever the outcome, as yet hidden from him, was going to be?

If 'foreknowledge' would have dislocated Jesus' prayer, the same dislocation would have marred every aspect of Jesus' relationship with others. We would have to conclude that Jesus' life was so unreal, so insincere, that in some sense he knew what was going to be said to him and to happen to him before the event; that he had to behave *as if* he was ignorant, like a priest or doctor who *knows*, but has to act the part of an uninformed, impartial witness. By such criteria, not only Jesus' growing up but his whole life and his death were a piece of play-acting. The 'drama' was all written in advance. Jesus had only to give a satisfactory 'performance' and utter words prepared for him. Jesus would have been in the absurd position of consulting, even *memorizing* the future!

There remain, besides, many old chestnuts, such as, if Jesus knew Judas was to betray him, why did he choose him in the first place? The correct philosophical answer, I believe, is: If Jesus knew for certain that a disciple, Judas, was going to betray him, then he had by *logical* necessity to choose him as a disciple. No one could change the future if it were known already, any more than he could change the past!

But let us stay with Aquinas' presuppositions: Jesus would have been forced to choose Judas so as to bring about his treachery, foreknown by and communicated to Jesus' human mind by the Word of God. This is equivalent to saying that Jesus was not in a reasonable sense as free as the rest of men. For freedom is not just accepting the inevitable. Essential to freedom is the capacity to *fashion* and to decide the future. A man who can in no way change the future, *not even his future thoughts*, is not free in any sense.

On the matter of Jesus' suffering, scholastic theologians were equally bewildering. Arguing from the divinity of Christ and the evidence in the fourth gospel that Jesus was in complete accord and continuous dialogue with his Father, they maintained that Jesus, in the central core of his being, was beatifically happy. They could not deny the reality of Jesus' suffering since the gospel clearly states he suffered; besides, it was through his sufferings that he expressed his love for us and saved us. Even Jesus couldn't undergo a painless passion.[60] If Jesus' passion were not genuine, the salvation he won for us would not have been genuine either.

To account for suffering in Jesus' beatifically happy soul, Aquinas postulated a miracle. For a time, the Word withheld the flow of beatific joy from the high point of Jesus' soul, thus enabling him to taste the bitterness of agony and death. This solution is very drastic. Normal human beings require a miracle to stop their agony, not to initiate it. As with Jesus' igorance, so it was with his sufferings; earlier theologians could not harmonize the apparently conflicting data of the gospels.

The dilemma is far easier to resolve today. No need to segment the manhood and especially the mind of Jesus, leaving us with a creature of a different species from ourselves. All we have to do is to recognize that the gospels were written (i) from the standpoint of the resurrection and newly attained Lordship of Christ and (ii) to initiate fresh disciples into the Christian faith.

The gospels are not biographies of Jesus; it is misleading even to say they are about Jesus, period. And it is certainly not possible to make a film about the book! The subject of the gospels is Jesus who became Christ. Speculation about various 'layers' in Jesus is futile; a more subtle appreciation of the literary form in which the gospels were written is all that is required. Not for us to solve the intricate problems of our predecessors, only to dissolve them. The medievals attempted to answer, with matchless metaphysical ingenuity, questions which for us do not arise.

22. DID JESUS WALK ON THE SEA?

As a result of modern scripture studies, Christians are now in a better position to appreciate what are known as the nature miracles of Christ, such as the walking on the water, the stilling of the storm, the miraculous draught of fishes, the multiplication of the loaves.

Exegetes, for a long time, found these miracle stories perplexing. The reason is obvious. It is one thing for Jesus to work wonders which depend upon the response of faith, quite another for him to operate, as a magician purports to do, on inanimate objects or fishes or the elements of Nature.

To illustrate the modern approach, it is worth examining in detail the story of Jesus walking on the water.

To the question, 'Did Jesus really walk on the water?' the first response must be a qualified 'Yes'. An unqualified negative would eliminate the story altogether and, thereby, the vehicle of faith itself. Nevertheless, a further question arises: 'In what sense did (or does) Jesus walk on the water?' Here, the examination of the meaning of the story may give us a clue as to whether the story is to be taken as the literal report of an event or not. No affirmative or negative decision can be made on the literalness of the story prior to a careful analysis of the gospel texts in the light of faith.

At the outset, all we can say is that fresh insight into the fundamental literary cast of the gospel has led to a reassessment of long-cherished ideas about Jesus' knowledge and passibility. A similar reassessment of the stories of the nature miracles may be forced upon us by the texts. Certainly, it is not easy to stifle the suspicion that a man who walks on water hardly lives and dies as other men. But, first, let us rid ourselves of certain dogmatic approaches to the literalness or otherwise of this story.

Did Jesus really walk on water? One reply is: He didn't, because he couldn't. Water is not an element for walking on. No further argument is required. If a man tries to walk on water, either gravity operates, in which case he falls in; or gravity doesn't operate, in which case he cannot properly put one foot in front of the other. Besides, if there were interference with gravity at any single spot, the whole universe – tightly knit system that it is – would be put out of gear.[61]

The argument is admittedly, from the scientific and psychological standpoints, very strong. However, it is methodologically inadequate. A believer can always counter it by pointing out that because Jesus is divine, no general reasoning about the nature of the universe is relevant. It is wrong to limit in advance and without humble inquiry the workings of the deity. Normal expectation is no safe guide to what God can do if and when he so wishes.

The second reply to the question, 'Did Jesus really walk on water?' is, 'Yes, he certainly did.' But what is the basis of this reply? It usually is: The gospels say so; and it is more reasonable to accept *either* all of Jesus' miracles *or* none of them. What justification could a Christian have for picking out the miracles that appeal to him and rejecting others he finds repugnant to his modern scientific mentality?

This reply also has its attractions. But it, too, smacks of dogmatism. Here, as in the first instance, no attempt is made to examine the literary question, to look at the gospels as they were meant to be looked at: in the light of faith in Jesus risen.

It is true that the evangelists depict Jesus walking on the water, but how did the authors mean this incident to be understood? Is it a description of what Jesus once did in the days of his flesh? Or is it their way of portraying the significance of Jesus the Christ for all his disciples today? In brief, is this story a piece of history or is it symbolical, a kind of parable of Easter, the purpose of which is to represent the nature of Jesus as Lord and Christ?

It is a mistake to insist, without looking at the texts, that all the miracles are alike, and that someone who denies that some miracle stories are descriptions is undermining Jesus' wonder-working capacity altogether. In the infancy narratives, the Magi, at first reading, appear to have as much historical reality as Mary. Deeper thought shows that they stand for the universalism of the gospel message. This discovery in no way undermines our belief that Jesus had a mother.

The biblical story must be examined, as far as possible, without dogmatic preconceptions.

23. THE JEWISH ATTITUDE TOWARDS THE SEA

Who can be master of waves
That smash the tallest ships to pulp?
Who can tame wild seas
That swallow crews up in a single gulp?

One there is who walks on waves
As on a quiet, furrowed field.
Demoniac seas,
At the touch of his gentle feet, are healed.

Cruel all death-dealing things,
But none as cruel as the sea.
Who is this who speaks
One word of peace and claims the victory?

Jews of biblical times had a tendency to express what they believed in story form. Whereas we might say, 'I suddenly saw', or, at best, 'I saw in a flash', they would tell a story in which appears the phrase, 'I saw a flash.' Whereas we might say, 'I dreamed I saw', they would report, 'I saw this in a dream.' They spoke, that is, in a more vivid, concrete manner than we usually do. Jesus' own way of speaking is the best instance that could be found of the Jewish mind at work.

To understand further the story of Jesus walking on the sea (Mark 6:47–51; Matt. 14:24–33; John 6:15–21) we must try to grasp the Jewish attitude towards the sea. Jews thought of it, especially in moments of storm and tempest, as the unmasterable element. In their imagination, it figured as the haunt of the sea-beast and it was, in every way, capricious, menacing, restless. It was death-dealing on an unsurpassable scale. The generally peaceful lake of Galilee is not without its victims, for, due to the configuration of the surrounding hills, fierce storms have a tendency to rise there unexpectedly.

The Jewish Bible is full of references to what the sea symbolized for Jews. In no way a maritime people, they had no pretensions, like Britannia, to rule the waves. At heart, they remained gypsies, unable to cope with the tideless Mediterranean, let alone the turbulence of the English Channel. They normally saw the sea not as a friend but as a potential destroyer. The mouth of the sea was for them an image of mortal peril. The depths into which it sucked its victims without trace were very close to the pit of Sheol, the abode of the dead. This is why the Psalms, in figurative language, frequently ask God to save Israel from deep water. Psalm 69 is a good example of this; it is a psalm that clearly influenced the composition of the passion narrative. Jesus was represented as the just man who came into the deep waters of his second baptism in which there was no foothold. To him in his distress, the words of the psalmist could fittingly be applied: 'They gave me poison for food, and for my thirst they gave me vinegar to drink' (v. 21). Psalm 69 reads:

> I sink in deep mire,
>   where there is no foothold;
> I have come into deep waters,
>   and the flood sweeps over me.
> I am weary with my crying;
>   my throat is parched. . . .
> With thy faithful help rescue me
>   from sinking in the mire;
> Let me be delivered from my enemies
>   and from the deep waters.
> Let not the flood sweep over me,
>   or the deep swallow me up,
>   or the pit close its mouth over me (vv. 2–3, 14–15).

It was a natural image of salvation to say of God, 'He reached from on high, he took me, he drew me out of many waters. He delivered me from my strong enemy' (Ps. 18:16–17). The sea symbolized any strong enemy whom Jewish people feared. Sometimes, however, God, who had the sea in his control, used this element to turn the tables on Israel's foes. Not only did the Euphrates overflow Assyria and the Nile the traditional enemy, Egypt, but, most memorably, the Red Sea, in the

Exodus saga, became a friend and avenger by opening a dry path for the Hebrews and subsequently swallowing up the Egyptian hosts. Here, they claimed, was God the Saviour snatching his people from the mighty waters and drowning there instead the implacable foe. Of God it was said: 'Thy way was through the sea, thy path through the great waters; yet thy footprints were unseen' (Ps. 77:19). The Lord walked dryshod over the menacing and death-dealing waters of the deep. If the Lord withdraws his help from his chosen ones, the flood sweeps over them, the torrent takes them, and the raging waters suck them down (Ps. 124:5). But if he comes near, there is no danger. 'Stretch forth thy hand from on high, rescue me and deliver me from the many waters' (Ps. 144:7).

There are many other indications in the Bible of how Jews thought about the sea. For instance, it is amusing that the author of the Apocalypse, taking no chances, allows no sea in paradise (21:1), except perhaps an artificial one, a sea of un-menacing crystal (4:6). The real sea, symbol of destructiveness, is inadmissible at the new creation, when there is to be a new heaven and a new earth.

I have limited myself to extracts from the Psalms because they were the daily prayer of the pious Jew. By their use, the earliest disciples of Christ would have understood implicitly the symbolic meaning of a storm at sea and of someone walking dryshod upon the heaving waters of the deep.

24. WALKING ON THE SEA: A RESURRECTION STORY

Having examined the literary background to the storm at sea, we have to recall briefly the theological background.

The gospel is essentially a passover narrative. Jesus, the man from Nazareth, went down into, was baptized by the waters of death. He sank ignominiously into the watery pit where all human help is unavailing. But the Lord came to his help and drew him out of the deep waters. Jesus, who before had been weak and mortal, was made strong and immortal. God bestowed on him his own title 'Lord'. Henceforward, this was how his disciples thought of him, as the Lord who had mastery over the stormy, capricious seas of death. Never would he sink again.

There is a contrast in Mark's story between the disciples' distress as they rowed helplessly on the sea in the face of the opposing wind, and Jesus walking effortlessly by them as though he were in a field. He is as much at home on water as on the solid shore. Here, surely, is the Lord whose feet cannot even be made wet by the most death-dealing element there is: the stormy sea. Here is one who is beyond life's sorrows and the agony of death.

The disciples, in their terror, think of him – as in the more explicit resurrection accounts – as a ghost. He assures them that it is he; there is no cause for fear. He gets into the boat and the storm ceases immediately.

This is a wonderful, poetic image: the disciples of the risen Christ are rowing fearfully and without success against the tempest. In their distress, they find consolation in having with them in the boat one who has mastered death. In the story, the sea symbolizes every destructive force; and Jesus has tamed the sea.

There is another version of the story – the moral is the same – in which a storm arose while Jesus was asleep on a cushion in the boat (Mark 4:37–41). Jesus is apparently oblivious of, or unconcerned about the plight of the little boat that is carrying him and his disciples across the stormy sea. In a wonderful and moving question, the disciples ask, 'Teacher, don't you care if we are perishing?'

This story probably arose at the time when Jesus, himself beyond death, seemed to be far away from them, lost in a deep unmindful sleep. He was the Lord and it was right to address him in terms of Psalm 44:23:

> Rouse thyself! Why sleepest thou, O Lord?
> Awake! Do not cast us off for ever.

The disciples were still trapped in the evening storm, rowing without his help and being dragged overboard one by one into death's murky waters. And then he awakes at their summons;

he shows them he is there and is the master. Once more, words from the more obvious resurrection story: 'Peace. Do not be afraid.' And there was no storm any more. Only an immense calm. Jesus chides them for being fearful, for not having enough confidence in him. Awe came over them, awe that becomes men in the presence of the divine. Jesus is Lord, the one who commands the restless and voracious sea. 'Who then is this, that even wind and sea obey him?' To this, there can be only one answer: he is the victor over death.[62]

This particular Markan story of the storm at sea is followed by the curious tale – perhaps originally the elements of it were part of local folklore – in which Jesus comes to the land of the Gerasenes. There he casts out an evil spirit from a fettered man living among the tombs. Jesus, who has come to bring wholeness, restores this man who is dwelling among the dead to full communion with the living. The evil spirit goes into a herd of swine – abhorred by Jews as unclean animals – which promptly hurtle down the slopes into the sea.

The proximity of this story to Jesus' calming of the storm makes us realize that Mark thinks of the calming in terms of an exorcism. The sea, with its writhing, crested waves, has the appearance of an epileptic rolling uncontrolled with foaming mouth upon the ground. The sea, too, is tormented by a demon. Jesus' words of rebuke addressed to it, 'Peace, be still', are words he sometimes addressed to people possessed (cf. Mark 1:25).

Mark says in the former story, Jesus the Lord is capable of exorcising the unwholesome demon-possessed sea so that it obeys him and serves him. In his story of the Gerasene demoniac, the unclean spirit who is legion goes into its proper place, the accursed pigs, who themselves go where they are most at home: into the sea of death.

25. PETER WALKS ON THE WATER

Re-focusing on the story of Jesus walking on the sea, we notice that only Matthew mentions that Peter also walked upon the sea. If the gospels were recording a historical incident, the omission in Mark and John would be astonishing. It is improbable that such a marvel escaped the tradition that Mark was relying on and was found by Matthew elsewhere. Besides, Matthew clearly treats Jesus' and Peter's walking on the water as part of a single story. He has copied verbatim Mark's phraseology, showing how indebted he is to Mark for the story of Jesus walking on the water; but he has embellished it on his own initiative.

On other grounds, we know that Peter was the dominant figure in the early Christian community. Had Matthew's tale of him walking on water been a factual report, it would have appeared in all the traditions. Nothing would have been better calculated to emphasize his leadership. The more reasonable supposition, however, is that Peter's primacy gave rise to many stories in which Peter played a prominent role, and this is one of them. Matthew's story of him walking on the sea towards his Lord who saves him from sinking seems to be a pictorial and symbolic elaboration of a deeply held conviction about Peter.

Matthew first develops Jesus' words in Mark: 'Take heart, it is I; have no fear.' He seizes the opportunity of representing in story form Jesus' constant request to his disciples to show not fear or anxiety but only faith. Peter wants convincing that it is Jesus on the waters and not a ghost. 'If it really is you, Lord,' he says, 'tell me to come to you on the water.' A daring experiment on Peter's part! If it fails, the consequences for him will be disastrous. His act has the semblance of foolish trust, or irreversible commitment. That is what faith is: it is walking on water, even though water is not an element for walking on. Faith is doing at the bidding of another an absurd thing which, on his own, a man could not begin to do. A far cry from the nonbiblical idea of faith as an assent to 'supernatural' truths on the authority of someone else!

'Come!' says Jesus. At this, Peter climbed out of the boat and actually walked on the water towards Jesus. At the last moment, the ferocity of the wind and sea made him afraid. He began to sink. He cried out, 'Lord, save me', and Jesus immediately stretched out his hand and caught him. 'O man of little faith, why did you doubt?' Afterwards, when Jesus and Peter got into the boat together, the wind ceased and everyone worshipped Jesus as the Son of God, that is, the Messiah. Matthew alone has given his story a messianic ending. The disciples' confession of faith is further evidence of Matthew's tendency to develop his teaching in a pictorial way.

In its theological density, this is one of the most superb stories in the gospels. Peter was the leader in the early Church. Most probably, he was marked out for that role by Jesus himself. His faith and fidelity had been enormous. He had been prepared to follow the carpenter of Nazareth to death if need be. But at the literally crucial moment, he with all the rest – and more seriously than they – failed lamentably. He lost heart and deserted. The storms and perils of the passion had been too much for him. He began to sink. He needed convincing that Jesus who had died so shamefully was the Master of death; that he could and did walk dryshod upon the stormy waters; that he was no powerless ghost out of Sheol, no figment of the imagination, but his living Lord. In the very moment of distress and failure, the moment of infidelity, Peter cried out to his Lord, 'Save me, Lord.' This prayer of faith in unfaith was answered. Christ immediately took his hand and saved him. Jesus proved he was the Lord who stretches forth his hand and saves those whom he loves from deep waters.

Peter's faith had broken down at the cross; in the same place it was mended. He grasped that Jesus had not been swallowed up by death for ever but through death had become the Lord and the Christ. It was when Peter believed that Jesus was risen that he came with the Lord to the storm-tossed boat which then found a new calm. Through Peter's faith, the Lord was able to present himself to all his disciples as no ghost, no pale and ineffective remnant of a man, but as the Son of God in power.

J. C. Fenton laconically writes that the story of Peter walking on the water is 'best regarded as a preacher's elaboration on a theme by means of a story'.[63] I agree. Nonetheless, underlying it there are known facts about Peter, his leadership of the community, his loss and recovery of faith. The recovery or, better, the transformation of Peter's faith at the crucial moment was the condition of Jesus being worshipped as Messiah, the Son of God, by his disciples.

I can imagine Peter himself, after the resurrection, preaching something like this: 'I was nothing very much, only a fisherman. He called me all the same. I dropped my nets there and then to follow him. I would have followed him even if it meant walking on the sea. Or so I thought. But when he got himself crucified, I lost heart altogether. I began to sink. Soon, I knew, I would be lost without a trace. I realized he was dead and yet, like a fool, I cried out to him, "Lord, save me." And he answered me. He wasn't a ghost, you see. He was very much alive. He came to me across the waters, took me by the hand and saved me. Then he put me – a fisherman, mind you! – into the boat, and all of us worshipped him together. "You", we said joyfully, "are the Son of God." '

Matthew's story makes explicit in imaginative form what the rest of the gospels assume. Peter has precedence. He is always mentioned first in the otherwise diversified lists of the apostles. (Only Judas, besides, keeps a consistent position in those lists. He is always mentioned last.) It is Peter's boat from which Jesus preaches. He is the spokesman, in times of anxiety, for all the others. His faith is eventually to confirm the weaker brethren; it is the rock of his confession on which the Church is built. He is the first to whom the Lord appears (Luke 24:34), at least in the order of importance. It is Peter, in other words, who first grasps the reality and significance of Jesus' resurrection.

We will return to this all-pervading presence of Peter in the early Church. This influence, and especially his foundational belief in the resurrection, lies behind this story – superbly told and abounding in symbolism – of a courageous fisherman who one day walked with his Lord upon the sea.

26. A BACKWARD GLANCE

A comprehensive glance backwards over the terrain most recently covered may here prove beneficial.

We have noted both the excellence and extreme complexity of the literary form of the gospels. In the light of this, it is not easy to sustain the view that the story of Jesus walking on the water will pass as a description of an event.

From the literary standpoint, why did Matthew alone record the staggering fact that Peter walked on the sea? The scientist wants to know what happened to the laws of physics, the properties of matter. Theologically, it is hard to maintain that someone who in his lifetime walked nonchalantly on the sea was ever a serious candidate for death. (Back again with a Jesus who would need a miracle to die?) As to Peter, if he walked on water at Jesus' bidding, why was he so afraid for his own and Jesus' safety when the passion loomed ahead?

The problems, exegetical and otherwise, are numberless. To insist, despite them, on the literal character of this miracle, betrays other fears and preoccupations. Perhaps the need to prove something about the divine nature of Jesus; or to put faith on a sure, scientific footing; or to cling to old-fashioned ideas about the character of gospels as exact descriptions.

In response to this: Christian faith cannot result from scientific investigation, for that would contradict the nature of faith. Nor should we look on the miracle stories of the New Testament as referring to unrepeatable wonders of a bygone age. The story we have been investigating, considered simply as a description of an event, would be of little use to us: it is impossible to watch Jesus of Nazareth walk on water and unlikely that we shall emulate him in this remarkable feat.

But what if we are here confronted with a unique and breathtaking literary form which, in this instance, holds, in a fruitful tension, Jesus and the Christ? In the stories of the storms, we find Jesus tender, comforting, so human as to fall asleep. But here, too, is the Lord and Christ, immortal, master of living and dead. The harmony of composition is superb.

In the first place, the story contains general memories about Jesus. The sea, no doubt, was an element which the apostles as fishermen were by and large more capable of dealing with than he. Jesus was probably not much of a sailor. Sometimes perhaps he did not feel too good upon that sometimes stormy lake. Could it be that on occasions he tried to sleep on a cushion in the bottom of the boat just to be on the safe side?

Apart from these surmises, we recalled the general Jewish attitude to the stormy seas from the figurative point of view. The sea was the enemy, always opening its mouth and licking its venomous lips; a thing possessed; the destroyer.

The genius of the evangelist was to put these elements together in an unforgettable story form so as to preach the gospel to every age and to evoke the supreme confession of the Christian faith.

This confession is: Jesus crucified is alive. Peter twice calls Jesus 'Lord'. In the context, this is an emphasis on Jesus in so far as he is risen and endowed with divine honours. This profession of faith conditions the gospels from beginning to end. The resurrection does not make its entry into the Christian Bible at the moment when, in the theological narratives, the tomb is found empty but from the very first sentence the evangelists wrote.

Matthew has shown, in his own way, that the whole gospel is, in a sense, according to Peter. His was the faith that first revived after failure; his was the love for Jesus that won through. By reason of Peter's faith Jesus received the worship due to him as Lord and Son of God.

There can be little doubt that Peter first started formulating the gospel message in its fullness. Jesus had been obliged to act that message out; his was the death and the resurrection that brought in the kingdom. But it was left to Peter – and to his fellow disciples, subsequently – to *present* the gospel, to show the meaning of Christ's death and resurrection. Peter's renewed faith reversed the greatest infidelity. Only then was he able to preach the good news of Jesus' Lordship through crucifixion.

The story of the storm at sea in which Jesus and Peter walk together on the water is not a symbol of an eternal truth. It is the pictorial expression of particular truths. It could be said that this miracle story is really a parable, provided the word 'parable' is understood in its proper sense. A gospel parable is not a religious story made up about an abstract, everlasting truth: it is a pictorial presentation of a very definite truth about Jesus and his life-situation which becomes for us the light by which we walk through life. As some of Christ's miracles are parables, so, too, many of his parables are truly miracles. I mean that the parables of the Good Samaritan, the Lost Sheep, the Prodigal Son, have the power in them to work wonders in the lives of Christ's followers when even the miracles leave them untouched.

The concrete facts expressed by the stories of the storms at sea are these: In the first place, Jesus is risen; he is the Lord. He is the divine presence among men. God, according to Job, is master of the sea: he shut the doors on it when it burst forth from the womb; he gave it limits, saying thus far and no further, and here your proud waves must stop (Job 38:8,11). God, says the psalmist, rules the raging of the sea and stills the waves when they rise high (89:9). And here, says the gospel, is one who has the same control over the unmanageable sea. But the image demands that such a one has attained already the mastery of death. Only at his crucifixion could Jesus have reached the Lordship which the story ascribes to him.

Next, we see that the story represents genuine facts about Peter. He did fail. He did say, 'I will follow you, Lord' – and then ran away. But he was converted, and he confirmed his brethren so that they, too, confessed the Lordship of Jesus. But those same brethren, even after the resurrection, had to ride out stormy seas in a fragile boat. Still, when they implored Jesus' help, he was there, alert, alive and ready to help.

Since this story is gospel, it is Christ's word, which means, his *presence* today. Jesus is here and now in our lives the Lord who walks on water. He cannot sink; and this is not because he contravenes the iron law of gravity but because he has vanquished the more tyrannous law of sin and death. This explains

why the attitude with which the disciples greet him is one of
awe. Men always feel a quietness in the presence of death. An
even greater awe is to be expected in the presence of death's
conqueror. Jesus is as omnipresent as death and more powerful. He brings peace to his disciples and the confidence that he
is saving them from all the forces of destruction. The evangelists are elaborating Paul's terse phrase: death which, sea-
like, swallows everything up is itself swallowed up. No wonder
the Apocalyptist, in his vision, says there is no sea any more.

This, then, is the Lord who calls to us, the gospel-readers,
across the violent sea: 'Come!' Faith is walking safely over the
deep without fear of sinking into the pit. Faith is living in
death. But it requires a personal decision to let go, to leave the
relative security of the storm-tossed boat and to go where,
humanly speaking, there is no hope at all.

This approach to one of Christ's so-called 'nature' miracles
may encourage a more open-minded attitude to the rest of
them. They should all be read as 'signs' of the glory of Christ
which is revealed to faith alone.

The feeding of the five thousand, for example, seems to be a
eucharistic story woven out of Old Testament texts. Jesus'
disciples feed multitudes with the unfailing bread that Jesus,
like Moses before him, provides. It is reminiscent of nineteenth-
century rationalism to interpret the story as a miracle of charity,
with the crowds sharing out the sandwiches they had brought
with them! Exaggerated hypotheses of this sort will not reveal
the evangelists' intentions; only the examination of the literary
form will do that. The gospels, through a story, are making the
theological point that Jesus, the Lord, has greater capacity to
feed multitudes in the desert than Moses and Elisha (2 Kings
4:42-4). Indeed, he is himself the bread we feed upon in faith
(John 6).

The miraculous draught of fishes is a sign of the confidence
the disciples should have in their future mission as fishers of
men. Fuller says, faith is not committed to holding this
incident really happened. Faith consists rather in believing in
Jesus Christ as my Saviour, as the one in whom God has acted
finally for my salvation. 'To such a faith, the historicity of this

or that miracle in the gospel tradition is "comparatively irrelevant".'[64]

Richardson, a still more moderate scholar, does not scruple to suggest that Jesus' raising of Lazarus (John 11) is a literalization of the parable of Dives and Lazarus (Luke 16) in which a man come back from the dead fails to persuade his fellows of the truth of Jesus' message.[65] John Marsh, also, acutely observes: 'The real miracle is not that Jesus restored Lazarus to physical existence; to think so would be to join the Jews in their materialistic misunderstandings of Jesus' miracles throughout the gospel. It is far more wonderful when Lazarus, dead in the tomb, is in that condition brought to the only life that is life indeed, viz. when a man, dead or alive, hears the voice of the Son of God and lives.'[66]

Richardson suggests that Luke, too, constructed miracle stories like the raising of the widow's son at Nain and the curing of the ten lepers 'in order the better to illustrate the significance of the work of Jesus or the preaching of the apostles by means of teaching conveyed in story form'.[67]

All this may be strong meat to readers who have had no reason until now to question the literal truth of these miracle stories. A last word, therefore, to those who still cling to the older interpretation. If Jesus really did walk upon the sea, I don't think he would mind some of his followers taking this feat of his figuratively. Provided that they, in the power of his love, have the faith and courage to walk on stormier seas than Galilee's.

27. MIRACLES TODAY

An essential, distinguishing feature of Jesus' miracles is that they continue in the world. The risen Christ comes and works wonders among us still.

How does he do this? Through his disciples in whom his Spirit burns. Only those who live in and from Christ can demonstrate that he is not a dead figure in the past but alive and active now. The most valuable apologetics is faith, hope and charity.

People need to be practically convinced that the resurrection is continuing every moment. Jesus is, as it were, always dead and awaiting resurrection in us. He rises not once but every day like the sun. He is resurrected in us or he lies cold in the tomb of our hearts. Will we give Jesus new life? Will we show forth his glory today? Will we carry on his healing activity wherever we go? These are the questions provoked in us by the timeless, Christian gospel.

Without his disciples, Jesus is powerless and faceless, a beautiful corpse. An empty tomb holds little interest for people nowadays. They are far more interested in split atoms than in empty tombs; in spacemen up there, rather than in Christ who is up there or out there – somewhere else, anywhere, but not here.

Jesus is alive in us. He will be among us wherever two or three are gathered in his name. He is here in the interchange of love between people, in the hope we inspire, in the joy we bestow. The Christian community exists only to show forth his love, his sensitiveness and concern, his longing for his Father's glory.

Christ may be present, as we say, 'in heaven and in the blessed sacrament of the altar', but unless he dwells among us, who cares? In the first Russian revolutionary novel, *Mother* by Maxim Gorky, someone says: 'Just think – there wouldn't have been a Christ either if people hadn't died for him.' And later: 'There would have been no Lord Jesus if people had not given their lives to bring him glory.'[68]

Whenever Christ's work is done, whenever someone is recovered from despair or cared for and loved, Christ is risen and we can sing our Alleluias. Without love, there is a perpetual requiem around the garden tomb.

Jesus was an extraordinary human being, full of God. He did work wonders through the faith he evoked. But the first question posed by the miracles is this: Is the living Christ still working in us what those miracles signify? Are we ourselves, in Christ's name, miracle-workers?

I was lecturing once in Victoria, British Columbia, on the subject of miracles. Afterwards, a lady with Celtic fire asked me: 'Can *you* work miracles?' I like to think her belligerence was somewhat softened when I replied: 'Yes, of course. I often work them. Don't you?' We are not Christians (or human beings) unless we continue Christ's work of performing miracles.

Someone might object: 'What I want to know is: Can you work *real* miracles?' My answer to this is: In my view – and I believe it is the New Testament's view – I *have* been referring to 'real miracles'. I cannot conceive of anything more miraculous. When a disciple of Christ holds out the hand of true friendship to a stranger, the withered hand is healed. When he gives someone a reason for living when he had none before, or when he so demonstrates the power of Christ's Spirit that someone believes, then he has raised the dead. (To say that faith is death and new life is to speak of *real* death and *real* life!) When someone is an outcast, and Christ's disciple brings him 'home to the human race', he has healed the leper. God's rule is thereby extended.

The living Christ does all these things through his disciples. Moreover, he makes a promise – we do not take it seriously enough – that his followers will do greater works than he did. 'He who believes in me will also do the works that I do; and greater works than these will he do, because I go to the Father' (John 14:12). Having passed over to the Father, Jesus sends his Spirit on us.

If the kingdom is really present in its fullness so that the least of those who belong to it is greater than the Baptist; if to belong to the kingdom is to participate in the new life consequent upon the overthrow of sin and death, then, in the name of Jesus risen, his disciples are able to offer this life, victory and healing to others.

28. JESUS' PARABLES

Jesus spoke in parables. His manner of doing so was original.
Joachim Jeremias writes: 'Jesus' parables are something
entirely new. In all the rabbinic literature, not one single
parable has come down to us in the period before Jesus.'[69]
This is why, in reading Jesus' parables, we are in close touch
with his character and personality. Jesus did not use examples,
as other rabbis, to illustrate his teaching: his parables *were* his
teaching. They do not simply enlighten the mind; they demand
involvement and response. Jesus' listeners become part of the
parable. By making the correct response, they gain entrance
into the kingdom.

The usual caution must be given: Jesus' teaching comes to us
through the medium of the gospel preaching. The parables
of Jesus which belonged to his own particular situation and
spoke, often dramatically, of and to that situation, in the course
of time were modified to suit the new circumstances in which
Jesus' disciples found themselves.

Jesus' parables are his way of making the kingdom present.
They were initially addressed to those who criticized his
message of divine forgiveness offered freely to sinners and
outcasts. They were also spoken at a time when Jesus was
trying to make the crowds aware of the impending catastrophe,
the hour of judgement which was in process of coming through
his words and action. But, for the most part, the parables in
their present form are addressed to the early Christian fellowship and are sometimes annoyingly allegorized. These disciples
had, of course, to adapt themselves to a new situation: Christ
had not come to them with the speed they had expected, so
that on them fell the tremendous missionary task of spreading
his name among Jews and Gentiles.

The parables exemplify what is now recognized to be one of
the most striking aspects of the gospels: a fidelity to Jesus'
original teaching, combined with considerable flexibility in
applying that teaching to fresh situations. In all situations,

Jesus presents himself as the Christ. Straightforward reporting of what Jesus had said would not have been relevant to the changed circumstances encountered by his disciples. On the other hand, a response to the new situation that was in no way connected with what Jesus had taught would have implied that he was not the Christ nor still personally present among them as Lord and Master.

An investigation of the final form of Jesus' parables reveals that considerable alterations were made to Jesus' own words, alterations sometimes helpful and sometimes not. But these changes resulted not from the disciples' inability to reproduce Jesus' stories without embellishment but from their conviction that Jesus Christ was still with them. His word is always a contemporary word. What Jesus once said must not be dissociated from what he is saying today and every day.

All the same, it is useful sometimes to get behind the modifications made by the community and find the original situation as well as the parable's application which Jesus himself intended. Then we can see the two (or more) 'layers' and judge, firstly, what Jesus himself meant; secondly, whether the usage of the early Christian tradition was adequate to Jesus' meaning; and, thirdly, how God's word judges and saves us to-day.

With this plan in mind, let us look at one of Jesus' most important parables, The Lost Sheep.

In Matthew's gospel, Jesus is in the company of his disciples. He is telling the leaders of his flock how careful they should be lest any of his little ones are lost.

> What do you think? If a man has a hundred sheep, and one of them has gone astray, does he not leave the ninety-nine on the hills and go in search of the one that went astray? And if he finds it, truly, I say to you, he rejoices over it more than over the ninety-nine that never went astray. So it is not the will of my Father who is in heaven that one of these little ones should perish (Matt. 18:12-14).

This is a simple and beautiful story whose theme is divine joy at the lost sinner's recovery. God's joy is compared to that of a shepherd who, having left ninety-nine other sheep, seeks and finds the one that was lost.

At first glance, the parable's conclusion raises no difficulty. A shepherd might well rejoice more over one sheep recovered than over ninety-nine that never strayed. A mother once said: 'My eldest daughter joined a hippie colony. She went in for all kinds of experiments in community living and got hooked on drugs. But after six months, she returned. Let me tell you, that was the happiest day of my life. None of my other children ever gave me the joy my eldest daughter gave me on the day she came home.'

In the parable, as Matthew relates it, joy predominates. Doubts begin to arise when we consider the assiduous search undertaken by the shepherd. He does not wait for the sheep to come back to him. The implication is, the sheep is so lost, it cannot find its own way home. This is why the shepherd leaves the ninety-nine to carry out his search. But is it reasonable for a shepherd to leave ninety-nine sheep unguarded, while he goes to look for one that is lost? To continue the parallel with the unhappy mother, would it be right for her to leave her growing family unattended while she spends six months searching for a daughter who had left home?

Luke's account of the parable lends support to these doubts.

Luke begins by putting the parable into an entirely different context. Jesus was preaching to tax-collectors and sinners. At this, the pharisees and scribes were angry and they said accusingly of Jesus, 'This man is receiving sinners and eating with them.'

A change in the context of the story often results in a very different story. In Luke's presentation, the parable is intended as Jesus' defence of the gospel. Essential to the gospel is God's promise of free pardon to sinners and outcasts, a pardon of which Jesus is the herald and the guarantor.

The parable is not addressed, as in Matthew, to the disciples as a warning to them to be careful shepherds of the flock. It is directed to the pharisees and scribes, Israel's shepherds in Jesus' own time, and it is meant as a bitter attack on some of them for not perceiving the true character of God. God is good, generous and anxious to forgive. The teachers of Israel should all have presented God in these terms to the people. Instead, some of them were counter-images of God, proud, overbearing, ungenerous. They did not preach a merciful God, nor were they, as was Jesus, heralds of that mercy. On the contrary, by their imperious attitude towards sinners, they made God out to be as sectarian and legalistic as themselves. Only this situation can explain the vehemence of Jesus in this parable. He is defending what is closest to his heart: the grace, mercy and love of God his Father.

Luke's interpretation runs like this: Jesus is talking to some of the current teachers of Israel who never question their worthiness before God. They insist that Jesus should explain and justify his friendship for sinners and law-breakers. Isn't he becoming contaminated by contact with them and proving in the process that he cannot be from God? Jesus, in reply, tells the parable of a shepherd who leaves behind ninety-nine sheep of his flock to seek out one that was lost. At a certain point in the parable, the pharisees and scribes might have been willing to accept the legitimacy of Jesus' ministry. Somebody had to go to sinners and preach God's word of repentance to them. As Jesus was telling the story, they were, no doubt, happily identifying with the ninety-nine sheep safely housed in the fold. But Jesus' parable has a sting in the tale: 'I tell you, there will be more joy in heaven over one sinner who repents than over ninety-nine righteous persons who need no repentance' (15:7).

In Luke's context, this is not an expression of God's joy when a lost sinner is recovered: it is a bitter denunciation of the scribes and pharisees who fail *to see themselves* in the one lost sheep, classing themselves with the ninety-nine instead. But these are the sheep whom the Shepherd (God) leaves behind and finds no joy in. It is their failure to acknowledge they are lost that prevents the shepherd from searching for them and finding them.

Luke's interpretation of the parable is probably correct. It is a parable directed against Jesus' opponents and shows the superb irony of which he was capable. It describes well the hostility and self-righteousness which, for so much of his ministry, surrounded him and which he needed all his courage to confront. It explains why Jesus was so hated. Maxim Gorky tells how he once met on his travels a man who was trying to account for a widespread and puzzling phenomenon: the fear of saints, the desire to exterminate holy men.

> At the cost of tremendous effort, people have built themselves a life of sorts. They've gotten used to it. And then some solitary soul revolts, says their life isn't right. Not right? Why, we've put the best we've got into this life, may the devil take you! And they strike out at the teacher, at the saint. There! Leave us alone! And still, the truth is with those who say, 'Your life isn't right.' The truth is on their side.[70]

Jesus had come to shatter the comfortable old life that people had built for themselves on the foundations of their own achievements and to replace it with the new life of the kingdom. A teacher, a saint of extraordinary quality, he naturally met with tremendous opposition.

In the face of this opposition, he went on preaching without wavering the message of divine forgiveness which he himself embodied in his pursuit of the lost sheep of the house of Israel.

29. CAN WE KNOW ANYTHING ABOUT JESUS OF NAZARETH?

Let me formulate an objection on the basis of our findings: Is it really possible to know *anything* for certain about Jesus of Nazareth?

Scholars say that, on the part of all four evangelists, there is a great deal of theological elaboration. For instance, Jesus was certainly baptized by John but the baptism, like the temptation in the desert, has been written up in such a way as to bring out more vividly the early Christian community's understanding of his person and his role. This means we cannot be sure how

Jesus himself understood his baptism. In some miracle stories, such as the story of the storm at sea, Jesus is credited with traits that only really belong to the Lord of glory. The parables of Jesus have come down to us worked over very often by the first Christian preachers for numerous purposes: to instruct, to respond to contemporary problems, to convert the unbeliever. Later happenings, such as the mission to the Gentiles and the fall of Jerusalem in AD 70, have led to 'prophetic' utterances being put on Jesus' lips. What Jesus said about the imminent crisis of the kingdom is altered subsequently so as to refer to the imminent end of the world.

To continue the objection: In John's gospel, we find Jesus speaking in a solemn, hieratic fashion, making direct and personal claims for himself quite incompatible with what we know of Jesus from the synoptic gospels. In John, there is even complete silence about Jesus' main preoccupation, the kingdom of God; instead, Jesus speaks continually of 'eternal life'. Obviously, we cannot 'harmonize' the Jesus of the evangelists, for in each of them he speaks differently, displays different traits and interests. In particular, John's Jesus is linguistically unlike the Jesus of the synoptics. But more significantly, John seems to have uncovered the psyche of Jesus, allowed him to think aloud, as it were, before the reader. The nature of this thinking is as much out of keeping with a normal human life as is walking on water.

We may have progressed considerably in solving the theological problem by pointing to the creative tension within the gospel between Jesus of Nazareth and the Christ of glory. But what if the conclusion of the exegesis is that we do not really know the man at all? If Jesus has been merged without trace in the Christ, have we any longer a Jesus to follow, a Lord with distinct features whom we can love, serve, revere?

Once, the response of some scholars was to say: We ought to admit we can know nothing at all about Jesus' personality. In the gospels, we possess the complex phenomenon 'Jesus-Christ'. We cannot strain out the 'Jesus-part' and inspect that separately. We cannot 'unscramble the egg'. As Bultmann wrote in 1926: 'I . . . think that we can now know almost nothing concerning the life and personality of Jesus, since the early Christian sources show no interest in either, are moreover fragmentary and often legendary; and other sources about Jesus do not exist.'[71]

Most scholars now agree this view is exaggerated, but it would be well to emphasize the positive element in Bultmann's early exposition. It is true that, by and large, the evangelists are not directly concerned with Jesus' personality or development; they are more interested in what Jesus – or God through him – has accomplished. This is to say, they focus on *Jesus Christ*.

Jesus' inner development is assumed by the whole of the New Testament; Jesus is really a man as we are, is subject to the same kinds of trials and temptations we ourselves have to face. But the only material the evangelists had at their disposal was a series of isolated stories, translated from Aramaic into Greek by any number of people and not always accurately. The manner in which they edited these stories often obscured further, rather than assisted the discovery of Jesus' thoughts and developmental processes. Scholars, we saw, are unable to say for certain whether Jesus, who often spoke of the Son of Man, really identified himself with this heavenly figure endowed with triumphant traits.

In spite of these qualifications, it is no longer thought unscholarly to assert we know a great deal about the human personality of Jesus. As Dennis Nineham remarks, the gospel picture may be taken as 'fair comment' on the historical Jesus.[72] There is a continuity between Jesus and the Christ which the Church recognized from the beginning in its fusion of his name (Jesus) with his function (Christ) in 'Jesus Christ'. The portraits of each evangelist, while differing quite noticeably from each other, are substantially true to the man. The Jesus of John is no exception to this.

It would have been ridiculous had the disciples, after the resurrection, attributed Lordship and mastery of death to a kind of Nazareth mouse who had hardly squeaked in his lifetime. The Christ they worshipped and whose coming they looked forward to was the same Jesus who had proved himself already – although they had been blind to it – to be worthy of worship. Mark's so-called messianic secret, the literary device by which Jesus, after working a wonder, frequently warns, 'Go, and tell no one', is perhaps Mark's way of saying that Jesus, even in his ministry, was in very truth the glorious one. John made the same point in an even more direct and theological way throughout his gospel.

Unless we have in the gospels an authentic picture of the man from Nazareth, Christianity evaporates into a system of ideas or legends, and salvation consists, as one ancient heresy affirmed, in a kind of interior illumination. The fact is: Christianity is about a man. We are not saved by ideas; we are saved by him.

30. THE PERSONALITY OF JESUS

We know a very great deal about Jesus of Nazareth who became Christ. Apart from the essential facts of his life – that he was baptized by John, worked wonders, preached God's kingdom, spoke in parables, acted out a great deal of his teaching in symbolic actions like the cleansing of the temple, suffered and died on the cross – we know him as a distinctive individual.

He was, above all, a man who felt himself to be in a position of such unique intimacy with God that he dared to address God as 'Abba, my Father'. He fostered this intimacy in a life of continual prayer.

Jesus preached the kingdom. But the kingdom (or rule) of God was not something from which he himself could be detached. Through his own words and wonderful deeds the kingdom was in the process of drawing near. Here is a man so close to God that he is doing, on God's behalf, the most important thing his race had ever been called to do. Naturally, as a Jew, Jesus could not imagine anything more important than what was to be accomplished by his own people, God's elect. When, in John's gospel, Jesus preaches not God's kingdom but himself as the resurrection and the life, as the source of eternal life to all who come to him, we see this as a legitimate extension of Jesus' own preaching. Jesus was quite clearly conscious of his oneness with God and of the identification of his work with God's work. When the kingdom came in Jesus' death and resurrection, what was more natural than to point to Jesus, the exalted one, who exemplified God's rule in his own person?

Strengthened by his intimate communion with God, Jesus spoke with a sovereign authority that Moses himself, the most renowned leader in Jewish history, could not equal. The scribes and pharisees were certainly no match for him. Jesus was a man completely sure of himself because he never doubted his loving relationship to God his Father. He claimed to be so much greater than Moses that he felt entitled to correct his law – not even Isaiah or Jeremiah had dared to do this – as in the question of the indissolubility of marriage. This claim was the most important single cause of the antagonisms Jesus aroused and, ultimately, of his death. He did not try to resolve all problems by resorting to Mosaic texts but, like a heretic, claimed: 'Whatever the Bible may say, this is what I say.' Paul Tillich was surely right to point out that every word of Jesus challenged and disturbed the mind of both wise and simple, a characteristic marking 'the difference between him as the originator and the dependent interpreters, disciples and theologians, saints and preachers'.[73]

A man of God, he attacked, often with deep irony and prophetic vehemence, the inhuman, legalistic system which was frustrating the word of God. The law, intended to express the saving will of God and to set men free, was at that time being used by lawyers to undermine the prophetic principles of mercy, justice and truth. So clearly did Jesus perceive the absolute, constantly original demands of God, he insisted that even the Sabbath – most sacred to Jews – had sometimes to be put aside if love was to prevail. In his sense of the priority of human need, in his emphasis on loving care especially for the indigent, we see the figure of a man pre-eminently free and holy.

Jesus, holy and undefiled. This was how his disciples

remembered him. He was a man who could not be deflected by
so much as an inch from the sacred will of God. And, strangely,
while he was undefiled himself, his single aim in life was to
search out sinners. These became his special friends: the
prostitutes, the publicans, the lowly. He who lived out the
beatitudes of meekness, poverty, purity of heart, never ceased
to tell the outlaws of Jewish society that God loved them. He
was *showing* them God's love in his own loving quest for them.
And he ate with them to show in the most vivid way he could
the interchange of life he wished for. He who was identified
with God in his saving and forgiving love was identified with
the poor and the wretched in their misery. He was, he said, so
identified with them that to refuse them food and drink was to
refuse food and drink to him (Matt. 25).

Despite the fact that the gospels proclaim Jesus as Lord and
Son of God in power, his sheer humanity – so accessible and
so vulnerable – shows through all the time. He was a man of
faith, indeed the pioneer of our faith (Heb. 12:2); a man of joy
who had given his whole self for the kingdom's sake. He was
a man of deep insight into human nature. He was a man of
such personal attractiveness that people detached themselves
from the dramatic figure of the Baptist to follow him. He was
always full of peace and confidence in the future. When doubts
were cast upon the outcome of his ministry – so narrowly
based, it seemed, on a group of fishermen, publicans and
prostitutes – Jesus spoke parables of the kingdom's growth
being as certain as that a mustard seed will grow into a big
bush, and that a pinch of leaven will ferment a whole mass of
dough. Never did Jesus appear to doubt that, though the
harvest which is God's kingdom may take a long time, require
immense patience and seem sometimes to be non-existent, it
was coming inexorably. Out of small, secret beginnings, God's
glory was in process of being manifested.

Jesus, on occasions, is lonely and surprised. He asks questions to discover things he does not know, and is surprised
at some of the replies given him. He is tempted. He fasts and
feels hungry. He prays throughout the night. He loves his
friends and needs them, especially in times of tiredness and

trial. He is courageous and deliberately faces up, an unknown Galilean with a rough provincial dialect, to the authorities in Jerusalem. He can be angry and sarcastic as well as bitter in that prophetic fashion that perhaps Jews alone, through their reading of the prophets, could recognize as love. He is disappointed when a trusted friend betrays him. He is terribly afraid and alone in the presence of death. He asks to be released from death if it is possible. But he goes on trusting in God in the immense desolation and darkness that floods his soul.

The judgement scene before Pilate is, of course, a literary construction of an event that no one could have witnessed. The ruthless, military governor would scarcely have held a dignified, early-morning interview, through an interpreter, with an obscure Galilean rabble-rouser, as Pilate must have imagined him to be. In his ten years as procurator, Pilate was to see too many such Christ-figures come and go: he wanted not to speak with them but to be rid of them. Nevertheless, the story is true to the man Jesus was: under judgement, he judges everyone else by the innocence and purity of his life. Later, when he was nailed to the cross, we witness a free man whose whole bearing declares, 'I lay down my life of myself. No man takes it away from me' (John 10:18).

Jesus is, in every way, a man among men. Yet he is a man of such stature that preaching him as alive after being dead, as being Christ (Messiah) despite his crucifixion, did not invite derision but fashioned fresh disciples.

Jesus is not a neutral, anonymous human being, a man whose manhood has been blotted out by glory. Nor is he, as he is depicted so often in academic writings, someone who shares our essence but not our existence; someone who possesses our nature but none of its problems, its history, its experience. He was a man who led a very individual life and was involved in the history of a very individual people, his Jewish brothers.

31. DO WE KNOW TOO MUCH ABOUT JESUS OF NAZARETH?

When the form of the gospels as the proclamation of Jesus as the Christ is appreciated for the first time, the initial fear is we may not know anything about Jesus of Nazareth. The gospel is not about 'Jesus according to the flesh' whom Paul claimed he never knew or wanted to know, but about the Crucified made Lord and Christ.

Further reflection often leads to the opposite apprehension, namely, that we know *too much* about Jesus. He was fully a man. This means he was a first-century Jew; his appreciation of life, his vision, his hopes, his political involvement or lack of it, belonged to the first century and not to ours.

He believed, for example, in demon-possession. He thought of human beings, even the sea, as subject to supra-natural, demonic forces. He presumed that when he cast out these demons from the possessed, he was giving the most convincing sign he could of the coming of the kingdom.

Jesus thought in the apocalyptic terms of two aeons, one of sin and death which was passing, and the other aeon of lasting glory and joy. He believed most probably that the end of the old aeon was near and before long there would be a great cataclysm followed by the general resurrection of the dead. In some theological circles – not well acquainted with exegesis – it is still considered temerarious to say that Paul thought the 'parousia' (coming) of Christ would take place in his lifetime. It is hard to imagine how they will react to the suggestion that Jesus himself thought the age was to end in a conflagration very soon.

As James Robinson expressed it:

The shock of seeing the all-too-familiar Christ of the traditional gospel within the context of Jewish eschatological sects is comparable to that experienced in portraits, e.g., by Picasso, where half the face is the normal full-face mask, while the other half is cut away, providing insight into what is going on within the head; when one returns to the traditional half of the portrait, one must recall that this conventional view and that 'subliminal' view are together the reality of the person.[74]

Jesus' first-century cultural setting is not necessarily attractive to us. Previous generations of Christians 'overcame' Jesus' historical and cultural limitations by more or less forgetting Jesus was a Jew and repeatedly affirming 'Jesus is God'. God, it might be plausibly argued, is outside all cultural settings. However, the *idea* of God is always culturally conditioned, as an examination of the history of the idea of God in the Bible soon reveals.

We have seen that to concentrate on Jesus as God and to forget the man he is runs counter to the correct idea of revelation as 'the divine disclosing itself in and as the human'. A Christian who is not interested in Jesus of Nazareth is not interested in God. Equally, not to be interested in Jesus' *limitations* is to be uninterested in Jesus. I should not care much to hear someone say, 'I'm very fond of Peter De Rosa. Not that I'm in the least concerned about what he thinks, about his being a Christian, an Englishman, a lover of the sun and the sea, an avid reader of Russian literature . . .' When this person says he is fond of Peter De Rosa, can he mean anything at all when he does not want to know about my way of seeing and experiencing the world? Maybe he is only interested in his idea of me or in human nature in general. His indifference to me as *this* individual with all *these* limitations makes nonsense of his claim to be fond of *me*.

Past indifference of theologians to Jesus of Nazareth was equally disconcerting. They were more interested in analysing abstract notions (nature, person, trinitarian processions) and in arguing from the power of his miracles to his divinity. But scant concern was shown for Jesus, for the kind of man he was as is evidenced by his words and actions, all of which were in keeping with his severely conditioned existence as a first-century Jew. His humanity, in so far as it was dealt with at all, was analysed in terms of generic characteristics, hunger, thirst, capacity for pain. The particular characteristics, the particular fears, narrowness of interest, hopes, misapprehensions, joys, anguish, habits, vehemence, of a first-century Jewish prophet received hardly any attention. It was taken for granted that errors and misapprehensions could not be revelatory of God and, therefore, Jesus could not have suffered from them.

Was there a certain wisdom in this way of dealing with Jesus of Nazareth, namely, paying no attention to him as *this* man of *this* age? It is at least plausible to say so. Jesus, after all, is separated from us by two thousand tumultuous years. Maybe it's better, considering Jesus' finiteness, to forget he belonged to any particular age and concentrate on his 'divinity'!

But to surrender like this without a struggle whenever the problem of cultural relativism is raised is to deny the incarnational principle altogether. Jesus is not a man in general but this man, a member of this race, at this particular moment of history and no other. His manners, his sense of humour, his lack of concern for proprieties and hygiene[75] were aspects of his age not of ours. We are very fortunate, in my opinion, in having no picture or portrait of Jesus. We might not have liked what we saw. There would, at least, have been considerable differences in people's appreciation of it.

It is worth remembering that had Jesus lived in the nineteen-seventies, preached about God in our terms, he would be just as 'outdated' in the year 4000 as he is now – probably much more so. If God comes to us, it *must always be* in a limited, time-conditioned human fashion because the human race is ceaselessly altering. Therefore, the task of making Jesus contemporary, of updating his message and his work, of seeing what is essential and what is not, is endless. Mere repetition of what Jesus said and did is a betrayal of his work. There is always a danger in reinterpreting the New Testament; the danger of non-interpretative repetition is far greater.

To summarize what has been said about the problem of knowing Jesus of Nazareth: Christianity is not a philosophical or ethical exercise; it is the following of Christ. The gospels, despite their character of proclamation, are true to the man he was.

Jesus is the melodic theme of the gospels. The resurrection has raised the music to a higher key; the evangelists have orchestrated it and, here and there, slightly misread bits of the score. There is no problem in this. The evangelists were only human, and when they say something out of keeping with what Jesus obviously meant, this jars on the ear. (We might say, Jesus quite certainly existed because he was so evidently mis-quoted and, in part, misunderstood!) But Jesus, the melodic theme, the sole inspiration of the gospel music, is there all the time and unmistakably. The world has never heard music quite like it.

Another example, from literature. (The same, I presume, would be true of sculpture or painting.) An author may be the founder of a new school or a new style. He is the inspiration behind it. His spirit guides it, a spirit that is easily detectable. It is extraordinary that an author can sometimes be recognized through a single sentence that he wrote. Who but Jonathan Swift could have written, with such a mixture of irony, pity and rage, these few, spare words in *A Tale of a Tub*: 'Last week I saw a woman flayed, and you will hardly believe how much it altered her person for the worse.' Even if someone else had written it, we would still see Jonathan Swift's spirit there. The Spirit of Jesus is no more difficult to recognize than Swift's, even in John's elaborations.

Jesus' human personality shines through the gospels, but this is not simply a reference to his manners, his culture, his speech.[76] Still less is it a reference to his looks or physique. These are all time-conditioned things. (Who is to say what good looks are or good manners?) But through these time-conditioned things, the essential man, *the Spirit* of the man does shine through. His action, his dream of God, his teaching on the kingdom and human brotherhood, make him very real. The essential Jesus is the man who, on being asked, 'How often must I forgive, seven times?' replies, 'No, seventy times seven times', that is, times without number. The essential Jesus is the man of whom it makes sense to report that he promised paradise to a dying thief as a reward for one kind word.

Despite his inevitable, historical limitations, Jesus of Nazareth who became Christ is still for us the revelation of God. Käsemann writes, 'There are still pieces of the synoptic tradition which the historian has to acknowledge as authentic if he wishes to remain a historian at all.'[77] 'Biography', says Barclay, 'we do not have; characterization we most certainly have.'[78] After all the critical study, remarks C. H. Dodd, 'the more sure we become that here is a real Person in history, many-sided, often perplexing, certainly too great to be reduced to any common type, and not fully intelligible to us; but, for all that unmistakably individual, strongly defined in lines of character and purpose, and challenging us all by a unique outlook on life'.[79]

Part 3
PASSOVER

1. THE BASIC CHRISTIAN MESSAGE

The Christian message, after initial crises in the Church, received early on a basic, organic structure. Later developments remained true to this structure: Jesus, the man of Nazareth, who was crucified, has been raised by God to be the Lord and the Christ (Acts 2:36). He is the coming One.

There are other ways of expressing this fundamental message. Paul speaks of Jesus who shared our condition of 'the flesh' – that is our mortality, with the accompanying subjection to pain, weakness, the harshness of the law – being constituted the Son of God in power, according to the Spirit of holiness, by his resurrection from the dead (Rom. 1:4). The fourth evangelist writes in Exodus terms of Jesus passing over from this world by means of his exalting death to God the Father.

In every exposition, there is a movement (or change) in Jesus' existence. While he was among men, he suffered the same lot as the rest of us. He was weak as we are weak; he endured pain as we have to do; he was lonely as we are. But now he is glorified, exalted, beyond the touch of mortality. He is the Lord and the Christ. He is so filled with the Spirit which is the power of God that Paul can simply refer to him as 'the Spirit'. As Jesus is identified with God and shares his title of sovereignty, 'Lord', so he is one with God's Spirit of life and renewal and can be called 'Spirit' (2 Cor. 3:17).

Christianity always centres on the idea of Jesus' passover. Since he was a man like us, his life was a process that, in the nature of things, could not be completed from the beginning. He needed to be perfected by all the trials and joys of life, and ultimately, as the author of Hebrews puts it, by his passion. That was when he really proved his love for God and his fellow-men. This is why, having humbled himself and emptied himself so completely as to die upon the cross, he was exalted by God and given the new name 'Lord'.

In the creed, no mention is made of Jesus' life and ministry. We simply say that he suffered under Pontius Pilate, was crucified, died and was buried. What is implied in this is that Jesus' whole life of dedicated service was summed up and brought to fruition in his saving death. It is as if the ripe fruit of lifelong love was offered in that single, all-sufficing gift of himself to God on the cross.

Theologians once had a tendency to think of Jesus in non-biblical terms. He was 'God who died and won infinite merits for us' on the cross; on rising from the dead, he applies these merits to us for ever afterwards.

According to the New Testament, Jesus is God's Son who himself had to be made perfect by his passion. He needed for his own sake to pass over from this mortal world to reach the glory that was truly his, and, after that, he was able to bestow the Spirit upon us. In other words, the scriptures concentrate first of all on what the death and resurrection meant for Jesus himself. Christianity is not primarily what Jesus did for us but what God did to Jesus for our sakes. God raised and glorified Jesus; our salvation does not consist in the application of 'merits to our souls' but in a personal communion between us and Christ who, as the risen Lord, is near to each of us.

Jesus' resurrection is not a miraculous proof designed to convince us of Jesus' divinity. It is the supreme source of life for Jesus, and so for us, too, because he is our wisdom and righteousness before God (1 Cor. 1 : 30).

Without the resurrection, there would be no Jesus Christ and so no Christianity. Christianity is not a system of ideas or holiness, but fellowship with Jesus Christ. Without the resurrection, there would have been no life for us or in us. Who would preach a glorious but dead Jesus? What life could a corpse communicate? What confidence could we retain in God's fidelity to his covenant had Jesus remained forever dead?

Paul says: 'If Christ has not been raised, your faith is futile and you are still in your sins' (1 Cor. 15 : 17). Paul is not operating with a theology of infinite merits. Had Jesus, the Son of God, suffered on the cross and not been raised, Paul claims, his followers would not have benefited in the least. What would have become of these 'infinite merits' if he who is supposed to be the source of them had been extinguished by death? Only the resurrection provides us with the full basis for faith and a satisfactory image of God. Unless Jesus had been raised, we would have lost all confidence in God and ceased to look on him as Father.

2. JESUS' DEATH AND RESURRECTION

> If he died but did not rise,
> Speak to me not of triumph but disaster.
> If he rose but did not die,
> Worship with me a ghost but not our Master.

It is almost impossible to over-emphasize the closeness of Christ's death and resurrection in the scriptures.

The resurrection does not cancel out or, in any way, annul the cross. It is not as if after Easter we need only preach the resurrection. Without the cross, the resurrection would be a piece of make-believe, an imaginary triumph over sin after an imaginary death. Equally, without the resurrection, the cross is nothing but a ghastly, unredeemed and unredeeming tragedy.

It makes no sense to say: In earlier times, Christians tended to preach the cross exclusively; we preach only the resurrection. Unless we preach both simultaneously we preach neither. It is true that, like Paul, we stress sometimes one aspect rather than the other. At one moment, Paul tells us: 'If Christ has not been raised, our faith is futile and we are still in our sins.' At another, he cries: 'Far be it from me to glory except in the cross of our Lord Jesus Christ' (Gal. 6:14).

In our lives, there is the cross aspect: discipline, self-denial. But we experience at the same time the resurrection, since it is not merely afterwards but *in* the discipline and self-denial that we can find God, hence life, joy and self-surrender.

John's gospel, too, in its characteristic way, tells us that the death and resurrection of Christ are one mystery of faith. The resurrection is not only what happened to Jesus after he was dead; it is the glory of the death. With splendid ambiguity, he speaks of Jesus being exalted (raised up) on the cross, at once crucified and glorified. John also anticipates the moment which Luke delays until Pentecost by making the bestowal of the Spirit coincide with Jesus' death. Jesus, at his consummation, breathed forth his Spirit (19:30), clearly the Pentecostal Spirit. His dying is our living; his expiration is our inspiration; the breath by which Jesus lived is henceforth in the world. Likewise, the waters of new life – these waters represent the Spirit – come from the fountain in Christ's side pierced by the soldier's lance (19:34. Cf. 7:38).

According to John, there is in Jesus a glory that death cannot extinguish. This means, of course, that in the Christ there is a humanity and a force of love that is not erased by the divine glory. Jesus was, we said, most true to himself in death when he surrendered himself for our sakes in love to God; and he lives on forever as the obedient Son of God. This is what his perpetual stance is. This is his eternal reality in which he is consummated (or made perfect) forever. In pictorial fashion, John shows the risen Christ retaining the marks of crucifixion on his body. Just as the mortal Jesus was transfigured, so the immortal Christ is transpierced. The imagery is basically the same. The resurrection wounds show that Jesus and the Christ are one; the crucified Jesus is the glorified Christ.

Christian devotion, it bears repeating, has never found this idea perplexing. Jesus, crucified in weakness, is adored as the Lord. In the Eucharist, the crucified One is present, offering us life and pledging himself to come in glory.

Belief in the resurrection is belief that Jesus on Calvary was loved and not cursed by God. When the disciples, after initial failure, grasped this and its consequences, they 'saw' their risen Lord. It took a little while for them to grasp it, and this is why we speak biblically of the resurrection in chronological terms as taking place 'on the third day'. But theologically – and this is John's position – the resurrection is the very death of Jesus

seen from the divine standpoint: Jesus crucified is already with
God. This, too, is why Paul can say with strict theological
accuracy: 'Far be it from me to glory except in the cross of our
Lord Jesus Christ.'

Belief in Christ's resurrection is far from being the consequence of scientific investigation. It entails abandoning ourselves to the God of Jesus crucified; and he alone, our Father,
the God of the living, is able to show us the face of the risen
Christ.

3. JESUS THE SON OF GOD

Death and resurrection constitute a single mystery of faith.
Our whole treatment so far illustrates that the same is true of
the human and the divine in Christ. The human is the expression
– the Bible speaks of the 'word' – of God. The human is
distinct from the divine, but this does not mean the human and
divine are juxtaposed to constitute an amalgam of two infinitely
diverse realities (or natures). It is not as if we could get 'behind'
the human or 'underneath' it or 'on the other side' of it to
reach the divine. The human *is* that by which alone we encounter God and by which God embodies himself and so
approaches us. This is the law of the incarnation.

God the Mystery comes to us through a man, like ourselves
in everything except that he did not fail his Father. It is dangerous to think in terms of 'the manhood' of Jesus being, as it
were, inconsequential in comparison with 'his divinity';
rather, Jesus Christ is our meeting point with God. In him, we
find God and are reconciled to God. Failure to focus on Jesus
of Nazareth who became Christ is a failure to know God.

Christ is, in a sense, the oldest and newest revelation of God.
He is the oldest revelation in that he shows how man has
always revealed God to his fellow-men. He is the newest
revelation in that, before he came, it was taken for granted
that no man can really mirror God: God in all his attributes is
in no way like man. I suggest that Jesus makes God both
familiar and strange at one and the same time. What is truly

familiar is thought to be strange, and what is truly strange is thought to be familiar. Let me explain.

So often the approach to Jesus has been: We all have a clear, ready-made idea of God. He is immortal, impassible, eternal, invisible. We find this idea 'made flesh' in Jesus who, mainly through miracles and especially through the resurrection, the greatest possible miracle, showed that he is God the almighty and immortal. Jesus thus proves himself to be one with the God whom we have always known, presumably through inferring his existence and attributes from the beauty of nature, the succession of the seasons, the order in microcosm and macrocosm.

There are still books of apologetics that follow this line of argument: Firstly, prove the existence of God; next, show that miracles, especially the resurrection, are proofs that whoever does them is God; then point out that Jesus both claimed to be God and performed miracles to substantiate this claim. *Ergo* . . .

These apologists would do well to heed Bergson's remarks about the philosophers' notion of God acquired by reflection on the world:

So remote is this conception from the God most men have in mind that if, by some miracle, and contrary to the opinion of philosophers, God as thus defined should step into the field of experience, none would recognize him. For religion . . . regards him, above all, as a Being who can hold communication with us; now this is just what the God of Aristotle, adopted with a few modifications by most of his successors, is incapable of doing.[1]

In the apologists' approach, Jesus appears familiar when he ought to appear strange. It, surely, is a strange thing that God should reveal himself in the lowliness and, ultimately, in the death of a son of man. Jesus brings in a new idea of God. We do not know, in advance of Jesus, what God is like, namely, Father. Otherwise, we would not call Jesus 'the Word of God'. We could dispense with his services.

Jesus does not simply corroborate the notions of the Greek

philosophers. He tells us, or, better, since he doesn't aim to provide us with 'information', he *shows* us what God is like. God is Love and Forgiveness. The philosophers found these characteristics so alien to the deity that *they never thought of attributing them to God*. After Jesus, it isn't possible for Christians to picture God except as the merciful and all-forgiving Father of our Lord Jesus Christ who loves and justifies the sinner. All this helps explain why Jesus is termed Emmanuel, God-with-us, and God-for-us. He is our Way to God, a new way that does not depend on philosophical arguments. H. R. Mackintosh expressed all this in a passage that is worth extensive quotation:

> The full truth cannot be expressed by saying that Christ simply corroborates an idea of God long familiar to the average man; rather it is in Christ that for the first time we perceive the true character of God and know, without reasoning, that nothing other or less than this could satisfy. And when we have seen in Christ what we know is God, we are then able to call Christ divine with some complete reality of meaning. Athanasius, a great man if ever there was one, appears to have supposed that *ab initio* he could give an account of God in agreed and tolerably simple conceptions, since it was quite possible to formulate a statement of his chief attributes which Greek philosophy would have had no difficulty in countersigning. People who take their religion from the New Testament discover that we have first to let Jesus show us what the Father is like, and that forgiveness, about which philosophy as such does not concern itself, is his characteristic gift. As we contemplate Jesus presented in the gospels, we discern not merely that God is love, but what *kind* of love this is. On that crucial point our true thoughts have all been overheard from Christ.[2]

It has always struck me as odd that theologians should go on considering God, in the manner of non-Christian philosophy, as immutable and impassible,[3] especially when they want to maintain, firstly, Jesus is the exact Image of God, and, secondly, he was most himself when he gave himself up in agony on the cross. Not that I want to claim that God *as God* suffers. Only, I believe that to say that God does not suffer is not merely unhelpful but positively misleading. A stoical, unfeeling God – what other image could impassibility in the face of human misery conjure up? – is not attractive to us.

Someone might ask: If you are not proposing that God as such suffers or does not suffer, what are you trying to convey? My answer is: God is Mystery to whom our categories do not apply; but I am a Christian because the only model that satisfies me when approaching this Mystery is Jesus Christ. I believe him to be the Word, the manifestation (or epiphany) of God. Jesus most exactly models and corresponds to God at the moment when he suffers lovingly on the cross for us. I consider it wrong for a Christian to say that what Jesus, God's Image, suggests to me by dying on Calvary is that God is impassible! In Jesus, God surfaces to show he is involved in all the sufferings of mankind.

Jesus brings in this strange, new idea of God: through those aspects of human life usually thought to be most distant from God – in fact, the challenge to the very existence of the deity: pain, failure, humiliation, death – the divine is manifest in Christ's own life and thus mediated to us.

Having said that what many people consider to be familiar is really very strange, the converse need not detain us long: what is thought to be very strange is, in fact, familiar. Jesus shows that what is authentically human is already the divine expressing itself. Jesus is the supreme, not the sole instance of this. He is unique not by being abnormal but by being the supreme realization, indeed, the criterion of the normal.

Holiness is sometimes confused with inhumanness; the 'supernatural', as it is called, is expected to be weird, abnormal, unattractive.[4] Jesus has completely reversed this expectation. The Son of God was no different from other men, except he lived human life most humanly, most intensely and most caringly. I return to this basic standpoint: the human and divine in Christ are distinct but do not constitute two. The human in Christ is the divine expressing itself in the only possible way. Jesus is the supreme instance of *man* being the

Lord of creation (Gen. 1:26). Were the divine to express itself in any other way than the human, we who are only human would not be capable of apprehending it.

4. THE OBSCURITY OF JESUS OF NAZARETH

In his story, 'The Procurator of Judea' (1892), Anatole France presents a Pontius Pilate grown obese and old, his mind unimpaired though his body is tormented with gout. At the famous watering-place of Baiae, he meets up with an old crony from his Judean days, Aelius Lamia. On their couches in the evening, they chatted together – after interchanges on the subject of their ailments and the best known remedies for them – about the great events they have lived through. Pilate recalled great engineering feats – the construction of bridges, canals, aqueducts – before expressing bitter regret that the Jews whom he had wanted to like but eventually detested had not taken at all well to the Imperial Eagle of the occupying power. In Jerusalem, Pilate ruefully admitted, there had been nothing but intrigue, accusations, rebellions, which he had tried at first to mollify and later to extirpate by force.

For his part, Aelius recalled a voluptuous Jewess there, a dancer, who had given up her 'profession' to attach herself to a group of men and women surrounding a Galilean wonder-worker. Aelius continued:

'His name was Jesus; he came from Nazareth, and he was crucified for some crime, I don't quite know what. Pontius, do you remember anything about the man?'

'Jesus?' he murmured, 'Jesus – of Nazareth? I cannot call him to mind.'[5]

Jesus was not someone worth remembering.

For the Christian, in Jesus' pain, obscurity, death, God is to be found and the glory of God. Something terrible died in Jesus: the sin that obscures God from men, the old world of self-reliance which Jesus 'repented of' upon his cross. In so doing, he made way for the 'glory'.

Christians reckon Jesus to be God's last word to men, in the sense of God's decisive word. This is why the evangelists make the voice from the cloud of the divine presence say: 'This is my beloved Son. Listen to him.' If a friend were to say, 'Listen very carefully. This is the last thing I shall ever say to you', we would give him all our attention. Christians want to give their whole attention to Christ and his message. He is not any word of God; he is the fulfilment of Israel and God's decisive word.

It is a startling word. It tells of strength in weakness, wisdom in folly, success in failure, divine in the human at its most human, redemption through the scandal of the cross, life in death – hence, meaning in everything, even the apparently meaningless.

Because of the indivisibility of death and resurrection in Christ, we do not centre on death for its own sake, for that would be joyless, morbid, defeatist. We centre on God's vanquishing of death, on Christ's passover by means of death to new life. This is why Paul and John can proclaim this paradox: the Crucified is alive. We, too, through faith, pass through Christ's death to new meanings, new wonders, new worlds.

It can be put like this: we focus on Christ's death only because of the evidence there of a love stronger than death, a love that broke the bonds of death and overcame death's absurdities.

The gospel is good news only if it proclaims that death is vanquished. This is why some crucifixes are indefensible from the Christian viewpoint: they depict only the loneliness, the anguish, the death. They do not express anything of the communion and the glory. Their 'realism' is unrealistic.

The gospel tells us we have died with Christ; and there is one sense in which we must remain dead, dead to the old world of self-reliance. 'The old aeon' is a situation of reliance on our own resources, our own systems of theology or holiness. We have to remember that Jesus, the Jew, died excommunicate for 'heresy'; Judaism, as a system of sanctification, failed him at the crucial moment, as any other system, Christianity included, is bound to fail. Jesus ultimately proved that he had always relied on God alone, the gracious God, the living God who raises the dead. Jesus went down into the pit (death) where only God can help.

True religious experience is to be had wherever there is dependence on God alone and mistrust of all systems as such. Christians, being dead to 'laws and systems', even those of sacred origin, should rejoice in communion with the God of resurrection. We share in Jesus' death to all the enslaving forces: sin, the impotent 'flesh', the 'world' which is systematized opposition to God, the 'law' which claims superiority over love.

Jesus' disciples were still enslaved to the law and incapable of grasping Jesus' originality: his total and immediate dependence on God alone. Only this can explain why even in death on a cross – reputedly a curse according to the law – the glory shone through him.

It was hard enough for the disciples to accept that God's presence can betray itself as absence. Their theology had no place for a crucified Messiah. Jesus' own problem, it seems, was to hold on to the conviction that apparent abandonment by God was not desertion but a still more loving presence. The whole gospel story is told in the unshakeable belief that Jesus retained this conviction to the end.

This is the reason why Arthur Koestler's story, 'Episode' is unacceptable. In this story, Jesus is surprised that his Father allows him to be crucified, a reasonable hypothesis, I consider, in view of Jesus' prayer in the garden. (On Aquinas' supposition, Jesus, knowing in advance the events of Good Friday 'ought not' to have offered that prayer in Gethsemane.) 'Now is the time,' says Koestler's Jesus, 'now is the time to call it off, to stop this frightening make-believe.' On Calvary, the Father does not intervene, so that Jesus thinks: 'I must not faint. I must not look into his eyes if he has eyes to see. Eloi, eloi, how can you bear watching this? Thou dumb spirit, vapour of the desert, ignoble absence, thou art not, hast never been. Only a parable. And my own death another parable; they will remember it and twist its meaning. They will torture and kill in the name of a parable. And thus will your will be done, not mine.'[6]

This story – if I understand it correctly – runs counter to the basic assumption of the New Testament writers which is that Jesus, despite the temptation to despair, did not yield to it.

The cross, said Paul, is both a stumbling block to non-Jews and stupidity to Jews. Jews ask for miracles; non-Jews waste their time on metaphysics. In Christ crucified is divine power and wisdom. There are no stupendous signs, however, and nothing much to arouse intellectual curiosity. Paul does not mention a single miracle of Christ. He never talks of puzzling exhibitions of power on Jesus' part, only of a paralysing display of weakness. It is this weakness that saves us and shows the ultimate truth about God.

In Bernard Malamud's *The Fixer*, Yakov, a most unhappy Jew, deserted by his wife and a prey to every misfortune, is addressed by his father-in-law:

'Yakov,' said Shmuel passionately, 'don't forget your God!'

'Who forgets who?' the fixer said angrily . . . 'We live in a world where the clock ticks fast while he's on his timeless mountain staring into space. He doesn't see us and he doesn't care. Today I want my piece of bread and not in Paradise.'[7]

Jesus cried out on his cross like any atheist, 'Why have you abandoned me, God; why have you forgotten me; why don't you see and care?' I know he was reciting a psalm. He recited it because it put into words the temptation he was undergoing and the desolation of his soul, even though, and perhaps *because* that same psalm ends with a triumphant expression of confidence in God. Jesus first had to descend into hell, the hell of death, and discover for himself more painfully than any psalmist that 'if I make my bed in Sheol [hell], thou art there' (Ps. 139:8).

Jesus' descent into hell became part of the confession of the creed. For Jews, hell was Sheol, the place where God is absent, where there is no life or joy or communion. Jesus' descent into

Sheol represents pictorially Jesus' cry of abandonment on the cross. He, too, experienced the dreadful absence of God, and yet he gives to his fellow-sufferers the good news of God's love.

At the crucifixion, God didn't 'do anything'; he didn't step in and put things right. He 'only' let himself be found. Jesus shows to Israel and to his Church that in the condition of this sinful, fragmented, war-torn world, God's love often comes in the form of suffering. When suffering is made into a means of expressing love and even joy, it redeems. What Christ guarantees is that God himself can always be found, even in the suffering. This explains why there is not really a 'problem of evil' in the New Testament as there was in the Old. There is 'nowhere where God is not'.

This is the sense in which God does not change. He is not the untarnished, imperturbable, stainless steel God of Greek philosophy. Rather, he is unchanging in his covenantal love and fidelity. And he promises to sustain us in all our trials so that in the end we win through.

5. ATONEMENT AND THE CHARACTER OF GOD

'In this the love of God was made manifest among us, that God sent his only Son into the world, so that we might live through him' (1 John 4:9). 'For God so loved the world that he gave his only Son, that whoever believes in him should not perish but have eternal life. For God sent the Son into the world, not to condemn the world, but that the world might be saved through him' (John 3:16–17). 'So we know and believe the love God has for us. God is love . . . We love, because he first loved us' (1 John 4:16,19). 'By this we know love, that he [Christ] laid down his life for us' (1 John 3:16). 'Greater love has no man than this, that a man lay down his life for his friends' (John 15:13). 'I do as the Father has commanded me, so that the world may know that I love the Father' (John 14:31). 'Father . . . I made known to them thy name, and I will make it known, that the love with which thou hast loved me may be in them, and I in them' (John 17:26).

In the New Testament, there is no developed theological theory of the atonement. Certain images are used. There is the legal image of paying back a debt, of redeeming or ransoming a slave. There is the ritualistic image of Jesus offering a sacrifice pleasing to God.[8] The Johannine passages quoted above stress what underlies all these imperfect models: God loves us; he is faithful in his love. Paul's own image of God justifying the sinner rests on the same basis of God's prior gratuitous love for the sinner. 'Justification' is a word that may give Westerners the impression of a legalistic approach to atonement when really it stands for the priority of God's love. Faith is accepting this priority, the acceptance itself being seen as the first gift of God's love. Faith is in no way a human work taking precedence over the loving action of God. It is despair over self as the originator of new life, hence death to the old self-seeking, death-seeking, self-justifying self. Faith gives God his true glory, recognizes his sovereignty, and so brings abundant joy.

God is Love, not 'just', legalistic, severe. He is not a God who requires, even demands, a repayment of a debt or some readjustment of the scales of justice. He is Love proven in the action of 'sending' his Son. He sent Christ because and only because he loved us. To speak in the only terms we can, God's only 'motive' was to save us. His love is always prior to ours. Our love is response to the love which he essentially is; he is the Love underlying everything.

Christ is the parable of God. He is the Image, the perfect mirror, the complete model of God. He, too, in all his dealings with us and his attitudes towards us is love and forgiveness. His message in word and deed was always that God loves and is gentle towards the sinner who humbly acknowledges his sin. Not that a person can recompense God for the evil done. God simply forgives without payment anyone who responds with love to his own unfailing offer of love. How did Jesus come to this startlingly original idea?

Jesus didn't know it all in advance, as it were. He didn't come 'from outside' with a clear understanding of our problem and a ready-made solution to it. He came from within Judaism, discovered what the problem was and assumed responsibility for it. He found God in human need. He perceived God's will in the response he felt called upon to make to this need. He recognized God as Father. He came to this recognition because he took his fellows to his heart as his brethren. He so identified with sinners that he himself experienced God's gentleness with sinners. God's graciousness to them was first experienced as graciousness to himself who bore the fate of sinners. Jesus, the reconciled man, the man who did no sin, knew God's forgiveness best of all because he knew it as God's forgiveness of himself *as our representative*.

In a deep sense, we, though sinners, mediated God the Father to Jesus. Only men can mediate God to their fellowmen. This was not less but more true of Jesus than of us, even though he was to mediate God to us in the plenary sense of embodying, of expressing in himself, the forgiveness and fatherliness of God. The cross and resurrection are the expression of God's forgiveness of us, but they are expressed *in him* because of his oneness with us.

Christ, then, incarnates the love of God as well as the sinfulness of man as he lies there on the cross. Christ is suspended, in biblical imagery, between heaven and earth. He belongs to both parties; he sides with neither, *because* he sides with both. He is a man literally torn apart by his twin allegiance. It is hard to imagine how different Christian sympathies and devotion would be had Jesus been executed in a way other than that of suspension and exaltation.

Jesus' heart was so attuned to God that he must have suffered from evil in ways we cannot fathom. As Simone Weil writes:

Evil dwells in the heart of the criminal without being felt there. It is felt in the heart of the man who is afflicted and innocent. Everything happens as though the state of soul suitable for criminals had been separated from crime and attached to affliction; and it even seems to be in proportion to the innocence of those who are afflicted.[9]

Jesus knew himself to be the faithful Israelite, the proclaimer of the presence of God's kingdom. His words were God's

words, as his deeds were the deeds of God. Moreover, his
offer of love and forgiveness to God's people was God's own.
On account of this identification, he experienced rejection as
the rejection of God. His crucifixion was the decisive refusal
of God's love. There on Calvary, through the Jewish leaders,
mankind was saying, and continues to say in every sin, 'I will
not serve.'

Jesus, the representative of God and men, is caught in the
cross-fire of the supreme offer of love and its rejection. On his
cross, Jesus embodies love and hate. Which of them will win
the mastery in his heart? Which will claim him for its own in
this great parable of the decisive exchange between God and
men?

The first Christian disciples believed that it was love. In
Jesus, the Image of God, the crucifixion became the expression
of God's love, precisely when, despite seeming to be abandoned
by both God and men, he kept on loving God and men. He
even prayed for those who nailed him to the cross. This was
not a plea for God to change speedily from wrath to mercy.
God is changeless love and eternally faithful to his covenant.
Christ is his perfect Image. The new covenant is in the blood
of him who is God's Word, faithful and true.

Paul sometimes uses terrifying phrases to describe Jesus on
his cross. He says of him, 'For our sake he [God] made him to
be sin' (2 Cor. 5:21), he 'became a curse for us' (Gal. 3:13).
Paul was bold in employing these terms because he was sure
that God's love had been able to master this embodiment of
sin, the cross. He mastered it by raising Jesus from the dead,
by 'justifying' the repentant, sin-laden man who, bearing our
sins away, changed the heart of the world. Jesus, the expression
of God, brings in a fresh love that did not yield to hate; this is
why God exalted him and made him glorious forever.

Jesus did not pay back a debt to God. Not even he was
capable of doing that. It is nonsense to suggest that God who
is love and who always freely justifies the sinner demands
'repayment'. Jesus is the Servant of God, the *unprofitable
Servant of God*. Contrary to some theories of atonement, Jesus
is special not because he alone is able to pay God back a debt

but because of his unparalleled response in love to the prior love of God *who alone is good* (Luke 18:19). Jesus recognized that God had given him the strength of his Spirit to love and serve him throughout his life and, above all, in his death.

It is wrong to picture a situation in which sin demands retribution – called 'justice' – if order is to be restored. God, in this view, insists on punishment for the sake of satisfying his sense of justice. In the event, the innocent Son willingly endures a more than adequate punishment when he substitutes himself for us. After the crucifixion, divine justice has been done, the balance is restored.

A cursory glance at the scripture texts at the head of this section shows this justice view has no biblical foundation. It is refutable on at least three grounds: (i) It makes God appear vindictive, insistent on an eye for an eye.[10] Jesus, on the contrary, tells us God is not like that, therefore we must not be like that either. Christian ethic is an imitation, and a participation in the gracious love (*agapē*) that God is. (ii) God appears to be not only vindictive but unsatisfied until he has punished an innocent man whom he knows to be innocent. The atonement, on such a supposition, would be an undeniable work of injustice. (iii) The justice view depicts God as loving us only *after* Christ died for us on the cross. The Christian Bible says the opposite: it was because God loved us while we were sinners that he sent his Son into the world (Rom. 5:8; 1 John 4:10).

The justice theory of atonement undermines the gospel of grace in that, according to it, redemption is paid for, even if paid for by Christ, rather than freely given. The theory distorts the incarnation, implying that Jesus loved us when God did not, which is to say that Jesus is not the model of God who is love. Finally, it caricatures the crucifixion, making it appear that God, not man was responsible for the death of Jesus, or, at least, that God needed men to put his Son to death to satisfy his justice.

Scripture represents the atonement from beginning to end as a work of perfect love and free pardon on God's part. God, in love, sends his Son and Word. In a loveless world, Jesus loves his way right through death – the death that sin demanded –

and for his pains, was raised by God. In death, his love overcame hate and won for him the Spirit of love. This Spirit he
now spreads in the hearts of believers, enabling them to master
sin through love and to imitate God as he did.

6. CHRIST THE REPRESENTATIVE

Jesus was put to death for our sins and raised for our justification (Rom. 4:25). The idea that Jesus acts *for us*, is *our representative*, is everywhere taken for granted in the Christian
Bible, though in this case, as with the atonement with which it
is closely connected, there is no developed theology to account
for it. It is experienced by the believer and yet it is hardly
expressible.

In the first place, Jesus is *God's* representative. As such,
Jesus is in no way God's substitute; he does not supplant God
or act instead of God. God works through him. This is how
God always works on men: through men.

Jesus is also *our* representative. Paul, above all, sees Christ
and all mankind, Jews and non-Jews alike, as constituting a
single man (or body). Christ, however, is alone sinless, the
reconciled man. This means that he died not for his own sins
but for ours, just as he was raised so that we may be justified
in God's sight.

Paul makes great play of the fact that Christ is the second
Adam but his form of argument needs careful analysis.
Remember how he reasons in Galatians that the promises were
made to Abraham 'and to his offspring', in the singular not the
plural, therefore signifying Christ! The rabbinic style of arguing
strikes us as amusing. In Genesis, to which Paul refers, 'seed'
or 'offspring' was obviously intended to refer to a multitude
and not to an individual. Paul is simply playing games with a
figure of speech in order to make a point. Likewise with
Adam. Paul uses the illustration of the first Adam who, in the
rabbinic literature of the time, was considered to have brought
sin and death into the world which each individual then
appropriates through personal acts of trespass. The risen

Christ, as the representative of a redeemed mankind, brings life which is more abundant than the universal death subsequent upon Adam's (mankind's) sin. Jesus, as the new Adam, the new Mankind, opened up the way of life by being the first-born from the dead whom the rest of men will eventually follow. Christ's obedience more than compensates for the disobedience of the former Adam.

Paul assumed we were reconciled to God and attain peace and righteousness through Christ. As a Jew, he was accustomed, as was Jesus himself, to the notion of representation. The Jewish people as a whole was a representative people and Abraham was the father, hence the representative, of many nations. But the theological question cannot be evaded: how were we so united to Christ that we really died to sin with him on Calvary and were raised to new life with him at Easter?

We don't take too readily to the notion of representation and yet, even in a supposedly individualistic age like ours, we cannot do without it.

For example, a father often represents his family in its decisions. A child may say, 'We drove down to the south of France', meaning his father drove the family there, or, 'We emigrated from Poland', meaning his grandparents did. Boxers represent their fans and supporters, showing that there is something in them that calls out to be represented even at a boxing match. We read in newspapers and magazines, 'We lost the Davis cup', or 'We won the Ryder cup.' Nobody quarrels with this way of putting things. It is so reasonable that some people who disagree with their nation's foreign policy object to the British or American 'presence' in territory not their own, even though they may be women or too old to be personally called up for military service there. If they disagree with a particular war, they object to being represented by their soldiers fighting it. They understand that their soldiers are fighting *for them,* on their behalf, and, therefore, that they themselves are fighting and killing through their military representatives. These objectors feel they cannot shrug their shoulders at what is done abroad and say their *nation's* presence is only a convenient fiction without any bearing on their own lives. Nor can anyone, be he a national or a foreigner, absolve himself from all responsibility and concern for the more obvious atrocities committed in a war in which his nation is engaged. I am not referring simply to the crimes known to be committed under stress and perhaps extreme provocation by the soldiers we happen to support. I am speaking, as well, of the crimes committed, under whatever provocation, by the 'enemy', too, whom Christ commanded us to love.

The Jewish-Christian faith has been saying for millennia that we all belong to one another; we constitute a single family; we are all responsible for one another. Each of us is Everyman, Adam, the Representative. Together we have built up a total system of iniquity – referred to in the Christian Bible as the 'world' – as well as a system of goodness and neighbourliness, the beginnings of the new creation, the kingdom. These two systems are forever in conflict even in the Church. It is the Church's tragedy when she is looked on necessarily and self-evidently as a zone free from sin and corruption, since pharisaism and triumphalism inevitably ensue.

So one is mankind that a particularly outstanding example of evil – for example, the mindless massacre of innocent, unarmed civilians in the midst of war – is only the point of the nail. There bears down upon that point the whole weight of the world's sin. Part of that sin at least, we, through our trespasses, are directly and immediately responsible for. All of it we are responsible for in the representative sense that we ought to accept responsibility for the faults of others, for we are all brothers.

Through the mass media; newspapers, radio, television, we are becoming more aware of the unity of the race at the very moment when its divisions are most plain. At the same time, we are conscious of the *representative* character of everything being enacted before us.

It is clear from this brief and inadequate examination that representatives bear, in diverse forms and degrees, the fortunes of those whom they represent. A soccer team will represent its college as far as soccer goes; in a sense, through its team, the whole college loses or wins. An army represents a nation in a deeper, moral sense: the nation's whole value system as well as its security is under scrutiny, and will be judged according to the justice or injustice of its military policies. But in everything we do, whether for good or ill, because we are members of a single family, we represent all mankind.

The Letter to the Colossians claims that Christ is the representative of all mankind and that it is he who constitutes the human race as a family. In its mixture of Greek pre-existence language and specifically Jewish resurrection language, the Letter says of Christ:

He is the image of the invisible God, the first-born of all creation; for in him all things were created, in heaven and on earth, visible and invisible . . . all things were created through him and for him. He is before all things, and in him all things hold together. He is the head of the body, the Church; he is the beginning, the first-born from the dead, that in everything he might be pre-eminent. For in him all the fullness of God was pleased to dwell [by his resurrection], and through him to reconcile to himself all things, whether on earth or in heaven, making peace by the blood of his cross (Col. 1:15–20).

The author is suggesting, in cosmic terms, that Christ did not come into the world and afterwards find himself man's choice of representative. Everything finds its significance in him; it was for him that it was originally made. He is the head of the Church which is his body; but the body exists because of him. He acts on behalf of the whole human family because it is he who makes it a single family. In everything he is pre-eminent, and the fullness of God dwells in him as the first-born from the dead. Whatever exists before or after him derives existence and meaning from him and his resurrection.

Such statements only make sense in the light of faith. No scientific proof can be offered to substantiate such claims. Each of us, through a personal act of discipleship, has to discover that Christ, in very truth, is 'the whole world to me' because he is Emmanuel, God-with-us. Nothing has any lasting significance outside him and the powerful new life he made available to us at his resurrection. Without him and his resurrection, the whole world is in darkness (Matt. 27:45). Faith clings to Jesus as the special representative of mankind. Very close to God, he bears the fortunes of the Jewish people, and so of the entire race, upon his shoulders.

Outside the poetry of pre-existence language, Jesus is looked on as the perfectly reconciled man; the obedient Son who fully lived a life of love in accordance with the Father's kingly rule. He is the new Adam whose influence extends to the entire family due to his intimacy with, and service of the Father-God.

We do not complain about Christ. We only object to our representatives when they let us down. But in Christ, we fought the right war and won it in the right way; we reached a lasting and honourable peace with God. Christ died for us and rose for our justification, which is to say, we died with him on Calvary and rose with him at Eastertime.

Christ is our representative, but unless we accept him as such, the world is not changed in any way. He did not act instead of us,[11] any more than he acted instead of God or as God's substitute. We must play our part; we are free to give (or refuse) him our support.

Christ acted for us at a time when we could not act on our own behalf. But he did this so that subsequently we, through faith in him, should not be dispensed from action but capable of action. He is fully our representative only when, influenced by him, we do what he does. Nothing – whether it be God, Christ or the sacraments – can work magically upon us, substituting some kind of 'spiritual' or 'supernatural' activity for our own response. God in Christ is with us enabling us to carry out his will.

Finally, we must become representative people in our turn. We have in us the first Adam, the man of dust who is obliged to accept guilt for, and involvement in the world's sin. We have in us, too, the second Adam, the man from God who speaks a word of hope to the world. Wherever there is a reconciled and reconciling person, to that degree *the whole world is different*. In this instance, too, Jesus is the prototype of all of us. Just as 'all Israel is in her Messiah', so in a derivative way the whole of mankind is in each of us.

7. JUDAS ISCARIOT

My face he presses with his lips.
With this, my sorrow rises to a flood.
His hand into my dish he dips,
This friend, who is the first to taste my blood.

There is no blacker figure in all literature than Judas Iscariot. Jesus chose him presumably because he loved him and saw potential goodness in him. The evangelists, however, seem not to have had a single kind word to spare for Judas.

When Jesus went up to Jerusalem in an open and courageous bid to have his proclamation of the kingdom accepted there by the officials of Judaism, Judas went to the chief priests and promised, for money, to betray Jesus to them at the opportune moment.

Judas' presence at the Supper is depicted as being a source of sadness to Jesus. He who knew what was in man realized that one of his own, who dipped bread in the same dish with him in fellowship, was a traitor. If, as was becoming so much clearer, he must be rejected and suffer, 'woe to that man by whom the Son of man is betrayed! It would have been better for that man if he had not been born' (Mark 14:21).

Later, in Gethsemane, Judas came with the crowd sent by the chief priests to apprehend Jesus. The sign he had given them was: 'The one I shall kiss is the man; seize him' (Matt. 26:48). It was with this kiss that Jesus was handed over to his enemies for trial and execution.

The information we have about Judas is makeshift and inconclusive. Why did he betray Jesus? Was the sum of thirty pieces of silver (Matt. 26:15) an adequate recompense for his treachery? What happened to him afterwards?

John's gospel reserves an absolute condemnation for Judas. He is 'the son of perdition' by whom the scriptures are to be fulfilled (17:12). He is accused by the fourth evangelist of being a thief who was used to stealing from the disciples' money box of which he had charge (12:6). Jesus is said to have foretold a long time before that one of his disciples had a devil and was to betray him (6:71). Judas was the one into whom Satan entered at the Supper (13:27). His departure from the feast occasions John's comment: 'So, after receiving the morsel, he immediately went out; and it was night' (13:30). This night into which Judas melted was the godlessness out of which came Nicodemus, a ruler of the Jews (3:2).

When reading John's gospel, we must always be aware of his tendency to contrast light and darkness and to theologize events. Therefore, his verdict on Judas shares in that absoluteness of judgement almost demanded, as it were, by the categories he is working with. Judas belongs to the other 'world' of sin, chaos, darkness, the devil. Further, the view that Judas was a thief, even if true, is hardly an explanation of his treachery. He was not likely to have made a large amount on the deal. Judas seems to have been an enigma to the fourth evangelist who selected, implausibly, avarice as his motive.

Matthew's gospel tells of Judas returning the money and crying: 'I have sinned in betraying innocent blood' (27:4). He threw down the pieces of silver in the temple and went and hanged himself. There are difficulties in Matthew's account, too, especially when we compare it with what Luke has to say.

The site where Judas threw down the money, the temple, is symbolic with a vengeance. The blood-money paid out for Jesus, scattered upon its floors, would have certainly marked out the temple for destruction. Matthew suggests that Judas hanged himself soon after he departed, and he states that it was the chief priests who bought the potter's field, called the Field of Blood at the time of writing. Matthew, as was his custom, revels in the fact that two rather irrelevant texts in Jeremiah and Zechariah – which he has doctored somewhat – are 'fulfilled' in this incident. He alone mentions the ironic amount Judas received, thirty pieces of silver, the recompense for a slave who had accidentally been put to death. A trivial sum. This is a barely disguised theological comment!

In brief, Matthew, with the help of biblical texts, has elaborated considerably on local Christian folklore in which the traitor's name had become associated with a field of some notoriety called *Hakeldama*.

Luke, in the Acts, makes Peter say that Judas himself bought the field, that he fell headlong (or peharps 'swelled up') and burst open so that all his bowels gushed out (1:18). There is no mention of any remorse or suicide on Judas' part.

We are left with these few hard facts: Judas, one of Jesus' closest disciples, betrayed him to the authorities for money. He came into the garden where Jesus was accustomed to rest and pray after leaving the city. There he betrayed him with a kiss.

About such a man all sorts of things could be imagined. He had betrayed a friend with a kiss, and such a friend. Surely he must have got his just deserts in the shape of a terrible death.

Possibly Judas saw even before the other disciples that Jesus was not going to be the messianic figure they had hoped for. If everything was to finish not in acceptance but in disaster, he wanted no part in it. It was perhaps his disgust and disappointment rather than any hope of considerable financial reward that put it into his heart to betray his master. The betrayal might be interpreted as flowing from Judas' despair over Jesus as the Christ. He fell over the stumbling block of the cross 'and got broken'.

Any final judgement about Judas the individual must be made in the light of Jesus' total message of forgiveness. Jesus said, 'Love your enemies and pray for those who persecute you' (Matt. 5:44). He told his disciples to forgive seventy times seven times (Matt. 18:22). He said that it was for the lost sheep of the house of Israel he had come (Matt. 15:24). Of Jesus, it was appropriate to tell the story of a dying gaolbird who, while hanging on his gibbet, repented and found peace. Judas, his betrayer, never ceased to be Jesus' friend. Jesus must have loved Judas and kept him specially in mind to the very end.

Judas, if true love never ceases,
How could you, my friend, have come to this:
To sell me for thirty silver pieces,
Betray me with a kiss?

Judas, remember what I taught you,
Do not despair while dangling on that rope:
It's because you sinned that I have sought you,
I came to bring you hope.

Judas, let's pray and hang together,
You on your halter, I upon my hill.
Dear friend, even if you loved me never,
You know I love you still.

While this is true of Judas the individual, we have to admit that the New Testament is really concerned with Judas *as a figure of sin*. This is why the evangelists do not speak at all well of him. He is a symbol of all the dark forces in the world and in each of us, dark forces that strain to betray Jesus and bring about his destruction. Similarly, Barabbas is a figure of the sinner who is acquitted by the Son of God who takes his place on the gallows.[12] Pilate is a figure of the iniquity of all human systems when they convict a man who has been declared innocent. And Judas the traitor also testifies to Jesus' innocence and to the wrongness of the slave's death he underwent.

The scripture's comment on Judas as 'the son of perdition' is theological rather than personal. Jesus is supposed to have said of Judas, 'It would have been better had he not been born.' This is again a theological comment, and a graphic way of condemning Judas' crime, which is, in some sense, the crime of all.

But the popular mind has not usually grasped the gospel form. The temptation was to take the condemnation in all literalness: Judas' life was totally meaningless; for such a crime he must surely have been flung into the blackest pit of hell.

All the more surprising that the temptation was not yielded to. What an astounding testimony it is to Jesus, the all-forgiving, that despite a generally literal reading of the gospels Christians have refused to say unconditionally even of Judas that he was damned.

In this paradoxical way, Judas the Betrayer, has been through the ages one of the best witnesses of the mercy of Christ. Not even the man whose hands are drenched in the blood-money which was the price of the crucifixion need die without hope.

The Christian instinct is unerring in that we, too, are parcelled up in Judas. We, too, are betrayers of the Lord. And if Judas, the individual, necessarily is lost, so are we all. The gospel is for today; to each of us who reads the story of Judas it could be said, even as we point a condemnatory finger: 'Thou art the man.'

8. THE REPENTANT THIEF

Hang him high between two dying thieves.
Hold him as cursed and outlawed on that rocky knoll.
Hang him high so everybody sees
That God himself can have no mercy on his soul.

Jesus was crucified between two thieves. Someone among the military had conceived a splendid idea: Jesus, of whom many Jews had messianic expectations, was to be crucified in the worst possible company. Let his friends and followers try to explain this away: how their master met a disastrous death indistinguishable from that of common criminals.

The jest – if it, like the cross's inscription, was intended to be such – could not have been more theologically apposite, as Luke was quick to discern. Jesus had always preferred the company of sinners, the outcasts of society. Was this an aspect of his death he cherished: to be surrounded at the last by the sinners he had been pursuing, in God's name, ever since his ministry began?

According to Jewish law, Jesus was thrice accursed and defiled. He had been inside the praetorium of a Gentile governor: this rendered him ineligible to partake of the feast of

passover, since now he was officially 'unclean'. He was
crucified: hanging meant he was irretrievably cursed. 'Cursed
be every one who hangs on a tree' (Deut. 21:23; Gal. 3:13).
He was crucified outside the city walls: nothing could symbol-
ize better than this that he was finally rejected and without a
home. He, the Christ, was excommunicated from the house of
Israel.

In these circumstances, it was good for God's Outlaw to be
strung up with other lesser outlaws.

Luke alone tells the tale of the repentant thief, as it is Luke
alone who relates Jesus' most beautiful parables of forgiveness.
He was the gentlest of the evangelists. Whereas Mark – and
Matthew, who followed him – wrote that both robbers joined
the crowd in reviling Jesus, Luke says that one of them rebuked
the other. ' "Do you not fear God, since you are under the same
sentence of condemnation? And we indeed justly; for we are
receiving the due reward of our deeds; but this man has done
nothing wrong." And he said, "Jesus, remember me when you
come in your kingly power." And he [Jesus] said to him,
"Truly, I say to you, today you will be with me in Paradise" '
(23:40–3).

Most likely, this story is not history but literature. Jesus was
known to have been crucified with a mockery of his kingship
pinned above his head in three languages. This fact provides
Luke with an opportunity to preach the gospel, the good news
of forgiveness through Christ's cross. He depicts an outcast,
crucified with Jesus, there and then drawing salvation from the
cross. To any one who repents, even though he be a murderer
in extremis, Jesus promises Paradise. No one need ever despair
at any time if he turns to the Crucified. Mackintosh records the
ironic saying, popular in parts of Germany, 'that Romanists
become Lutherans when they are dying; they come to God
then, not as One who calculates nicely the less or more of a
sinner's merit but as One who receives him, if only he be
willing, in simple grace'.[13]

The dying thief is like the virgin Mary in this sense at least:
he, too, shows us that God's goodness and kindness come to us
without merit on our part. He, too, is a splendid figure of the

gospel of grace. Luke's gospel is rounded off in the promise to the dying thief. To the Virgin, the woman without a future, it was said that her Son would inherit the throne of David his father and of his kingdom there would be no end. To the thief without a future pleading for a remembrance when Jesus comes into his kingdom, Jesus promises Paradise.

Luke's good-news story is true to the man whom Jesus had always shown himself to be. Luke has developed the passion story, certainly, but this is not 'fiction'. I would say there is hardly a truer or more precious picture in our possession than that of Jesus, the sinless One of God, and a thief joining crucified hand to crucified hand and walking together into Paradise.

9. PETER'S DENIAL

Proudly the cock began to crow:
They may desert you, Lord, not I, not I, not I.
Wherever you go, I will go,
Though I should die.

Peter, his Master sadly said,
Three times before the cock crows you will me disown.
Prepare to weep and bow your head.
I'll die alone.

There is a kind of massive presence of the apostle Peter in the gospel story. This is evident already from the analysis of Matthew's account of the storm at sea. In the context of Christ's passion, it is worth returning to Peter to reflect on the part he didn't play in it.

He was a 'bluff fisherman', a leader of men to whom Jesus gave the name of 'Rock'. He is frequently the spokesman for the disciples; he asks Jesus to explain a particular parable or to tell them what reward they can expect for leaving everything to follow him. With James and John he is represented as sharing with Jesus moments of wonder, when Jesus heals the ruler's daughter; moments of awe, on the mountain of transfiguration; moments of pain, when Jesus takes them apart to console him in his agony.

Besides being solid, reliable, Peter was also impulsive. This trait had its good side and its bad.

He does the apparently foolish yet trusting thing of casting nets into the sea at Jesus' bidding after having fished all night without success. He professes that Jesus is the Christ when there was scant evidence for it. It is even suggested in the text that Peter's confession, fraught with misunderstanding about the nature of messiahship and vacillating as it was to prove, gave Jesus the confidence to turn his eyes to Jerusalem where his greatest test and trials awaited him. Certainly, the resurrection has coloured the presentation of all this, but I'm inclined to think that the gospels are true to the man that Peter was, loyally impulsive.

On the other hand, Peter can speak thoughtlessly. He objects to Jesus mentioning failure and rejection, with the result that Jesus is afraid and shows how much Peter's words are an echo of his own inmost desires. Sharply he tells Peter he is Satan, that is, his tempter, and he orders him to get behind his back and stay there. When Peter boasts that he will always remain loyal whatever happens, even though all the rest run away, Jesus, not without a touch of mockery, insists that his boast is as magnificent and meaningless as the sound of a cock. Yes, even before the braggart cock crew in the morning, Peter would deny him.

Considering Peter's pre-eminence at the time when the gospel stories were circulating, we can only marvel at their honesty. Both Bibles, Jewish and Christian, would be remarkable religious documents if only for their self-criticism and their reverent but ruthless onslaught on God's representatives. The evangelists felt no pious need to hush up the failure of the chief apostle and witness of the resurrection. Only if his weakness was openly admitted, like that of Jacob, David and Solomon under the old covenant, could Christ's glory be revealed in him. A man who denies his master at the taunt of a serving maid has nothing to rely on, save the power of God. I forget who it was who said that the chief apostle was almost ostentatiously accused in the New Testament of what later came to be considered the unforgivable and capital offence: apostasy.

As with Judas, so in Peter's case, I offer one suggestion: Peter fled from the garden not because he was afraid to die but because there was no point in dying. There is in Luke's account of the passion, the superb, theological story of Jesus mending the wounded ear of Malchus, the high priest's servant. When Jesus' enemies approach and initiate all his calamities, here is Jesus speaking a word of peace. He heals the smallest wounds of his cruellest enemies. Clearly, the man has no enemies. But someone who has no enemies can hardly complain if he cannot keep his friends.

Perhaps there was a moment in the garden when Peter, exhausted by the meal, the late hour, the impending catastrophe, suddenly saw that Jesus was not going to defend himself, that it *was* going to end in disaster. Peter's insight into the situation was at last as accurate as Judas'. That was when he fled.

10. GENERAL APPROACH TO THE RESURRECTION

It will probably be helpful if I first outline my approach to Christ's resurrection as simply and honestly as I can. Subsequently, I will attempt to justify this approach in greater detail.[14]

The stories of Jesus' resurrection in the gospels are resurrection stories. Not, I hope, a useless repetition. I mean that the New Testament accounts of the resurrection are 'resurrection stories' in the sense in which the phrase has been used throughout this book: they are stories illumined, and to a degree moulded by belief that Jesus is alive. To assume that the accounts are throughout *descriptions of events* runs counter to what we discovered about the literary nature of the gospels in general. Time and time again, we have admired this facility of the evangelists to 'turn a belief into a story'. They were as adept at making up stories as we are at employing metaphors: it was done quite unconsciously, for the most part.

The gospels are proclamations of the good news of what God has done, is doing and promises he will continue to do for us in Jesus Christ. We noticed that what seemed to be straightforward description – for example, the Magi following a star, the transfiguration on the mountainside, Jesus walking on the water – was really a proclamation of resurrection faith. The Nativity stories themselves were forms that the resurrection faith put on to represent as vividly as possible the significance of Jesus' birth for believers.

It would be most strange to assert, after the previous analysis, that, while the gospels in general aren't biographies of Jesus, the resurrection accounts are in every detail biographical. In other words, what is said of Jesus' post-mortem life is a literal *description* of events.

There are numerous inconsistencies in the resurrection accounts which would be very worrying if these accounts were supposed to contain the history of what happened. It is much more satisfying, exegetically and theologically, to suggest that these stories are not intended to be accounts of how faith in the resurrection arose but how such faith clothed and expressed itself. The message of Jesus' being alive with God preceded the narratives which tried to convey this message. The disciples did not come to believe Jesus was risen by means of an empty tomb and subsequent physical appearances of Jesus. Rather, the belief that Jesus was risen gave rise to religious stories which were vehicles of that faith, the pictorial forms which faith used for preaching and teaching.

The stories of the resurrection are not descriptive of one phase – the post-mortem or Christ phase – of 'Jesus-Christ'. They are, like the rest of the gospel narrative, a fusion of Jesus and Christ. This means these stories are absolutely true to Jesus as he showed himself to be: the Christ.

It can be put like this: the story of Jesus is shaped and coloured by the belief that he is risen and is the Christ. Likewise, the story of the risen Christ harmonizes perfectly with the man that Jesus had proved himself to be, the one in whom the new world of God's kingdom had broken in.

The inconsistencies of the stories of the resurrection are

easily accounted for. While faith had considerable moulding to do throughout the gospels, much more creative work was needed to devise pictures to express the truth of Jesus' resurrection. Only in the infancy account was as much imaginativeness required. Further, only Matthew and Luke dealt with the nativity, whereas all four evangelists plus Paul wrote considerably about the resurrection, rendering all efforts at 'harmonization' extremely implausible.

Readers might feel that, having been told until now that the gospels are resurrection proclamations, they are finally expected to hold that the resurrection never took place at all!

My aim is not to deny Christ's resurrection but to interpret it. It is not a matter of a corpse getting up and living a second life. 'Resurrection' is a religious myth, hence a profound truth of faith, taken over by Christianity from pharisaic Judaism, to express, inadequately as must be the case, the truth that man's relationship to God continues even when he has died. Christians developed the myth by claiming that Jesus was already risen, that is, that he had anticipated and in some sense initiated the general resurrection so that 'the last times' had begun.

The Jewish myth is based on awakening from sleep. As Pannenberg writes: 'The familiar experience of being awakened and rising from sleep serves as a parable for the completely unknown destiny expected for the dead.'[15]

Resurrection from the dead differs from the Greek philosophical notion of 'the immortality of the soul', which the scholastics were so attached to, in that it stresses *communion* between people rather than the individuality of an enduring 'soul'. Also, it emphasizes the fact that man continues after death not on account of one intrinsically undying constituent (soul) but because of (i) God's power to raise up the whole man and (ii) his willingness to do this out of fidelity to his covenant.

In the New Testament, there are other images to express the irrefragable relationship between God and man. For example, the exaltation-ascension of Jesus in the fourth gospel is not an event subsequent to his resurrection, as it is in Luke; it is an alternative image to that of resurrection. Likewise, the image of 'going to the Father'. So, too, the cultic usage found in the Letter to the Hebrews in which Jesus offers his blood in the sanctuary of heaven. Again, in the original, shorter Markan ending, prior to the story-elaboration in the form of appearances, the gaping, empty tomb in the early morning light stands not as a historical preface to, but as the splendid *symbol* of Jesus' triumph over his crucifixion and death.

We should try to be more aware of the variety and richness of Christian imagery which is lost on us, worse, a source of worry to us, when it is treated as literal description. This tempts us to start indulging in high-flown, metaphysical speculation about how Jesus' corpse can be revivified by God after the physical horrors of crucifixion. Matthew Arnold's warning, if too global and severe, is relevant here: 'What is called orthodox theology is, in fact, an immense misunderstanding of the Bible, due to the junction of a talent for abstruse reasoning with much literary inexperience.'[16]

The resurrection of Jesus is, above everything, a truth about God and Jesus, his messenger, his Son. Faith holds that Jesus is alive, not dead; exalted by God and in intensest communion with him, not extinguished by crucifixion. But the faith, very sensitively, imposes no commitment as to the *way* God 'raises the dead', that is, it does not dogmatize about how God keeps open and transforms our communion with him when death comes. We must not pretend to know more than we can possibly know.

'The third day' of the resurrection is not to be taken as an exact dating of Jesus' being made alive. This was explicitly recognized by the fourth gospel which allows for the death, resurrection, ascension and imparting of the Spirit to take place on Calvary. 'The third day' is a Hebraism for 'a little while' which in time gave rise pictorially to a bodily revival on the Sunday after the Friday on which Jesus died. Jesus is said by Paul, quoting an early Christian creed, to have been 'raised on the third day in accordance with the scriptures' (1 Cor. 15:4). Hosea, referring to the affliction of his people under the Assyrians, writes of the Lord God:

He has stricken us, and he will bind us up.
After two days he will revive us;
   on the third day he will raise us up,
   that we may live before him.
Let us know, let us press on to know the Lord;
   his going forth is sure as the dawn (6:1–3).

Jesus' resurrection is foretold in all the hope and promise of the old covenant under which God never abandoned his people to final destruction and dissolution. The image of Jesus, the Christ and hope of his people, rising, going forth from the tomb bodily at dawn on the third day, is in perfect accord with Jewish eschatological expectations, very expressive of them and seen to be their consummation.

In so far as resurrection means that the faithful man will always be with God, it is quite correct to say that Jesus foretold his own resurrection. He was no soothsayer or fortune-teller. He did not speak of his resurrection as a detail added to other details, first betrayal, then crucifixion at the hands of the Romans, finally resurrection on Sunday. But in a sense, Jesus 'rose before he died'. He had attained in his lifetime so close a relationship with the faithful God of the covenant, the living God, the Father-God, that death could not shatter it. Instead, Jesus was to be more gloriously united to God by reason of his humbling death upon an 'accursed' cross. Jesus, the poor, the meek, the persecuted One, was already blessed with 'eternal life' while he walked the earth. Death would simply reveal and consummate that blessedness.

At this profound level, we realize that the gospel was not a form 'invented' by the evangelists, however delicate and nuanced their personal contribution may have been. It was the way the first Christians quite naturally expressed what they had really seen and recognized too late in Jesus of Nazareth.

II. INCONSISTENCIES OF THE RESURRECTION
ACCOUNTS

No evangelist says that there were any witnesses of Jesus rising from the tomb. The resurrection accounts begin when Jesus is risen already. This means that even if these stories are to be taken literally, we would still be under no compulsion to think of the resurrection in terms of the resuscitation of Jesus' corpse or of what is sometimes called 'the resurrection of the meat'.

As to the accounts themselves, we are already forewarned by the story of the storm at sea that what looks like pure description may not be so, in fact. The truth may be richer than the surface description indicates. It is wrong to assume that, in every instance, what seems to us a description was understood to be such by the author. Nor must we assume that, even if the author did think of it as a genuine description, he based his faith on the literalness of it. For example, even if, on the less likely hypothesis, Matthew thought that his description of the earthquake, the empty tomb, and the angel descending from heaven to roll back the stone and then sit on it – even if he thought all this was literally true, it does not necessarily entail that his faith *rested* on the literal truth of this description.

These preliminaries, though dry, may prove profitable when we start looking at the gospel texts on the resurrection. If only one text on the resurrection had survived, it might have been possible for a believer, with a certain amount of ingenuity, to take it as an exact, sequential description of what actually happened, a description which he was bound to accept humbly in every detail. But there are four accounts which cannot be put together like the pieces of a jigsaw to give a consistent picture, nor can we put the reported incidents in any historical or geographical order. It is not perversity or scepticism but the texts themselves that cause all the difficulties.

The attempt to find consistency in all the texts proves immediately fruitless. To prove this, we have only to put the texts of the resurrection narratives side by side. We cannot even decide from them whether the risen Christ was first seen in Galilee or Jerusalem. It would be no small inconsistency in a court of law if two witnesses agreed they were present at their mutual friend's fatal car accident, the first claiming it was in Oxford, the other in London. These discrepancies, easily perceptible in any newspaper reports, for some reason are not noticed when they occur in the New Testament or, at least, are not given their due weight by believers.

Who appeared at the garden tomb, one angel, a man, two men? And to whom, to Mary Magdalen and the other Mary, or to a crowd of women including the first two, or to Magdalen alone? To whom did *Jesus* first appear, to Magdalen and the other Mary, to Magdalen alone, to Peter? *When* did Jesus first appear, on Easter day or some days later? Was the Spirit given on the evening of Easter Sunday or fifty days afterwards? If the disciples were told to go to Galilee to see the Lord there, why did they remain in Jerusalem so that Thomas met the Lord in the upper room a week afterwards?

Apart from the order of events, there are problems about whether Jesus was recognizable or not; whether he always had the stigmata or not; whether he was material and able to eat fish or ethereal, materializing only on rare occasions.

When Jesus appears in the midst of his disciples while the doors are closed, the popular imagination immediately thinks of Jesus coming through the walls! It's hard to know why Jesus began on the outside and had to make such a spectacular entrance! John's gospel is surely saying that Jesus is among his disciples and sometimes they see him.

Pannenberg's conclusion about the texts is emphatic: 'The appearances reported in the gospels, which are not mentioned by Paul, have such a strongly legendary character that one can scarcely find a historical kernel of their own in them. Even the gospels' reports that correspond to Paul's statements are heavily coloured by legendary elements, particularly by the tendency towards underlining the corporeality of the appearances.'[17]

While there is no end to the difficulties raised by the texts, the most significant thing is that the evangelists do not seem to think of them as difficulties. It is commonly held that Luke had Mark's gospel in front of him while he was writing his own. His willingness to 'contradict' Mark indicates he had no intention of writing an inerrant, historical document; at least, he considered Mark hadn't written that kind of document. As Neill puts it: 'Neither Matthew nor Luke treats Mark as we would treat "inspired scripture". Each takes the utmost liberty to edit, to rewrite and to alter the material that is before him.'[18]

In particular, Luke read in Mark the young man's words to the women at the open tomb: 'Go, tell his disciples and Peter that he is going before you to Galilee' (16:7). Mark's intention is clearly to assert that it is in Galilee that Jesus will appear to the disciples. There they retired to ride out the storm of the passion. In spite of this, Luke writes imperturbably of the appearances of Jesus to the disciples at Emmaus (Judea) and to Peter in Jerusalem itself on Easter Sunday. The words Luke puts on the lips of two men are: 'Remember how he told you, while he was *still in Galilee*, that the Son of man . . .' (24:6). Mark said Jesus would be seen in Galilee. Luke prefers another version: Jesus was first seen in Judea. He 'justifies' this by referring back to words of Jesus spoken earlier when he was in Galilee.

Luke's purpose in doing this is strictly theological. He wants to show that the whole Christian missionary effort takes its origin from the centre at Jerusalem. How could this be if the Lord had not first appeared there and initially to Peter? Paul, incidentally, agrees in 1 Cor. 15:5 that Jesus first appeared to Peter but both are contradicted by the other evangelists (cf. Matt. 28:9; John 20:14).

It is fair to conclude that the evangelists had no misgivings about modifying the accounts of the resurrection they had received because they did not base their faith on them. Their faith was already sufficiently grounded on their personal meeting with the Lord Jesus. Their faith was this meeting. They were all convinced that Jesus was alive; his words, his healing activities were still in evidence among them. The accounts of the resurrection were subordinate to the fact of the resurrection, made this fact assimilable by the popular mind, and were designed to *serve* it.

If, in the service of the resurrection, they did not scruple to alter the order and timing of events, as Luke plainly did, the prospective believer is trying to walk in a swamp if he seeks to harmonize the events in all the gospels and makes this harmony a condition of faith in the resurrection.

12. DISPUTES ABOUT HOW CHRIST ROSE FROM THE DEAD

Jesus is alive. The Christian holds not that Jesus lives by his faith but that his faith lives by Jesus. And Jesus lives by the power of God. It was the God whom Jesus preached, not the faith of the disciples, that raised Jesus from the dead.

This common Christian conviction arouses no controversies until the manner and meaning of Christ's resurrection are discussed.

Some Christians think that if the tomb was not empty on Easter Sunday, faith in the risen Jesus is not possible. The scriptural accounts are literally true and Christianity itself is *grounded* on that truth.

This is a difficult view to sustain if the scripture scholars are correct in their surmise that the disciples came to faith in Jesus' resurrection in Galilee. They believed in the resurrection, that is, before they could have heard any stories of the empty tomb, stories in which, in any case, only the women figured.[19]

Other Christians think the tomb was empty, but faith is not based on that; faith is based on meeting first the risen Christ and then accepting that the scriptural account of the empty tomb has to be taken literally. According to this view, the witness of the New Testament to the empty tomb is literally true but there are too many obscurities in the texts themselves for anyone to prove from them that the tomb was empty, and make this the basis for faith. If we are certain that the tomb was empty, this is because Jesus was seen by the apostles to be alive; and if Jesus was alive, then the tomb *must* have been empty. They argue further, if the tomb had not been empty, this would have been pointed out by Jesus' critics.

This view naturally depends on a rather physicalist idea of Jesus' resurrection about which more will be said below. Further, despite its apparent moderation, the view contradicts the story sequence as told by the gospels. In the gospels, the conviction that the tomb is empty precedes belief in the resurrection and, as it were, prepares for it. Also, this view *presumes* that the whole story of the empty tomb arose on Easter Sunday and, therefore, verification of its emptiness was both reasonable and feasible. But what if the story of the empty tomb arose on the basis of Mark's account, in which it was only a symbol of Jesus' triumph over death, and that the story grew only gradually into its final form? By then, circumstances may not have admitted of verification, even should anyone have sought it.

A third opinion which I prefer is that the witness to the empty tomb in the New Testament is far from being conclusive. The stories about the empty tomb probably arose much later to 'explain' pictorially the fact that Jesus is alive with God to people who were only likely to understand this in the pharisaic, resurrection terms to which they were accustomed. These terms were of a corpse being made alive. But what looks like 'description' is not necessarily so. In this third view, the emptiness of the tomb as historical fact is not required for faith, nor is it imposed by a study of the gospels. Indeed, a tomb emptied by some miraculous intervention makes faith more not less problematical. Further, it should be continually borne in mind that faith cannot result from proofs, even though they are culled from the Bible.

The most I can hope to do is to clarify this issue a little.

When we say that the common Christian conviction is that Jesus is alive by the power of God, we mean Jesus of Nazareth is still alive. In other words, there was no substitution of a Christ for Jesus: Jesus is the Christ, and the Christ is Jesus now perfected and consummated by his passion and raised to glory by God.

But to affirm that Jesus of Nazareth is still alive does not mean that he has been granted an eternally extended lease of

life. He has entered into a new life. He has not, like Lazarus in
John's story (John 11), come back from the dead; he has gone
'beyond' death. He has gone to 'where' there is no death. It
seems evident to me that Jesus, beyond death and, therefore,
beyond history, cannot interact with people and things in the
way that he did prior to his death. This does not exclude the
possibility that Jesus, even after he died, made a tremendous
impression on his disciples and was their inspiration. This, in
fact, is what happened.

Jesus who is the Christ is fully alive as a human being. But
are we obliged to hold that, on Easter Sunday, Jesus' corpse
was revivified? Many people think so, and this may be the
main reason why they become anxious at any suggestion that
the tomb was not empty on Easter Sunday. The emptiness of
the tomb is, for them, not merely evidence of God's supernatural activity; it safeguards the identity of Jesus and the
Christ.

But perhaps identity has been purchased too highly if the
price is having to conceive the resurrection in terms of Jesus'
corpse being used again, as it were, after a fundamental repair
job done on it by God the Father. Was the resurrection a soul-
transplant on Jesus' corpse? Most medievals thought that
Jesus' 'dead body' – to use Aquinas' term, which is in open
contradiction to his whole philosophy of the human person –
was kept in a static condition while it was in the tomb by
reason of the Word of God still conjoined to it.[20] Even if this
were granted, the very moment of death would have wrought
havoc on Jesus' body. Did God repair all the damage caused
by his sufferings to the heart, to the cells of the body, and to the
brain which would have turned to jelly at death. And what
about all the blood he shed? Was that really reinfused by God,
as St Thomas said, after a complete, divine mopping-up
operation? What happened to the food remaining in the
intestines?

The view of the resurrection that rests on God raising Jesus'
corpse has another disadvantage: Jesus seems to come back,
like Lazarus, to his former, terrestrial life.

We, too, hope some day to be 'raised from death'. We will

retain our present identity; we will be, that is, the same people. But it doesn't worry us that our bodies may one day disintegrate altogether. We do not stake our eternal future with God on the reparation of our corpses, because personal identity does not depend upon any physical continuity with what are quite correctly called our 'remains', 'the mortal coil' of Shakespeare. St Thomas entirely agreed with this general standpoint, only, he could not apply it to Christ because he interpreted the scriptures too literally.

Our Christian forebears had generally a more physicalist notion of immortality than Aquinas. This is why, as Southern remarks, the importing of relics into tenth-century England was a major, competitive industry. Relics were the channels of supernatural power. 'On the Last Day they would be claimed by the saints and become an integral part of the Kingdom of Heaven.'[21] This physical continuity between the corpse and the resurrected body explains why the non-decomposition of the body of the saints, particularly of the virgin Mary, was considered God's greatest blessing.[22]

Our outlook today is very different! If so, why insist that Jesus' remains must have been continuous with his resurrected body, or better, his 'risen self'?

What does the Christian Bible have to say about the manner of the resurrection of the body? I'm afraid the answer is, many things. There are various accounts of Jesus' resurrection which are not easily if at all harmonizable and various views about what constitutes identity between the mortal body and the risen body.

13. CONTRASTING PAUL AND MATTHEW

I distinguished originally between faith in Jesus risen and different ways of thinking about how he rose from the dead.

To see a rather startling difference of viewpoint in the New Testament, we have only to contrast the writing of Paul and Matthew.

We tend to forget that Paul's Letters are the earliest Christian documents. Paul never mentions an empty tomb; he always centres immediately on the living person of the Crucified. His whole contention was that he had never known Christ according to the flesh. The only Christ he had met was the Christ of faith, the Christ who was Lord, immortal, imperishable.

Paul claimed to be an apostle and witness of the resurrection, yet not only does he show no interest in whether Jesus' tomb was empty or not, he seems to have taken no interest in the stories of the resurrection. These must have been circulating in the communities for some time before they appeared in the four gospels. If I were to hazard a guess, I would say that Paul found some of these stories exceedingly naïve. Christ was no longer in the flesh; he was sown perishable but raised imperishable. How could he have eaten broiled fish? How could people have touched him or wanted to touch him?

Paul, above all, wasn't able to think of Jesus' resurrection in terms of the revival of his corpse. The body was raised but not the body of flesh. The body of flesh, by definition, was marked out for destruction and it obviously perished *without trace*. What was raised was the spiritual body. Paul did not think, as we tend to, in dual terms of soul and body, with the soul surviving the body and one day being reunited with it. The body was the self. He spoke of the body (or self) being physical or spiritual. The physical body – what we call the remains – passes away entirely, while the spiritual body is raised imperishable.

Paul faced squarely the evident fact that the body that is laid in the tomb corrupts. It is not *that* which is raised. But the person continues; the same person that dies is raised. Hence the true self – not identifiable with what we call 'the remains' – is the spiritual body which exists entirely from God. The resurrection of Christ could not, therefore, have entailed for Paul an empty grave, unless, of course, the body of flesh had been snatched away by enemies or annihilated by God!

Turning to Matthew's gospel, we find ourselves in a different realm of discourse altogether. Everything is set out – as in the storm at sea – in a seemingly descriptive and, in fact, really symbolic way. One or two brief extracts will illustrate this:

Now from the sixth hour there was darkness over all the earth until the ninth hour. . . . And behold, the curtain of the temple was torn in two, from top to bottom; and the earth shook, and the rocks were split; the tombs also were opened, and many bodies of the saints who had fallen asleep were raised, and coming out of the tombs after his resurrection they went into the holy city and appeared to many. When the centurion and those who were with him, keeping watch over Jesus, saw the earthquake and what took place, they were filled with awe, and said, 'Truly, this man was a son of God' (27:45,51-4).

Matthew is using symbolic language here, as we understand symbolic language at any rate. While Jesus was on the cross, the whole earth was darkened, the sun was blotted out. In terms of literal description, his account is far-fetched but it would be pedantic to offer such criticism.

The veil of Jewry was torn. It is foolish to ask, 'How could anyone have known about this?' This is a splendid way of saying what only became clear to Christians a long time after Jesus' death, that the temple worship was now fundamentally over as far as they were concerned. Matthew had 'quoted' earlier Jesus' words which explain the subsequent pictorial use of language: 'I tell you, something greater than the temple is here' (12:6). Incidentally, John's gospel expresses the same thing through words placed on Jesus' lips: 'Destroy this temple [of Jerusalem], and I will rebuild it [my body, the new temple] in three days' (John 2:19).

The earth shook. Matthew was fond of seismic disturbances. He alone mentions the earth shaking at Jesus' death as he alone elaborates the resurrection narrative by introducing a great earthquake at the sepulchre (28:2). He even describes a storm at sea in terms of an earthquake (8:24), perhaps to give a clue that he is dealing with a passover story.[23] What Matthew means in the passion account is clear: Jesus' death is an earth-shattering event.

Afterwards, when Jesus was risen, the tombs opened and the bodies of the saints were raised and were seen walking about Jerusalem. Has Matthew here switched to an entirely different way of speaking? Is this exact description? What precedes it obviously is not, nor, therefore, is the report of the centurion's awe and confession of faith said to be *based* on those earth-shattering experiences. The centurion, in Matthew's story, is like the Magi, a figure of the Gentiles who were later to find faith in Jesus crucified.

Matthew is saying that after Jesus' resurrection, death as such has been mastered. The graves are emptied. But in the pictorial mode of expression he has chosen there are even witnesses to these dead men being alive again (27:53). But, of course, they are only literary witnesses. Matthew doesn't expect anyone to come forward and say: 'When Jesus rose from the dead, I saw the body of my father walking around Jerusalem.' The risings from the graves were literary, so were their appearances, so were the witnesses to those appearances.

While Matthew's image of dead bodies rising out of their opened graves is figurative, he takes it very seriously. He works out the details of a story in which the figurative language is not simply employed in a moment of metaphor or simile as, for example, 'There was an earthquake', i.e., an earth-shattering experience, or, 'It was like the whole world becoming dark', i.e., everybody ought to be in mourning. The images are treated as though they were descriptions and put into an ordered sequence. Within the story, each item is related to every other item, as the earthquake and the wholesale darkness are related to the centurion's faith as its cause or occasion.

In brief, Matthew cannot step back from his story and say, 'Of course, this is only a story, and I'm here using figurative expressions' – as if Matthew could or should have expressed himself differently, perhaps more accurately. Matthew found his own way of writing perfectly adequate to his religious purpose: to speak the gospel truth. He succeeded in this marvellously.

Proceeding to Matthew's account of *Christ's* resurrection, we notice that this, too, is depicted in exactly the same terms of a tomb being opened, a dead body rising and then being seen by the apostles who tell others what they have seen. This was the form in which belief in the living Christ was expressed, namely, in the *resurrection terms* of people brought up on the myth of pharisaic Judaism. In the story, an element seems to have been subsequently questioned by unbelievers or prospective believers: 'If the tomb was empty, that was because the body was stolen.' The evangelist's response to this is not, 'You haven't understood the way I write.' After all, Matthew has no other way of expressing the inexpressible, of capturing in some measure what Jesus' resurrection meant to faith. His reaction is to develop the sequence of the story.

Once this is grasped, the literary flavour of the following account is easily discernible:

Next day, that is, after the day of Preparation, the chief priests and the Pharisees gathered before Pilate and said, 'Sir, we remember how that impostor said, while he was still alive, "After three days I will rise again." Therefore order the sepulchre to be made secure until the third day, lest his disciples go and steal him away, and tell the people, "He has risen from the dead", and the last fraud will be worse than the first.' Pilate said to them, 'You have a guard of soldiers; go, make it as secure as you can.' So they went and made the sepulchre secure by sealing the stone and setting a guard (27:62–6).

This is manifestly Matthew's apologetic development of his story in answer to a criticism made of a part of the story. People were saying, 'Your story won't stand up. Anyone could have come between the day of his burial and the day the tomb was found empty and stolen the body away.' Matthew replies: 'Jesus' bitterest enemies thought of this, too. They remembered Jesus' prophecy' – a 'prophecy', incidentally, that no one, least of all the priests and pharisees, would have heard or taken seriously prior to the proclamation of Jesus' resurrection – 'and they told Pilate that if he wasn't careful, he would have a confidence trick on his hands too big to deal with. They advised him to guard the tomb against Jesus' disciples removing his body in the night and afterwards perpetrating a huge hoax. "These disciples", they said, "would do anything to obtain credence for their belief." '

Why the pharisees should be so circumspect when the disciples themselves were so absolutely shattered by the crucifixion is of no concern to Matthew. He brings in Pilate simply to confirm that in the judgement of this generally acknowledged harsh and efficient military governor, the chief priests and pharisees had enough men to deal with any prospective body-snatching.

Only Matthew reports that the chief priests and the pharisees posted a guard at the sepulchre. Apart from the silence of the other evangelists, it is very hard, for many reasons, to know how the priests could have so acted. A crucified Messiah was to all, to the disappearing disciples included, a contradiction in terms. The proclaiming of a crucified Messiah who had risen from the dead was equally inconceivable prior to the disciples actually meeting the Lord in some extraordinary experience. It could never have been anticipated – because it was contrary to all current Jewish theology – that a crucified Messiah could have 'lived down' his crucifixion. Besides, if Jesus rose from the dead, this could only be because the general resurrection was in process of taking place; and there were no signs of this happening. In short, the resurrection of a crucified Messiah was too implausible to pass even as a bad joke.

When all due comparisons are made, it is clear that Paul's way of considering Christ's resurrection is quite different from Matthew's. They are both firmly convinced that Jesus is alive. In Paul there is no story sequence to depict this, nor, if we consider his theology of the body, could there be a 'story'. 'For Paul, resurrection means the new life of a new body, not the return of life into a dead but not yet decayed fleshly body.'[24] Matthew, on the contrary, is very happy to launch into an account shot through with figurative expressions. This was his *way of expressing* the truth as he experienced it. This was the style his faith instinctively embraced. When objections are raised against his story, he reacts by adding further twists and turns to the plot of the story, not always stopping to consider whether the story becomes, in some measure, inconsistent as a result.

Our critical demands that descriptions should exactly coincide with fact cannot be met. This is because our demands are unreasonable. Why should Matthew have felt bound to write in a style that would satisfy twentieth-century doctrinaire critics in the West?

14. SEEING AND BELIEVING

Matthew's apologetic, to us somewhat unusual, is evidenced elsewhere in the New Testament. We noticed how Matthew himself used it in the infancy narrative where Joseph had a revelation in a dream enabling him to overcome the objections he had – read, 'Christian critics had' – to Jesus' legitimacy.

Historically, the apologetic was first employed in regard to the passover of Jesus. Once the conviction, 'Jesus crucified is alive', was put in story form, all kinds of objections were raised against the story. To the suggestion that even if 'Jesus' had been seen it was probably only a ghost, the reply, in keeping with the objection, was, 'He can't have been a ghost; he ate broiled fish.' Someone might have said, 'The story is very appealing, but seeing is believing; how can I believe unless I first see?' The tale of doubting Thomas would have been a good counter to this, especially with its parting retort: 'Blessed are those who have not seen and yet believe' (John 20:29). It is worth repeating: if the vehicle of religious truth chosen is the story, consistency within the story is more important than conformity between statement and fact.

Once belief in Jesus' resurrection is put in story form, seeings occur; and there arises, in consequence, a distinction between believing and 'seeing'. But even John 20:29 is really emphasizing that faith without any physical 'seeing' is most praiseworthy. This creates in John a tremendous problem: none of the foundation members of the Church, the apostles, would have had the better part. Not for them the privilege of believing without seeing. Not for them the blessedness of believing without proof. We shall return to this dilemma later. In praising the faith of all subsequent believers, John's gospel risks disparaging the apostles themselves, for, in the story, all of them, and not only Thomas, were faithless until Jesus appeared and was seen.

The texts insist we ask: Outside the story form, chosen by the early Christian tradition, then reported and developed by the evangelists, is there a need for any distinction at all between believing and seeing?

Have we any material for replying to this question? I think we have in the case of Paul. It is Luke in the Acts, not Paul himself, who writes of Paul's conversion in descriptive terms. It is Luke who records the light flashing from heaven and the voice which said, 'Saul, Saul, why do you persecute me?' (Acts 9:4). Paul simply and soberly says, 'He [the Lord] appeared also to me' or 'was seen by me' (1 Cor. 15:8). The word Paul uses to describe his faith ($\overset{\text{"}}{\omega}\phi\theta\eta$) is the same word which describes what happened to the other brethren and what the evangelists portray as Peter and the disciples 'seeing' the Lord in a material way.

This means it is most probably Luke who has built up Paul's seeing the Lord in faith into a story in which he sees a light and hears a voice from heaven. This is Luke's customary method of writing and we are far from having any objections to it. But it does raise the question of whether, in fact, we need to distinguish seeing and believing, and whether the seeings ascribed to the apostles in the gospels aren't a way of saying that the apostles *believed* in Jesus risen. There are both scriptural and theological reasons for thinking this may be so.

Firstly, from the scriptural standpoint, only believers see the risen Christ. There is so close a connection between believing and seeing that even in the story they often merge into each other. The word that covers both is 'recognizing'. Jesus is both believed in and seen *in one and the same act of recognition*.

The seeing is associated with believing in another way: all the stories issue in acts of worship on the part of those who see the Lord. Faith, worship, sight – this is the invariable sequence within the story. The story which requires – for there to be a story – a dissociation between seeing and believing, very quickly fuses them into a single experience. It is quite impossible in terms of the gospel to depict an unbeliever seeing the risen Christ as it was once possible for unbelievers to see the mortal Jesus.[25] In the apocryphal Gospel of Peter, unbelievers, in the person of the soldiers at the tomb, actually saw the risen Lord. Significantly, the first Christians rejected this idea.

From the theological standpoint, there are innumerable reasons for positing an identification between faith and seeing. The word 'theological' does not mean we are indulging in 'wishful thinking'. What is at stake is the gospel as a whole which would be seriously undermined if faith were a kind of *consequence* of seeing, or if seeing were a proof or inescapable sign by which faith is engendered.

My view is that many people are still trying to prove that Jesus must be risen because his tomb was empty on Easter Sunday. The only explanation they can find for this is a supernatural one: he left the tomb when he rose from the dead. This is not only a piece of rationalism; it is clean contrary to all the gospel teaching on the nature of faith.

If we can prove that Jesus is risen, even on the basis of what the gospels tell us – and no other evidence exists – faith is unnecessary; science becomes a substitute for commitment. On the other hand, if we cannot prove that Jesus is risen from the gospel records and yet continue as we do to believe it, proof in a scientific sense is not necessary for faith.

From time to time, there are newspaper sensations to the effect that, in some excavation or another, Jesus' body has been found. My conviction is that even if it were thought more likely that thieves did steal the corpse, faith would still be possible because faith in Jesus risen is not faith in the resuscitation of his corpse. Moreover, faith does not, and historically did not depend either on the tomb being empty or on *proofs* that it was.

Attempts to prove the resurrection are contrary to the New Testament notion of faith; they are also a misreading of the literary form of the accounts of the resurrection. These accounts emphasize only the consistency – at least, attempted – of a story.

Admittedly, the attempts at consistency, entailing as they did *ad hoc* clarifications of disputed points, are not wholly successful. There are inconsistencies not only between, say, Luke and Matthew, but also within each individual evangelist. For instance, in Luke 24, Jesus 'proves' to his disciples he is no ghost or shade out of Sheol by telling them to see and touch his hands and feet and by eating broiled fish; but he also vanishes while sitting at a meal in Emmaus, which is just what a ghost, in the popular mind, was expected to do. Likewise, the risen Christ in John breakfasts with his disciples by the lakeside (21:15) and materializes out of the thin air (20:26).

Nothing could be clearer than that the evangelists are not trying to base faith on the accuracy and consistency of their stories as we moderns might. They know they cannot prove Jesus is alive in that way, rather, it would never have entered their heads to think they could prove it even if it were required. This is why they are so free and easy in their elaboration and modification of the accounts. They are trying to convey by their story – whether it be accurate and consistent or not – that Jesus crucified is alive. Faith, and faith alone, enables the reader to communicate with the Lord.

15. WHAT IS CHRISTIAN FAITH?

The fundamental question raised by the resurrection accounts and by the gospel as a whole, since it is from beginning to end a proclamation of his resurrection, is: What is Christian faith?

The simplest and most impressive answer is: Belief that Jesus crucified is alive by the power of God. Christian faith is always a scandal and a stumbling block. We must never try to remove these by recourse to proofs, even on the basis of New Testament texts. No one has ever come to faith by the logical persuasiveness of the stories. Faith is always a walking on water by means of a power coming from God not from ourselves.

The major difficulty about holding a real distinction between seeing and believing in the risen Christ, outside the context of a story that requires such a distinction, is this: the faith of the apostles would not have been faith like ours, nor would it have been faith in the New Testament sense at all.

It is hard to accept that the apostles, having lost faith in Jesus at the cross, were subsequently dispensed from any need of faith because they not only came across the empty tomb but saw Christ himself in a flesh-and-blood experience or some inner experience quite different from faith.[26]

Some middle-of-the-road critics think that by taking the appearances of Jesus as his manifestations *within* the apostles they are being more faithful to a literal interpretation of the texts. They claim that no camera could have taken pictures of Jesus, no tape-recorder could have picked up his words. How many hypotheses, without any basis in the gospels, are needed to support the view that the resurrection appearances were real in the sense of *describable*, common to all the apostles at once, and yet in no other way *public*? As many as St Thomas propounded to justify his opinion that the Magi and they alone saw a 'star'. A wholehearted literal interpretation of the resurrection texts surely ought to insist that light and sound waves were transmitted by Jesus, making his appearances in principle, at least, open to public verification. Jürgen Moltmann's approach is, however strange, at any rate consistent. He maintains that the resurrection appearances are 'not merely dumb visions'. He writes: 'Without the speaking and hearing of words, it would have been unlikely – indeed impossible – to identify the one who appeared with the crucified Jesus.'[27] I prefer a more radical literary analysis on the lines I have attempted to lay down.

If the texts are to be interpreted literally, the apostles were given incontrovertible proofs that Jesus is alive. They escaped the scandal, and leaped over, in a single bound, the stumbling block of the cross. Things were made very easy for them.

Take the case of Peter. The gospel reports that prior to the passion he made a profession of faith in Jesus at Caesarea Philippi. Jesus said that it was not flesh and blood that had revealed this to him but his Father in heaven. Are we to suppose that after the passion Peter had his confidence in Jesus restored and his faith elevated by a real 'flesh-and-blood' argument?

And how is *this* genuine faith? It would follow that our faith was not, after all, a sharing in the faith of the original Christian community; they did not have or need faith. We, for our part, have to believe through the unseen revelation of the Father, while Peter and the other disciples were able to preach the results of clear, flesh-and-blood seeings for which they would not be counted blessed (John 20:29).

Once more, what is it to believe in Christ risen? It is to believe first in the person and entire message of Jesus of Nazareth. It is to believe that this man who both preached and lived that message – a message of God's fatherly rule of love and mercy – was not snuffed out by death. His life was not a waste. On the contrary, he is dear to the living, faithful God of the covenant; he is exalted by God and made the beginning of a new creation.

It is because the disciples – and Peter first – believed that God's Messiah had been crucified and was alive that they were depicted as seeing the Lord. They had believed the unbelievable thing.

The apostles had an indispensable role to play. Only they were capable of seeing Jesus as the Lord in that only they had been with him and heard his message since the time his ministry began with the baptism by John. Their witness is foundational for Christianity. They alone could fuse Jesus with the Christ, that is, give human features to the Christ and attribute divine glory to Jesus. They were not exempted from the obligation of facing the monstrous scandal of the cross by being granted some extraordinary sign, some irrefutable demonstration. They were the first to face successfully, in some tremendous faith experience, the scandal of the cross for which the Father gave them the light and the power. Had they failed, Christianity would never have got off the ground. The only remotely satisfactory language they had to express this is: Jesus appeared, was seen. This is not to say it was wishful thinking on their part, a 'subjective experience'. It had a genuine basis, namely, their contact with Jesus and the God whom Jesus brought near to them. I am simply asserting that while the risen Christ really manifested himself to his disciples, it was not through the kind of visual and probative experience that dispensed them from the *venture* of faith. The stories which include seeings are literary constructions which attempt to convey something of this faith experience.

Christians do not believe on the basis of the apostles' testimony but because they meet the risen Lord through stories, sometimes extremely inconsistent, in which the apostles' faith is embodied. We are not able to prove by any arguments adduced or stories told that Jesus is risen. We, like the apostles, must squarely face Jesus, his person, his message, and ask ourselves, 'Is this crucified Jesus alive and Lord? Is he alive for *me*, is he *my* Lord?'

Everything else is subordinate to this question. We do not get faith from the apostolic testimony. On the contrary, through faith, we see for ourselves that the apostolic testimony is true: Jesus crucified is alive. He is alive because, through him, I die and come alive again. I die to the old aeon to live in the new, the kingdom of God. Belief makes me a new man, indeed the whole world is changed for me. My experience is new, Spring-like, abounding in hope. I am forgiven my sins and taste life of a fresh, deathless and divine quality. This is because, as Paul stressed, I go through the same cross and resurrection experience as Jesus himself.

No one can absolve me from the scandal of the cross, from having to risk all by walking on the waters towards the outstretched arms of the Lord who has conquered death. The Bible nowhere admits that we can come to faith through something like textual argument or empirical verification. The only way is by surrendering ourselves completely to the Crucified and discovering for ourselves that he is the Lord of our lives. No one can become a Christian without paying the price, without daring and risk, without total self-surrender.

16. PETER, THE FIRST WITNESS OF THE RESURRECTION

I hope that what has been said explains to some degree the inadequacies and obvious figurativeness of so much of the resurrection narratives. As historical reports, they cannot be harmonized. If we had to ground our faith on their accuracy as reports we would never have faith. Faith can, in fact, be grounded only on Jesus crucified who is alive by God's power; and he proves he is alive by enabling us to pass with him from death to life in our day-to-day experience.

Further, what I have said helps account for what I called the massive presence of Peter throughout the gospel narratives. Not only was he chosen for a special task, he fulfilled that task. And if he failed at the passion, it was because, as Luke puts it, he was to be converted and to confirm his brethren afterwards.

The resurrection was first proclaimed when Peter came to believe fully in Jesus. Let me recall briefly the precedence of Peter in his crucial role as witness of the resurrection, a role accorded to him by the main New Testament authors.

Paul follows the earliest Christian tradition in detailing the order of Christ's appearances. He writes that Christ 'appeared to Cephas, then to the twelve' (1 Cor. 15:5). Mark ends his gospel with a young man in white at the sepulchre telling the women, 'Go, tell his disciples and Peter that he is going before you to Galilee' (16:7). Matthew relates the resurrection story of the storm at sea with Peter walking on the water to show how, through Peter's recovery of faith, the disciples worshipped Jesus as the Messiah, the Son of God (14:33). Luke agrees with Paul that Peter was the first to see the Lord. On returning to Jerusalem after having met Christ at Emmaus, the two disciples are greeted with, 'The Lord has risen indeed, and has appeared to Simon' (24:34). In the Acts of the Apostles, Luke again expresses the primacy of Peter. After the ascension, Peter is the one to make provisions for a replacement for Judas, Matthias, who had been in the apostolic company since Jesus' baptism and was able to witness to the resurrection. John's gospel, uniting closely the two originally distinct narratives of the empty tomb and the appearances, goes out of its way to stress Peter's pre-eminence. Peter is permitted to enter the tomb before Magdalen, who first noticed that the stone had been rolled away from the sepulchre, and before the

beloved disciple, who outran Peter and reached the sepulchre
in advance of him (John 20). Then in Chapter 21, we have the
moving meeting between Peter and the risen Christ, when Peter
is told to shepherd the whole flock.

Peter is especially contrasted with Judas at passover time.
Judas betrayed Jesus and the betrayal ended in disaster. Peter
fell asleep three times in the garden; he denied Jesus three
times, not before Pilate or the Sanhedrin, but in front of a
serving maid; he cursed Jesus, for that seems to be the force of
Mark 14:71 rather than that he invoked a curse on himself if
he were lying. But after all this, he was converted. Luke once
more demonstrates his superb talent for using the narrative
form. Matthew and Mark are content to say that Peter remembered the words of Jesus foretelling the denial. Luke makes a
significant pictorial addition: 'The cock crowed. *And the Lord
turned and looked at Peter*. And Peter remembered the word of
the Lord . . . And he went out and wept bitterly' (22:60–2).

Luke is the one most true to Peter's conversion. It was the
Lord's glance that made Peter repent and weep. The glance of
the living Lord fell upon Peter again after the crucifixion so
that he was able to believe.

Peter went through a most tremendous experience of conversion and faith which is described, inadequately it must be,
as Peter has 'seen' the Lord. He had failed lamentably but he
was forgiven by Christ who was, therefore, *alive* to forgive.
The preaching of the resurrection by Peter was first of all the
proclamation that the Lord had saved him and drawn him out
of the deep waters.

Peter had been very close to Jesus throughout his ministry.
No one had perceived better than he how close Jesus was to the
living God, how faithful, how obedient. No one had assimilated
better Jesus' message of forgiveness. Jesus' followers must seek
out the lost; love their enemies; forgive, if need be, seventy
times seven times.

This was the master Peter had deserted in the garden and
denied in the cold courtyard afterwards. And now that Jesus
was dead, there was no hope of forgiveness. Then the miracle
took place: he *was* forgiven. He 'saw' Jesus, the friend of

enemies, the searcher after the lost sheep. Jesus was alive – because Peter experienced his forgiveness.

Peter's first preaching must have been, 'I am forgiven. The Lord is risen.' There is no other way for us to come to faith in Jesus risen than this. We, too, must be converted and transformed into new beings by our crucified Lord. Our baptismal faith is, 'I was dead and now I live. Alleluia.'

The story of Jesus' meeting with Peter by the lakeside after the resurrection is a construction of superb artistry. In place of the threefold denial, Jesus asks for a threefold profession of love. Peter, the braggart, has learned a loving humility and a new kind of silence:

Why do you ask me if I love you, Lord?
You know I do.
You know that in the garden, when I raised that lonely
    sword,
I only thought of you.

Will you ask, Lord, about my love again?
Then hear my plea:
Did I not try to walk on roaring waves in pounding rain
To you across the sea?

Do I love you, Lord? How right of you to ask.
Your little flock
Would not be scattered now had I kept faithful to my task.
I am a splintered rock.

'Frail Simon,' Jesus said, 'when I depart,
My love will keep
Your love for me alive. For I chose you – I know your
    heart –
As Shepherd of my sheep.'

The Christian message was first preached in its fullness when a humiliated and humbled Peter saw his crucified Lord looking upon him supportingly, forgivingly, lovingly, as he walked across the sea of death.

17. THE LAST-BORN APOSTLE

'Last of all, as to one untimely born, he [Christ] appeared also to me. For I am the least of the apostles, unfit to be called an apostle, because I persecuted the church of God. But by the grace of God I am what I am, and his grace toward me was not in vain' (1 Cor. 15:8-10).

We saw how these sober words of Paul were developed into a beautiful story by Luke. Most probably Saul was once on the road to Damascus threatening with death Christ's disciples, men and women. A light from heaven flashed about him and he fell to the ground. A voice said, 'Saul, Saul, why do you persecute me?' And Saul said, 'Who are you, Lord?' 'I am Jesus, whom you are persecuting.'

The two accounts Luke gives of Paul's conversion differ slightly. We read: 'The men who were travelling with him stood speechless, hearing the voice but seeing no one' (Acts 9:7). We also read words put into Paul's own mouth: 'Those who were with me saw the light but did not hear the voice of the one who was speaking to me' (Acts 22:9). Once again, we see that Luke has more important things on his mind than consistency in telling a story.

Since Luke is using figurative language, we may interpret, in our turn, what happened as follows:

Saul, the devout, even fanatical pharisee, was hounding Christians to death. He had been present at the stoning of Stephen and acquired there both a taste for blood and a curious unquietness of soul.

Christ's disciples were saying, 'He is alive; he is risen.' Saul, a pharisee, believed in the resurrection of the dead, but it would not happen until the consummation, when all the just would rise together. Jesus was dead; and he, Saul, would put these heretics to death as well. They would join their master in Sheol.

It was noon on the Damascus road. The sun was at its zenith. Tired perhaps from riding in the heat, he made a catch: a Christian. He looked into his victim's eyes, the eyes of a man of faith. And then, in a flash, Saul saw in those eyes the face of Christ.

Saul, by hounding Jesus' disciples to death, was simply proving beyond a doubt that Jesus was alive, after all. He was so alive, so powerful, that men and women were willing to lay down their lives for him. He realized that it was not possible to extinguish the spirit of this man of Nazareth. All the unquietness that had been gathering in him since he first tasted Christian blood now reached a climax. He was converted. He was blinded by the glory in the eyes of his victim.

Saul was thenceforward a new man. He had himself been hounded to death by Jesus: from now on his new name will be Paul.

If readers object to this account of Saul's conversion it can only be because Luke's artistry with words is greater than mine. I simply wanted to give an example of what is done repeatedly in the New Testament by all the evangelists.

Paul learned from his conversion experience that Christ is one with his followers. Jesus gives life to the community; the community also gives him life, shape, existence – Paul's word is 'body' – in the world. The Church is the body of Christ. To persecute Christians is to persecute Christ.

We tend to miss the meaning of Paul's words or deliberately dilute them. By Paul's standards, to say that the Church is Christ's body was the most daring thing he could do. After all, Christ is immortal, imperishable, pure. The disciples of Christ are very mortal, as he knew, perishable, sinful. To say the Church is Christ's body seems positively blasphemous and exceedingly unhygienic. Paul, who would have found it intolerable to say that Jesus' physical body (his remains), once sloughed off, could be resurrected, is proud to call Jesus' poor and often persecuted followers Christ's 'body'.

Further, if we take Paul's words seriously, we have to admit the inseparability of Christ and his Church. Just as I cannot be dissociated from my body and my bodily performances, neither can Christ be dissociated from us. Just as I have no independent existence apart from my body, neither does Christ have independent existence apart from us. This is difficult to understand and to accept.

We continually think of Christ living on his own, as it were, in heaven, a long way away. Paul is trying to say: Christ is never on his own; he is not far away but as near as any Christian. Jesus meant the same when he said that he suffers and rejoices wherever there is suffering or gladness. As Jorge Luis Borges wrote in one of his parables: 'We may see Christ's features and be unaware of it. A Jew's profile in the subway is perhaps that of Christ; the hands giving us our change at a ticket window perhaps repeat those that one day were nailed to the cross by some soldiers. Perhaps some feature of that crucified countenance lurks in every mirror; perhaps the face died, was obliterated, so that God could be all of us.'[28]

We are tempted to turn Paul's direct words into simile: the Church is like Christ's body. We do not use such imprecise language of the Eucharist. Then, even more importantly, we ought not to say it of the Church.[29] The Church is not like Christ's body: it *is* Christ's body. Christ exists, but he cannot exist without, or in isolation from his brethren.

This is not to say Christ doesn't really exist or he only exists in the minds and hearts of believers. Paul means that we are necessary to Christ as our bodies are to us; our bodies constitute us. Christ is a member of the human family and therefore, incomplete, a non-entity, without his brethren. Only through them was he able to love and serve God in his lifetime. And God never envisages Christ in isolation from us, or us in isolation from Christ. We are all one in Christ Jesus.

Following Paul's terminology, we should say that Christ, after his resurrection, is *more embodied* than before, though not in any crude, fleshly sense. The body is the principle of communion between men. By means of our body, we see and are seen; we communicate with others. The communion and the communication so far known to us are essentially imperfect. This is because we walk in the flesh, that is, in a state of mortality and weakness and general opaqueness. Jesus, too, in Paul's estimation, knew all about this: he, like us, lived in the flesh, though he did not walk according to the flesh. Jesus knew the frustrations of being unable to communicate. He was more powerless than was to his (or any man's) taste.

The New Testament adopts throughout the same view of Jesus. He is the solitary isolated grain of wheat that must die in its aloneness; but, once it dies, there is a rich harvest of communion. Once he had passed over to his Father he was able to bestow the Spirit.

For Paul, the resurrection took place when Christ became a living Spirit. Now he diffuses his very being among his brethren without restriction. He is powerful. He communicates, through his Spirit, in ways quite closed to him when he was in the flesh. He is less distant from the world now than he ever was.

This new embodiment of Christ is the communion of believers. Here is Christ's life-giving communication in the Spirit of resurrection. Here is that fresh radiation of the glory of Christ that he won at his passover. The Church or Christian fellowship is Jesus Christ made visible and near, provided, of course, that the community manifests the same dying and rising as its Lord.

Paul has given a distinctive orientation to problems of the resurrection of the body. We spontaneously ask: Where will all these bodies be at the day of judgement? For Paul, this was too gross and materialistic (physical) a question. We know so little about life with God after death that we can do no more than qualify it with predicates that are contrary to those we apply to life now. 'What is sown is perishable, what is raised is imperishable. It is sown in dishonour, it is raised in glory. It is sown in weakness, it is raised in power' (1 Cor. 15:42–3). In other words, Paul knows nothing about what is called 'the after-life'. He only trusts in God, the giver of life.

However, Paul has richer insights to share with us than that. The body is essentially the principle of relatedness and communion between human beings. To be alive after dying must mean that these relationships are not severed but raised to a higher level than before. Christ's own resurrection showed this. Christ, not distant now but near, not remote in what concerns his followers and needy people, but immediately accessible to everyone. He lives in them all as they live in and by their own bodies. This is to say, they *are* him. They are his body.

What the risen Christ proves is that death leads not necessarily to the end of communion but to the restructuring of human relationships. This is why the question, 'Where will the risen bodies be and how will they all fit into heaven?' is not Paul's question. In the first place, Paul never says we will go to heaven, but that Christ (heaven) will come to us. Secondly, human relatedness, human bodiliness, will be enhanced, but to ask, '*Where*?' does not make sense. Or, at any rate, all we can do is trust God that we will be embodied in each other just as Christ is embodied in us today. That is quite enough for us.

The focal point of Christ's new manner of communication and bodiliness is the Eucharist. Here is the dramatic sign of the presence, the nearness and the sheer diffusion of the risen Christ. The Eucharist, like the Church, *is* the body of Christ. Here, in fact, the Christian fellowship becomes one in love, dying to the old ways and living anew, so that it can worthily be called the body of Christ. Where the fellowship is not truly the body of Christ or at least striving to be, it becomes a form of blasphemy to partake of Christ's body in the Eucharist (1 Cor. 11:27–9).

How and when did Paul begin to see the reality of Christ's living presence in all these forms? I suggest that, as in Peter's case, so in Paul's, the moment of seeing the Lord as risen was the moment of conversion and faith. Jesus personally looked on them both. But with Paul, Jesus looked out of the eyes of a persecuted Christian. It was then that Paul realized Jesus lives on wherever men and women are willing, in their different ways, to live and die for him.

18. THE MEAL AT EMMAUS

'Stay with us, Lord, the night is drawing on,
For we are hungry and our sun has gone.'
He stays, and, in the breaking of the bread,
They see their Master is alive not dead.
Then he who had escaped death's winding bands
Leaves them his sacred presence in their hands.

Luke, the story-teller of genius, relates how on Easter day two disciples were on their way to Emmaus. They were discussing the fact that the women had come back from the sepulchre with a tale about it being open and empty. Two men in dazzling apparel had said that Jesus was risen.

While the two travellers were talking, Jesus drew near and went with them. 'But their eyes were kept from recognizing him' (24:16). He seemed not to know anything of the events they were discussing. Sadly they spoke about Jesus' crucifixion. They had hoped, they said, that he was the one to redeem Israel. And now there was only this women's talk about seeing men in white and an empty tomb.

Jesus chides them for their slowness in believing the prophets. 'Was it not necessary that the Christ should suffer these things and enter into his glory?' Then Jesus, beginning with Moses and the prophets, interpreted to them what scripture said about himself.

At Emmaus, he seemed as if he were going further on, so they begged him, 'Stay with us, for it is toward evening and the day is now far spent.' He acceded to their request. At table, he took bread, blessed and broke it, then gave it to them. 'And their eyes were opened and they recognized him; and he vanished out of their sight.'

This book will have been to some extent successful if the reader readily sees that this beautiful story is not a piece of history, but part of the gospel of Jesus Christ. It is an early eucharistic story. 'The breaking of the bread' was one of the first terms used by the Christian community to denote the Eucharist. At the farewell meal in the Upper Room, Jesus had given his disciples a prophetic sign of the approaching kingdom. 'This is my body to be broken for you. This is my blood to be shed for you.' His body is himself; his blood is his life. The sign of eating and drinking is prophetic: 'Here and now, by eating this bread and drinking this wine, you have fellowship with me in my sufferings that are now beginning and in the life that comes from them.' This prophetic sign was to be repeated so as to commemorate Jesus until the present age was ended.

In Luke's story, the two disciples on the road to Emmaus, who had hoped so much that Jesus would redeem Israel, could not at first recognize their master in this stranger. He had first to interpret the scriptures for them. Far from the crucifixion being a disaster, he said, it was the fulfilment of everything that Moses and the prophets had written. The Christ had to suffer to enter his glory.

But still there was no recognition. The stranger makes as if to go on further without them. They cannot bear this; he holds out so much promise for them, he has such capacity to console and heal them. They plead with him to stay. They feel the darkness coming on.

It was only at table that they realized Jesus was alive and in their company through the prophetic sign of 'the breaking of the bread'. At the very moment of commemoration and recognition he was gone. What does all this mean?

Christ's death was not a mistake; it was not outside the providence of God. Christ needed to die for the sake of his glory. But he continues coming whenever his followers are afraid of the loneliness of the night. He is there at first unrecognized; as yet they are without faith. Faith is fostered at the Eucharist. Christ gives himself and then takes himself away. He goes away, leaving them with his 'presence'. He withdraws so that he can fulfil the request they made to him earlier on the road: 'Stay with us.' He departs, but only to assure them that he will be with them wherever they gather to break bread together. Today we would say he takes from them his physical presence so as to leave them his sacramental presence.

When they see him no more, what are they left with? A burning presence in their hearts; and in their hands, bread – broken and divided bread – which, when eaten, makes them one. This bread was put into their hands by their risen Lord himself. He has put himself into their hands. 'Into your hands I commit my body.' What are they to do with this bread but eat it together?

Luke's teaching is that the experience of seeing Jesus risen can take place at every eucharistic celebration. The Eucharist is the good news in action. 'Communication' occurs when a man's eyes are opened, when he sees Jesus' cross no longer as disaster, but as the way to the glory of the Christ whom we now feed upon in faith. Such a man is present at the coming of the Lord.

Notes

INTRODUCTION

1. Quoted by James Atkinson, *Martin Luther and the Birth of Protestantism* (Penguin, Harmondsworth, 1968), p. 51.
2. *The Nature of Faith* (Fontana, London, 1966), p. 59.
3. *What do we know about Jesus?* (SCM Press, London, 1968), p. 113.
4. *A New Quest of the Historical Jesus* (SCM Press, London, 1959), p. 95.
5. *Myth and Reality* (Allen & Unwin, London, 1964), p. 1.
6. *Faith and History in the Old Testament* (University of Minnesota Press, 1963), p. 63.
7. Mircea Eliade, op. cit., p. 168.
8. Rudolf Bultmann, *Jesus Christ and Mythology* (SCM Press, London, 1960), pp. 35–6.
9. *The New Testament in Current Study* (SCM Press, London, 1963), p. 18.
10. Ibid., p. 31.
11. Geoffrey Chapman, London, 1967.
12. I am reminded of an Anglican archbishop saying of Martin Buber that he 'can make himself incomprehensible in five languages; but he does not yet know English well enough to be incomprehensible in it'. James Parkes, *Voyage of Discoveries* (Victor Gollancz, London, 1969), p. 193.
13. Cf. O. Cullmann, *The Christology of the New Testament* (SCM Press, London, 1959), and R. H. Fuller, *The Foundations of New Testament Christology* (Fontana, London, 1969). These two works are of outstanding exegetical importance but any reader in search of wit or warmth would as well peruse a telephone directory.
14. *The Authority of the Bible* (Fontana, London, 1960), p. 222.
15. The question is Dietrich Bonhoeffer's. He formulated it in easily the most influential theological work of our time, his casual *Letters and Papers from Prison* (Fontana, London, 1959), p. 91. See also Eberhard Bethge, *Dietrich Bonhoeffer, A Biography* (Collins, London, 1970), pp. 767 ff. Our world has 'come of age'. This is not to say that it is morally mature but that, like an adolescent, it needs to be left free to solve its own problems

without constantly seeking religious 'explanations' or taking refuge under the tutelage of an intervening God.

16. Oliver & Boyd, London, 1965.

17. *The Two-Edged Sword* (Geoffrey Chapman, London, 1962), p. 70.

18. *Essays on New Testament Themes* (SCM Press, London, 1964), p. 20.

19. This is not the place to develop the evident truth that even to say that God is one – let alone is 'three' or 'three in one' – *can be* misleading. To speak without qualification of God in numerical terms can give the impression that divine reality is classifiable with non-divine reality and that God is objectified, that is, that he stands over and above his creation as another thing. If the danger is not real, why do theologians speak of *two* natures, *two* wills in Christ? The disastrous consequences of this manner of speaking will be taken up later.

20. Op. cit., p. 20.

21. Cf. Edward Schillebeeckx, OP, *The Future of Man* (Sheed & Ward, London, 1969). He writes: 'The correctness of these [new] interpretations cannot be tested simply by setting earlier formulas of faith against them since these too always require interpretation and have still to be *made* true' (p. 43). Ancient dogmas are answers to a different set of questions which, in our case, often do not arise. They are not so much wrong as irrelevant to the kind of search we are pursuing.

PART I

1. The same kind of technique was used in the novel and film, *Love Story*.

2. *The Last Temptation* (Bruno Cassirer, Oxford, 1961), pp. 333–4.

3. Karl Rahner rightly bemoans the fact 'that every text-book today offers a long treatise on Good Friday and disposes of Easter in a few lines' (*Theological Investigations*, vol. IV (Darton, Longman & Todd, London, 1966), p. 121). But what light does this cast on these text-books as a whole? Doesn't it suggest that their form and spirit hardly match the gospel?

4. *Jesus of Nazareth* (Hodder & Stoughton, London, 1960), p. 14.

5. A chatty yet scholarly account of the recent history of New Testament exegesis is given in Stephen Neill's *The Interpretation of the New Testament, 1861–1961* (Oxford University Press, London, 1966).

6. *My Early Life* (Odham's Press, London, 1949), pp. 10–11.

7. Lord Acton, *Essays in the Liberal Interpretation of History*, ed.

W. H. McNeill (Phoenix Books, Chicago, 1967), p. 310.

8. Ibid., p. xiii.

9. Peter L. Berger's *Invitation to Sociology* (Penguin, Harmondsworth, 1966) is an excellent introduction to the theme of the relativization of our value judgements – including those of modern sociological relativizers!

10. Op. cit., p. 16.

11. *The Apostolic Preaching and Its Developments* (Hodder & Stoughton, London, 1936), p. 94.

12. Bishop Neill, op. cit., p. 290, mentions the opinion of some scholars that the Christian faith would not collapse 'even if it could be shown that Jesus of Nazareth had never existed'. His amusingly restrained comment is: 'I am not in agreement with this view.'

13. *The Personality of Christ* (Longmans, Green, London, 1915), pp. 148–9.

14. *Summa Theologica*, 3/36/7 *in corp.* Aquinas, naturally, accepted Ptolemy's geocentric system, a fixed earth around which revolved the heavenly vault that bore the stars, the sun and the moon. Ptolemy's arguments that the earth must be stationary could have been disproved by the simplest of experiments. Only, prior to Copernicus and Galileo, strict scientific experiment was alien to the human mind. See Hans Reichenbach's *The Rise of Scientific Philosophy* (University of California Press, Berkeley, 1951), pp. 96–8.

15. *L'Osservatore Romano*, 21 January 1971.

16. Jesus' first Jewish disciples confessed him to be 'the Son of David', that is, the Messiah. This may have given rise to the idea that Jesus was related by blood to David and, therefore, was fittingly born in David's own town of Bethlehem. Alternatively – since precise information is impossible to come by – Jesus really was born at Bethlehem, a fact that might well have contributed to the development of his messianic consciousness.

17. *Poems* (John Lane, New York, 1916), p. 63.

18. *The Faith of the Church* (Fontana, London, 1960), p. 73.

19. *Thus Spake Zarathustra* (Everyman, London, 1941), p. 57.

20. Samuel Sandmel, *We Jews and You Christians* (J. B. Lippincott, Philadelphia and New York, 1967), pp. 78–9. Contrast Professor Sandmel's words with the beginning of *A Catechism of Christian Doctrine*, reissued in 1971 by the Catholic hierarchy of England and Wales for use in their dioceses: 'God made me to know him,

love him and serve him in this world, and to be happy with him
for ever in the next.'

21. It is extraordinary that the theology of virginity contained in Chaucer's Prologue to the Wife of Bath's Tale should have continued down to our own day.

22. The correct translation of Luke 6: 20 and Matt. 5: 3. William Barclay has pointed out that the Greek word for 'poor' is *ptochos*, meaning 'completely destitute', and it designates the man who has reached the end of his own resources and relies entirely on God (*The Plain Man Looks at the Beatitudes* (Fontana, London, 1963), ch. 3).

23. Canto 32, ll. 85–7. The text reads:
   Riguarda omai ne la faccia ch'a Christo più si somiglia,
   che la sua chiarezza sola ti può disporre a veder Christo.

24. *Collected Stories* (Penguin, Harmondsworth, 1961), p. 68.

25. From Theodore Morrison's modern translation, *The Portable Chaucer* (Viking Press, New York, 1958), pp. 179–80.

26. *Collected Poems, 1909–1962* (Faber, London, 1963), pp. 211–12.

27. Dante's 'Daughter of thy Son'.

28. Penguin, Harmondsworth, 1967, p. 138.

29. Fontana, London, 1967, pp. 28–9.

30. *Dogmatics in Outline* (SCM Press, London, 1966), p. 99.

PART 2

1. J. Epstein, *An Autobiography* (Studio Vista, London, 1963), p. 145.

2. Ibid., pp. 152–3.

3. *Early Christian Writings*, tr. by Maxwell Staniforth (Penguin, Harmondsworth, 1968), pp. 103 ff.

4. *Joan of Arc* (Hollis & Carter, London, 1950), pp. 111–12.

5. *Collected Stories*, p. 71.

6. Quoted by Henri Troyat, *Tolstoy* (Penguin, Harmondsworth, 1967), p. 273.

7. Gandhi, *An Autobiography, The Story of My Experiments with Truth* (Jonathan Cape, London, 1966), p. xiv.

8. As late as Pius XII's *Mystici Corporis*, 1943, we read, 'Jesus also enjoys [in his lifetime] the beatific vision in a degree both as regards extent and clarity, surpassing that of all the saints in heaven' (sect. 46).

9. *Summa Theologica*, 3/7/12 ad 3.

10. Those who think that because St Thomas was a genius his teaching can profitably be repeated in our days would do well

to follow me in a recent experiment. I reread the whole of *Tertia Pars* of the *Summa Theologica* (Marietti edition, 1948), pp. 1–365. Whoever goes through this will, no doubt, be as surprised as I was, not only at the utter impossibility of assenting today to Aquinas' theology of Christ, but also at his frequent inconsistencies. Time after time, he is forced to compromise his basic philosophical principles because of his literalistic reading of many key passages in scripture. This is not meant as a criticism of St Thomas, only of some Thomists (of whom Aquinas was not one).

11. We cannot over-emphasize the fact that most Christology in the past was written on the basis of a view of John's gospel that has only recently been demolished. Neil writes, op. cit., p. 340: 'The fourth gospel cannot be treated in the same way as the first three . . . it is primarily a theological restatement of the meaning of the manifestation [of God in Christ].' If true, this calls for more than a slight adjustment of Christology, which is all that most Christian theologians are prepared to make.

12. Rahner agrees that Jesus' consciousness of being the Son of God developed from the implicit to the explicit. But while Rahner, to whom I am deeply indebted, is more liberal than earlier Thomistic theologians, he still sets out the Christological problems *in the old terms*. He gives the impression that the style of modern exegesis has made little difference to the way the problem is posed, and that he is trying to justify, with few modifications, what earlier theologians said *on the basis of totally false presuppositions about the nature of the gospels*.

13. 'The Everlasting Gospel', in *William Blake* (Penguin, Harmondsworth, 1968), p. 75.

14. Louis Golding, *The Jewish Problem* (Penguin, Harmondsworth, 1938), p. 11.

15. Guenter Lewy, *The Catholic Church and Nazi Germany* (Weidenfeld & Nicolson, London, 1968), p. 51.

16. *Poems of Robert Browning* (Oxford University Press, London, 1959), p. 272.

17. Op. cit., 'The Story of My Dovecot', p. 231.

18. *The Authority of the Bible*, p. 195.

19. *Literature and Dogma* (London, 1873), p. 80.

20. In my probably misguided view, the dilemma is not so difficult to resolve. It is self-evident that any length is mathematically divisible *ad infinitum*: it can be divided in half, then in half again endlessly. But this has nothing to do with *movement* as such.

When I move, I am not dividing up space mathematically. Nor is space composed of an infinite number of points all of which need to be traversed if I am to reach my destination. (An actually infinite number is a nonsense.) When I move, I am *by definition* never in (i.e. stationary 'in') any point of my journey, let alone obliged to traverse (and at the same time be stationary in!) an actually infinite number of points on the journey.

21. Quoted by G. S. Hendrey, *The Gospel of the Incarnation* (SCM Press, London, 1959), p. 93.

22. *The Death of Christ* (Fontana, London, 1967), p. 58.

23. *The Humanity and Divinity of Christ* (Cambridge University Press, London, 1967), p. 68.

24. Ibid., p. 71.

25. Had Christ been so well-developed in infancy, he would not have merited the report which the psychologist, C. W. Valentine, refers to as the gem in his collection. 'The actual report of a nursery-school teacher on a little boy of three years [was] to the effect that he was "lacking in leadership"' (*The Normal Child* (Penguin, Harmondsworth, 1964), p. 29).

26. 'At his age [two or five or seven], the little boy or girl is still learning to perceive external reality, and to understand that the mother has a life of her own, and that she cannot be possessed as she belongs to someone else [the father]' (D. W. Winicott, *The Child, the Family, and the Outside World* (Penguin, Harmondsworth, 1964), p. 191).

27. In *Christ For Us Today*, a symposium (SCM Press, London, 1968), p. 143.

28. Everyman's Library, London, 1967, p. 252.

29. *Commentary on Galatians* (London, 1830), Gal. 2: 20.

30. Quoted by H. R. Mackintosh, *The Christian Experience of Forgiveness* (Fontana, London, 1961), p. 186.

31. An elaboration of this theme is to be found in the important work of Friedrich Gogarten, *Christ the Crisis* (SCM Press, London, 1970).

32. Dietrich Bonhoeffer, *The Cost of Discipleship* (SCM Press, London, 1964), pp. 39–40.

33. It would be amusing, were it not so sad, to see Jesus' teaching on the *ideal of marriage* interpreted as a piece of *legislation on divorce*. As if, for example, the current Catholic discipline, namely, that a consummated marriage between baptized Christians is indissoluble, is an exact transcription of what Jesus meant! The self-deception here, on the part of some moralists, is

alarming. On their own fundamentalist interpretation of scripture, Jesus was talking to unbaptized Jews whose marriages are canonically dissoluble anyway! Further, the Pauline privilege, so called, just as much contradicts Jesus' words taken as a legal enactment as does the Orthodox discipline that, in certain instances, even consummated Christian marriages are dissoluble. Finally, are we really to think that Jesus had in mind the details of a law of marriage which included not only provisions for consummation and non-consummation, but interpreted consummation in terms of the purely biological phenomenon of 'intercourse with insemination'? Of course, these remarks leave aside the historical and social question of whether the Roman discipline on marriage and divorce was beneficial or otherwise to Western society.

34. Amos Niven Wilder counters this in his *Eschatology and Ethics in the Teaching of Jesus* (Harper, New York, 1950): 'Not the nearness of the end but the supreme significance of Jesus' errand and the resistance from the old order governs the world-renouncing claims' (p. 188).

35. Leo Tolstoy, *On Civil Disobedience and Non-Violence* (Signet, New York, 1968), p. 182.

36. *Sin, Liberty and Law* (Sheed & Ward, New York, 1965), p. 132.

37. Alfred Edersheim, *The Life and Times of Jesus the Messiah*, vol. II (London, 1900), pp. 780–3.

38. *The Provincial Letters* (Penguin, Harmondsworth, 1967), pp. 89, 94, 106, 145. It is a shame that this, the most brilliant treatise ever written against the pharisaic mind, was put on the Roman Index of Forbidden Books. After three hundred years, it is as fresh, incisive and entertaining as when it first saw the light of day. Interestingly, though I have inquired of nearly twenty Jesuit priests, I have yet to find one who has read it.

39. H. Davis, SJ, *Moral and Pastoral Theology*, vol. II (Sheed & Ward, London, 1963), pp. 60–1, 67, 399–400.

40. Op. cit., pp. 3, 9, 12.

41. Like Pascal, I prefer to keep silent about the moralists' teaching on sexuality.

42. *The Art of Loving* (Allen & Unwin, London, 1957), pp. 47–9.

43. *The Poems of John Donne*, edited by Herbert Grierson (Oxford University Press, London, 1957), pp. 337–8. I have altered the seventeenth-century spelling.

44. *The Anti-Christ* (Penguin, Harmondsworth, 1968), p. 160.

45. Nietzsche, commenting on the traditional relish for eternal

punishment, declares that Christians have proven themselves to be the greatest haters in history. Cf. *The Birth of Tragedy and the Genealogy of Morals* (Doubleday, New York, 1956), pp. 181 ff.

46. Joachim Jeremias, *The Central Message of the New Testament* (SCM Press, London, 1965), ch. 1.

47. See Ernst and Marie-Louise Keller's *Miracles in Dispute* (SCM Press, London, 1969) for a historical survey of the interpretation of Jesus' miracles.

48. *Interpreting the Miracles* (SCM Press, London, 1966), pp. 32, 39.

49. *The African Child* (Fontana, London, 1959), p. 12. Camara Laye's mother possessed the crocodile as her totem. She believed crocodiles could not hurt her and continued, unharmed, drawing water from a river that was infested with them (p. 62).

50. Ibid., p. 48.

51. Exegetes continue to discuss the extent to which the raising of the dead and the healing of lepers (like the nature miracles, cf. below) are really stories constructed by the community. Some argue plausibly that Jesus' words, quoted from Isaiah, about lepers being cleansed and the dead being raised (Matt. 11: 5) have been developed into miracle stories to parallel the accounts of actual historical healings of lesser illnesses and the expulsion of demons. This is not to deny that the raising of the dead and the healing of lepers are based on the disciples' rich experience of spiritual regeneration and healing in the presence of Christ, a change that far exceeded purely somatic cures.

52. *The Miracle Stories of the Gospel* (SCM Press, London, 1960), p. 102.

53. *Jesus and the Word* (Fontana, London, 1962), p. 124.

54. *Jesus* (SCM Press, London, 1963), p. 74.

55. Rudolf Bultmann, *Theology of The New Testament*, vol. II (SCM Press, London, 1959), p. 33.

56. R. H. Fuller, in *The Foundations of New Testament Christology*, writes: 'The implicit Christology of Jesus becomes the explicit Christology of the Church' (p. 143). The sparkling remark that 'Jesus was not a Christian' is not, therefore, true in any profound sense.

57. *Summa Theologica*, 3/45/1–4.

58. Ibid., 3/21/2 *ad* 2.

59. I would like to argue more forcefully, had I the space, that it is really *self-contradictory* to assert that the future as such is know-

able in advance. A man can no more know the future than he can change the past.

60. The phrase was Cyril of Alexandria's (ἀπαθῶς ἔπαθεν). In the Koran, Jesus alone is said not to have died. This was in accordance with Muhammad's teaching that Jesus did not really suffer or die, but, at the end, was taken by God himself. The only teacher I know who at present teaches that Christ was not able to suffer is Maharishi Mahesh Yogi. He maintains that Jesus had the additional status of Universal Being, unbounded by time, space and causation. Jesus spoke of the kingdom within and said, 'I and my Father are one.' He was all joy and bliss. 'It is a pity that Christ is talked of in terms of suffering. It is painless suffering' (*Meditations of Mahesh Yogi* (Bantam, New York, 1968), pp. 121–4).

61. H. G. Wells's story, *The First Men In The Moon*, relies for its effect upon the invention of Cavorite, a substance opaque to gravitation, thus preventing objects gravitating towards each other. Its first brief employment nearly depopulates the world. The unconventional scientist-inventor remarks calmly of his projected second experiment: 'If we can possibly avoid wrecking this little planet of ours, we will. But – there *must* be risks!' (Newnes, London, 1901, p. 39).

62. My interpretation substantially accords with that of D. E. Nineham, *Saint Mark* (Penguin, Harmondsworth, 1963), p. 146. See also A. Richardson, *The Miracle Stories of the Gospels*, pp. 90 ff.

63. *Saint Matthew* (Penguin, Harmondsworth, 1963), p. 246.

64. *Interpreting the Miracles*, pp. 121–2.

65. *The Miracle Stories of the Gospels*, p. 120.

66. *Saint John* (Penguin, Harmondsworth, 1968), p. 438.

67. Op. cit., p. 111.

68. Progress Publishers, Moscow, 1961, pp. 201, 212.

69. *Rediscovering the Parables* (SCM Press, London, 1966), p. 10. This is a shortened version of *The Parables of Jesus*. Jeremias and C. H. Dodd (*The Parables of the Kingdom*, Fontana, London, 1961) are the best modern exponents of Jesus' parables.

70. *My Universities* (Progress Publishers, Moscow, 1968), pp. 158–9.

71. *Jesus and the Word*, p. 14.

72. *The New Testament Gospels*, a symposium (BBC Publications, London, 1965), p. 35.

73. *The Shaking of the Foundations* (Penguin, Harmondsworth, 1963), p. 100.

74. *A New Quest of the Historical Jesus* (SCM Press, London, 1959), p. 86.

75. Dennis Potter's play, *The Son of Man*, aroused a good deal of controversy when it was shown on BBC television in 1969. One reason was that Jesus was called upon to belch. The critics, no doubt, presumed that Jesus' manners would have been considered unexceptional even in an English drawing-room.

76. According to Dibelius, a Galilean 'does not distinguish the guttural sounds clearly, he swallows syllables, and pronounces many of the vowels carelessly' (*Jesus*, p. 35).

77. Ernst Käsemann, *Essays on New Testament Themes*, p. 43.

78. William Barclay, *The First Three Gospels* (SCM Press, London, 1966), p. 33.

79. *The Authority of the Bible*, p. 217.

PART 3

1. Henri Bergson, *The Two Sources of Morality and Religion* (Doubleday, New York, 1954), p. 241.

2. *The Christian Experience of Forgiveness* (Fontana, London, 1961), pp. 77–8.

3. An example of what Whitehead called, 'paying metaphysical compliments to God'. Quoted by Norman Pittenger, *God in Process* (SCM Press, London, 1967), p. 100.

4. One is reminded of Molière's *Tartuffe*. Orgon, having been taken in by the holy impostor, explains to Cléante, his brother, all the benefits Tartuffe has brought him:

   Orgon:
   Oui, je deviens tout autre avec son entretien;
   Il m'enseigne à n'avoir affection pour rien,
   De toutes amitiés il détache mon âme;
   Et je verrois mourir frère, enfants, mère et femme,
   Que je m'en soucierois autant que de cela.

   Cléante:
   Les sentiments humains, mon frère, que voila!

   Oeuvres Complètes de Molière (Oxford, 1941), p. 244.

5. *Great French Short Stories*, selected by Germaine Brée (Dell, New York, 1964), p. 206.

6. In the magazine *Encounter*, December, 1968, p. 38.

7. Penguin, Harmondsworth, 1969, p. 19.

8. In the patristic period, these images were often enlarged and

distorted. For example, the repayment image is interpreted dualistically as God paying a debt *to the Devil* to recover his enslaved children.

9. *Waiting on God* (Routledge & Kegan Paul, London, 1951), p. 66.
10. In the Old Testament legislation an eye for an eye was a distinct improvement on what had gone before. We know that when we are attacked, the tendency is to take two eyes for one, a whole mouthful of teeth for a single tooth.
11. Cf. H. A. Hodges, *The Pattern of Atonement* (SCM Press, London, 1963), p. 43. This idea is developed in Dorothy Sölle's difficult but rewarding book, *Christ the Representative* (SCM Press, London, 1967).
12. In Pär Lagerkvist's *Barabbas* (Chatto & Windus, London, 1952), Barabbas is reflecting on how much closer he was to Jesus than were Jesus' disciples. 'They spoke of him having died for *them*. That might be. But he really had died for Barabbas, no one could deny it! In actual fact he was closer to him than they were, closer than anyone else, was bound up with him in quite another way . . . He was chosen, one might say – chosen to escape suffering, to be let off. He was the real chosen one, acquitted instead of the son of God himself – at his command, because he wished it' (p. 41). What is here said of Barabbas as an individual is intended by the evangelists as a gospel comment on the liberation of all mankind.
13. *The Christian Experience of Forgiveness*, p. 137.
14. My present approach was substantially complete before I read Willi Marxsen's *The Resurrection of Jesus of Nazareth* (SCM Press, London, 1970). However, his book undoubtedly coloured my presentation. I can only recommend his book as providing the best general exegetical treatment I know of this thorny subject.
15. Wolfhart Pannenberg, *Jesus, God and Man* (SCM Press, London, 1968), p. 74.
16. *Literature and Dogma*, p. 181.
17. Op. cit., p. 89.
18. *The Interpretation of the New Testament*, p. 118.
19. G. Ebeling, *The Nature of Faith*, pp. 66–7; W. Pannenberg, op. cit., pp. 104–5.
20. *Summa Theologica*, 3/54/3 ad 3.
21. R. W. Southern, *Western Society and the Church in the Middle Ages* (Penguin, Harmondsworth, 1970), p. 31.
22. It also explains some macabre devotions. In a classic work, *The Waning of the Middle Ages* (Penguin, Harmondsworth, 1955),

J. Huizinga wrote: 'During the lying in state of St Elizabeth of Hungary, in 1231, a crowd of worshippers came and cut or tore strips of the linen enveloping her face; they cut off the hair, the nails, even the nipples. In 1392, King Charles VI of France, on the occasion of a solemn feast, was seen to distribute ribs of his ancestor, St Louis; to Pierre d'Ailly and to his uncles, Berry and Burgundy, he gave entire ribs; to the prelates one bone to divide between them, which they proceeded to do after the meal' (p. 168).

23. 'And behold, there arose a great *seismos* on the sea.'

24. W. Pannenberg, op. cit., p. 75.

25. See W. Marxsen, op. cit., ch. VII.

26. St Thomas Aquinas perceived this difficulty and answered it by claiming that some kind of faith was still required of the apostles despite seeing Jesus risen, namely, faith in his divinity.

27. *Theology of Hope* (SCM Press, London, 1967), p. 198.

28. 'Paradiso, XXXI, 108', in *Labyrinths* (Penguin, Harmondsworth, 1970), p. 274.

29. Cf. J. A. T. Robinson's excellent study of Pauline theology, *The Body* (SCM Press, London, 1952), p. 51.

INDEX OF
NAMES AND SUBJECTS

Index of Names and Subjects

INDEX OF
BIBLE REFERENCES

Index of Bible References

Also in the Fontana Theology and Philosophy Series

A Historical Introduction to the New Testament
ROBERT GRANT

'This splendid book is a New Testament introduction with a difference ... All students of the New Testament will welcome this original and courageous study.'
Professor James S. Stewart

The Historical Geography of the Holy Land
G. ADAM SMITH

'A classic which has fascinated and instructed generations of students. This masterpiece among the vast literature on the Bible ... will continue to delight readers as well as to inform.'
H. H. Rowley

The Dead Sea Scrolls 1947-1969
EDMUND WILSON

'A lucid narrative of the discovery of the scrolls which soon turns into a learned detective story; then an account of the excitement, the consternation and the intrigues.'
V. S. Pritchett, New Statesman

The Gospels and the Jesus of History
XAVIER LEON-DUFOUR

'This book is far more than an introduction to the study of the Gospels. With its detailed study of the Gospels and of the other New Testament books it is an excellent introduction to the Christology of the New Testament.' *William Barclay*